A Sandwich Short of a Picnic

Janice Newnham

JANICE NEWNHAM BOOKS

Copyright © 2025 Janice Newnham

All rights reserved.

No part of this publication may be reproduced, distributed or transmitted in any form or by any means, including photocopying, recording or other electronic or mechanical methods, without the prior written permission from the publisher or author, except in the case of brief quotations embodied in critical reviews and certain other non-commercial uses permitted by copyright law.

A Sandwich Short of a Picnic is a work of fiction.

The author, Janice Newnham has undertaken extensive research and investigation into the subject matter of this work. The content details a dark event in the history of the Upper Murray, which was extensively reported upon by newspapers of the time. These newspaper reports were a primary source of information to the author but since journalists of that time were not constrained by the strict ethical standards of reporting that we are currently familiar with, Janice Newnham makes no warranties or representations as to the accuracy of the information contained within this book. The assumptions and conclusions of the author are based on her own reasonable assessment of information sourced from her research; however, the work must be considered entirely fictional.

Unless otherwise indicated, all names of real people, real places, other characters, businesses, historical events and incidents in this book are either used in a fictitious manner or are the product of the author's imagination and are not intended to accurately depict actual events or to change the entirely fictional nature of the work. Any resemblance to actual persons, living or dead, or actual events is purely coincidental.

Cover Design:

Full credit for cover design is due to Duncan Blachford, *Typography Studio*.

I am most appreciative of Duncan's design skills, as he grasped my concept and efficiently turned it into a slick reality: A very striking book cover!

Janice Newnham - Author

Contents

Zol

This book is dedicated to "Zol" - Eugene Zolnierczyk, a colourful character, who, in 1986, was the Principal of Walwa Primary School. In celebration of the Centenary of the school, he enthusiastically led his students and staff in the pursuit of researching the local history of Walwa – Jingellic and district in the period since European Settlement. He and his staff, volunteers and students created a series of books which presented oral histories: snippets of recollections, anecdotes and some apocryphal stories, accompanied by verified facts relating to the early residents and the community of Walwa and Jingellic, in the Upper Murray, in rural Australia.

One of the books that was created during this school project was entitled:

He tried to Invent a Rabbit Poison.

The book was a collection of stories reflecting the darker side of the district's history. It was laced with murder and mystery. Claude Batson, the protagonist of this novel, is the character referred to in this title.

All small country towns have skeletons in their closets; events that are so dark and shocking that the community develops a degree of group amnesia. The tale of Claude Batson's brain snap and subsequent progression to infamy is typical of such a skeleton. According to newspaper reports of the day, the Batson case was "scandalous and shocking" but with the passage of time, community memories have faded and hardly any of the "old" families have any real or "inherited" knowledge of the events which roused a small army of vengeful civilians to take to the hills in the late summer of 1924. The men were bristling with firearms and intent on hunting down the fugitive who was considered to be:

The Last Bushranger of the Riverina.

Batson's heinous crime may well be one of the first copy-cat crimes of Australian history, or perhaps an unfortunate coincidence. He could have been a deranged sociopath, turned psychopath, or he might just have been a marginalised, lonely young man who was pushed to a mental breakdown after a prolonged period of bullying underpinned by a history of childhood trauma.

It would have been enlightening to have read Batson's case notes after his arrest, both police reports and medical records, but in the absence of these, I have based my interpretation of events on archival records, a few anecdotal recollections and numerous newspaper reports sourced by trawling through the rabbit warren of information which is the Trove website. (*https://www.trove.nla.gov.au*)

I have extrapolated from the available facts and have reimagined the folklore, settings and characters to create this novel:

A Sandwich Short of a Picnic.

There are many phrases in the Australian vernacular which indicate that someone is in the throes of a mental breakdown, or somewhat cognitively challenged. They might be described as: '*not the full quid,* '*not firing on all cylinders* or, *has a cuppla 'roos loose in the top paddock* but I think the selection of this idiom, *A Sandwich Short of a Picnic*, as a title of this book and to indicate Batson's brain snap, is fitting, considering the setting of his crime. I am aware that the use of the idiom in the dialogue within this novel may be a little ahead of its era of common usage... forgive me, and let's call it creative license!

I am so grateful to Zol for re-discovering this skeleton in the closet of the Upper Murray and thank you, too, dear reader, for discovering my novel!

I live in Australia, this book is set in Australia and hence, I have utilised Australian English as the medium for my narrative. This has meant endless arguments with spellcheck in the software program, that was utilised, but I will not be bullied by artificial intelligence to adopt an uncomfortable version of the spelling of common Australian words, nor will I participate in arguments with pedantic readers!

So put that in your pipe and smoke it!

Melbourne, 24 January 1924

Emma Payne's fingers paused. She stretched and gazed at the black letters which marched in an orderly procession across the crisp white paper spooling from her typewriter. A headache thumped persistently behind eyes which glistened with tears. She had been in the employ of the Repatriation Department for just a few short months, yet she was already overwhelmed, spent.

As she typed up the documents associated with applications for *Repat* financial assistance, she found herself vicariously experiencing the traumas of the clients, the returned ex-servicemen and their families. She was endlessly horrified by the details of their struggles to readjust to civilian life, a now shattered life. Which was the consequence of the ex-servicemen's efforts for *King and Country* during conflicts on foreign shores, during the dreadful years of the war... *The War to end all Wars, The Great War.*

The brutal impacts of war on the minds and bodies of Repat clients were further exacerbated by their confusion and dislocation after demobilisation. Emma's typing captured the fact that most returned servicemen were distant shadows of their former selves. She recorded physical disabilities - loss of limbs, poisoned lungs, disfiguring facial injuries, sensory impairment and the hidden psychological impacts which slipped under the official euphemisms of *war strain* and *shell shock.*

The war-time Australian Prime Minister, WM "Billy" Hughes had confidently assured the valiant troops:

"When you come back, we will look after you!"

His words were immortalised in newspaper headlines, radio reports and dispatches and later, in the years since Armistice, these same words had been thrown back at the staff on the Repat enquiry desks, often multiple times a day, by disillusioned and distressed clients.

The Repatriation Department had been established to provide War Pensions to service personnel and their dependents and to facilitate the promised benefits of healthcare, education, and training to assist the returned service personnel to adapt back to civilian life. Supported housing, soldier-settler land schemes, memorials and remembrance activities were also assured. Emma had read the pamphlets that were provided to the veterans of war. It all sounded positively encouraging in theory, but in practice, there were significant issues – it was not all as rosy as the brochures depicted!

Repat was the colloquial term applied to clients of the Repatriation Department but in the years since Armistice, the term had been bastardised to become a dirty word. The erstwhile heroes were now viewed as *bludgers* by the unsympathetic and ignorant public. The system and the department were overwhelmed. Newspapers featured depressing images of the long lines of dejected men at the demobilisation depots with headlines that sniped: "Hurry up and Wait".

To top it all, Australia was not spared the impacts of a growing global financial crisis, and unemployment and poverty were rife as Australia slid inexorably towards the Great Depression.

In Emma's workplace, the staccato rhythm of a roomful of typists recorded the agonies and despair of thousands of Australian Imperial Force (AIF) service personnel as their repatriation issues were documented, reported upon, and referred up the endless administrative chain for assessment. The most disturbing case in Emma's in-tray, and for which she had to transcribe a cold and formal official letter of "apology", was that of Corporal George Rodgers. Even as the words spilled across the page from her rapid-fire keystrokes, she was able to reflect on the details of the case which she had absorbed over the past weeks of departmental deliberation and documentation. In consideration of these facts, Emma realised that the letter she was typing would prove to be poor compensation for the trauma created by the Department's appalling mismanagement of the unfortunate Corporal Rodgers' case. She couldn't help but be affected by the tragedy of it all. She paused again as emotion crushed her heart, and she thought about the details of Rodgers' ruin.

Rodgers had endured the terror and misery of the misguided but heroic Gallipoli campaign as an infantryman with the ANZAC troops. He was one of the "lucky" ones. He had survived the conflict and was evacuated after suffering a relatively minor injury to his knee. He was sent to Egypt for initial medical care and then on to England for rehabilitation, before being unceremoniously sent back to the trenches of the Somme. Eventually, in the wake of Armistice, he returned to Australia on one of Monash's crowded Repat ships.

General Sir John Monash had been transferred to London after Armistice and was appointed Director General of the AIF Department of Demobilisation and Repatriation. He had commandeered merchant ships to assist his purpose, and, at the height of the activity, five hundred servicemen and women were dispatched back to Australia each day.

On his return to Australia, Rodgers' injured knee deteriorated and erupted into a painful and disabling ulcer. The elation of returning home to his young American wife and small child, was crushed when Rodgers' condition was misdiagnosed by an overworked and inexperienced doctor. The doctor's assertion that the ulcer was a consequence of syphilis caused Rodgers' world to implode. His wife was horrified by his presumed infidelity as demonstrated by his supposed affliction with a venereal disease. She refused to listen to his denials and entreaties, and she abandoned Rodgers, returning to her family in America with their small child in tow.

Rodgers was left a broken man. His hero status was sullied, his family life shattered, his body and mind were irreparably damaged. The diagnosis of venereal disease also excluded him from eligibility for a war disability payment. Even the reversal of the initial diagnosis failed to provide a reprieve - he was worn down and wrung out by multiple medical examinations and a lengthy battle with the Repat Department. Peace had been declared over five years ago, but Emma doubted that Rodgers would ever find personal peace - he would never recover from battle trauma compounded by the struggle of battling the Repat Department.

The enormity of the error and sheer disrespect shown to the man, an honourable returned serviceman, crushed Emma. It was intensified by the fact that Rodgers was not an isolated case, there were so many more...

Another disturbing aspect of the Repat assessment process was the controversial 'value' applied to the victim's degree of disability. How could the system ever make an accurate quantitative assessment on suffering and how to put a monetary value on that suffering? There was an increasing gap between *need* and *aspiration* in terms of the Australian Soldiers Repatriation Act of 1917, and the Repatriation Committee was established to grapple with decisions on cases that had been referred up the administrative chain. The Repatriation Committee struggled to identify and rank deserving cases, creating further delays in assistance being delivered. A Royal Commission was promised later in 1924, but many in the community, wondered what, yet another committee, was going to achieve. Most felt that the funding to support the work of the Committee and the Commission, would be better spent on the actual victims of war.

Emma's initial enthusiasm for her work had ebbed as she felt increasingly powerless to adequately assist the people whose details spewed from her typewriter keys for eight hours per day.
1

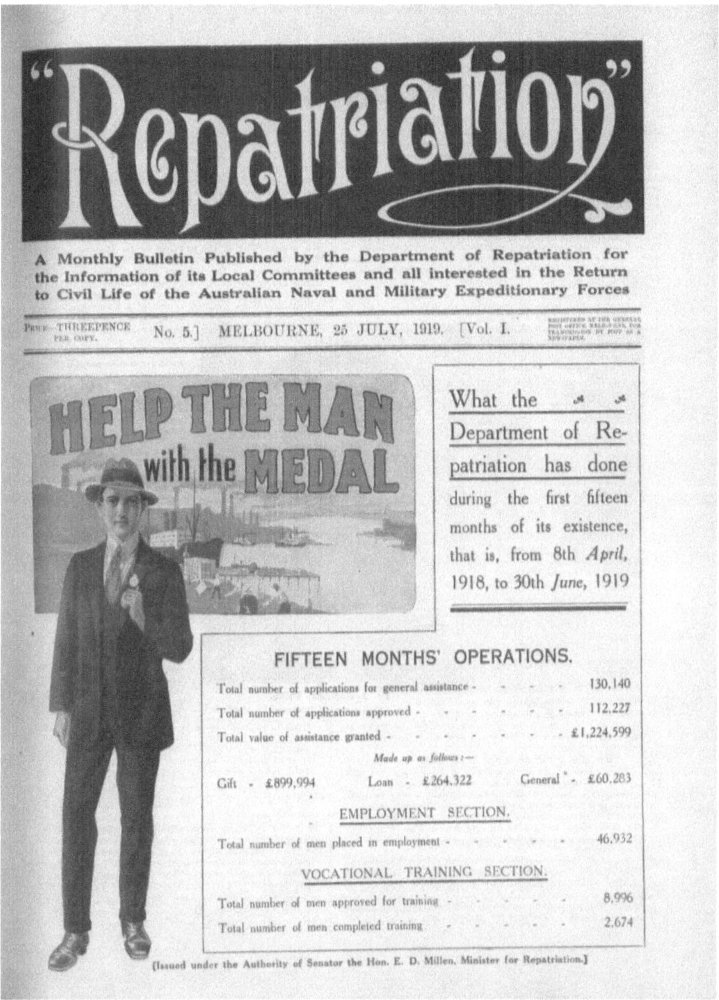

Inaugural issue of Repatriation Magazine, July 1919 - National Library of Australia.

1. A reference used and recommended by the author to explore the difficulties of the repatriation of troops post WWI was ***Repat : a concise history of repatriation in Australia*** / *Philip Payton Department of Veterans' Affairs Brisbane, Qld 2018*

CHAPTER 1

Who would bring a rifle to a picnic?

The typing pool of the Repat Department was a stuffy and uncomfortable environment as Melbourne sweltered through the searing summer of 1924.

"Time Ladies! Good evening!" announced the typing pool supervisor.

Emma glanced up at the clock on the wall, confirming that it was indeed 5pm. She felt relieved to be escaping. She tidied her desk, gathered up her handbag, gloves and hat, and called, "Goodbye, girls!" to her colleagues before bolting to the door.

She rapidly descended the stairs to the ground floor and emerged onto Martin Street. It was busy, and the crowds of commuters bustled and jostled Emma. She felt claustrophobic and anxious in the press of people. The thought of the crammed tram ride home was unappealing. The young woman yearned to immerse herself in green open space and slip between the delicate fronds in the cool environs of the Royal Botanic Gardens fernery. Nature always provided salve for her soul. She made a snap decision and Emma crossed two blocks, before hurrying across Domain Road, dodging between the rush hour vehicular chaos of trams, cabs, carriages, and motor vehicles. Her pretty face and slim figure attracted several ribald whistles and honks from drivers caught up in the snarl of traffic. She entered the Gardens precinct through the wrought iron gates and was immediately enveloped in a sense of calm.

The Botanic Gardens were filled with couples and families seeking relief from the oppressive summer heat. Picnic parties were scattered across the lawns in the cool shade of the expansive canopies of European specimen trees. Emma smiled, revelling in the clean air and freedom as she walked briskly along the path beside the lake where small children were feeding the ducks under the watchful gaze of young mothers. She crossed the Eastern Lawn and slipped into the fernery where she soon found her favourite bench. She loved the rich earthy smell in the cool shade-house. Inhaling to the extent of her lungs, she revelled in the fragrance, the calm and the silence.

Emma sat down, relaxing for the first time that day. Forcing her thoughts away from the misery of the Repats, Emma considered her options for the future. She longed to return to her roots, to the country, where life was more languid and to escape from the emotional burden of "her" Repat clients.

Taking a writing pad and a pencil from her handbag, Emma hesitated and gathered her thoughts, before starting to write a long-overdue letter to her aunt in country Victoria. She remembered with great fondness her last holiday in the small Upper Murray community of Walwa. She recalled waking up in the small bedroom of the farmhouse with kookaburras laughing raucously in the trees beyond her window and the enticing fragrance of fresh baked bread and bacon cooking in her aunt's simple kitchen. These memories intensified her desire to leave the city, to abandon the typing pool and to escape to freedom.

She had been labouring on her letter for some time when a sharp noise startled her. She froze and sat listening, her head cocked toward the direction of the sound. A frown furrowed her forehead.

"Was it a gunshot?" she thought to herself.

The noise was out of context for the city, and she assured herself it was just a vehicle backfiring. She was about to return to her writing, when another shot rang out. Emma flinched. She could hear panicked voices surging from beyond the cloisters of the fernery. Emma was confused and an aura of danger and dark foreboding prickled her senses. She slipped her writing pad and pencil into the depths of her handbag and quickly left the fernery. She kept close to the cover of the shrubbery, whilst searching the gardens for the source of the distressing sounds. She saw that the once idyllic scene across the Eastern Lawn was now chaotic. Picnic blankets were abandoned. People were scattering, running and screaming. She saw a body slumped next to a park bench and three small children standing alongside, wailing and clutching at one another. Movement caught her eye, just on the tree line opposite her position. A man in a grey suit was setting out along the gravel path towards the reservoir end of the park. He had a rifle nonchalantly hooked over his arm and was striding forth with jarring calmness. He had the appearance of a game keeper doing his rounds but was out of context: not in a suit, not in the city.

Emma's heart was pounding in her ears. She waited until the gunman was out of sight before hurrying across the lawns towards the victim and children. A man had beaten her to the scene: when Emma arrived, he was already squatting next to the body. He looked up at her with a grim expression and shook his head.

"She's gone...." he said.

Emma gasped, horrified. Her attention was drawn to the small children; three distraught, pale faces gazed up at her.

"Oh God," she whispered and clutched the children to her skirts, hiding their faces from the horror before them.

The metallic scent of blood assailed her nostrils.

Several more gun shots rang out. The sound was distant, beyond the trees. Emma flinched and her stomach flip flopped, the children sobbed.

"Quick," said the man, "You pick up the little girl, I will take these two, we need to get them away to safety!"

They scooped up the children and, with the man leading the way, they scuttled towards a clump of dense shrubbery. They squatted amongst the low branches, hiding, trying to keep the children calm and quiet. Sirens and whistles howled and shrilled, heralding the approach of the police. Screams, shouting and an occasional gunshot revealed the position of the gunman and his terrorised victims. Emma was quietly sobbing, holding the children close. She was devastated that these innocents had witnessed their mother's violent death. It was such a shocking event.

"Why? Who was that?" she whispered.

The man reached out a hand and laid it gently on her shoulder.

"A madman!" he growled.

The children were shaking and sobbing. The eldest, a girl of about six, was pulling away, trying to get back to her mother.

"Mam, Mam!" she cried.

Beyond their hiding spot, armed policemen were appearing, moving cautiously across the lawns. The man turned to Emma.

"You stay here with the kids; I'll go and talk to the police."

Emma smiled encouragingly at the children and asked their names. The eldest girl hesitantly gave her name and pointed to her sisters, introducing them in turn in a high lisping voice.

Soon, the man returned.

"The police seem to think the gunman has gone ... escaped. They are allowing women and children to leave the Gardens after registering their details, but men are being questioned to ensure the gunman hasn't doubled back and is attempting to disappear into the crowds. The police are organising for these children to go into the custody of some nurses while they try to contact family. They will be here shortly, then I think, you can go home."

"Oh God, the poor little mites!" wailed Emma.

She was again distraught, reliving what the children had witnessed. She looked at their tear stained and now, grubby faces. The children were bewildered. She hugged them close.

"I don't know your name..." Emma said haltingly as her eyes searched the man's face.

She felt that the shared experience had created a bond. He smiled at her kindly.

"Jacob Miller," he said as he reached out and firmly shook Emma's hand whilst gazing into her eyes.

"Such kind eyes," she noted to herself.

"I only came for a stroll after a tedious day in a stuffy office, and then this.... This is just horrific! I suppose it'll turn out to be an unhinged returned serviceman. Some of us came home with more than physical injuries from that bloody episode overseas," said Jacob with a catch in his voice and a grim, haunted expression.

Emma nodded sympathetically.

"I'm Emma, Emma Payne. I work in the Repat office, so I know what you mean - I see so many broken men, 'hear some god-awful stories. Displaced, damaged, disrespected..."

She paused, her eyes prickling with tears.

"Are you going to be alright?" she added with a worried frown, looking at Jacob with genuine concern and wondering what impact this sudden violent event would have on the self-confessed veteran of the war.

"Nothing, a belt of Scotch won't fix!" said Jacob.

He grinned, but the warmth of his smile didn't reach his eyes.

Emma and Jacob emerged cautiously from the shrubbery, leading the small children by their hands. Once on the path, they waited quietly for the police to approach. Soon, a pair of nurses arrived, their crisp white uniforms stark against the green lawns. The nurses spoke briefly to the police officers who were clustered around the body of the victim before they hurried towards Emma and her charges. The rotund, more matronly of the two nurses squatted down to the level of the children and introduced herself in soft, kind tones.

"Hello, Pets. What a day you have had! I am Sister Kate, and this is Sister Elsie. We are going to keep you safe! We'll take you to our office and give you chocolate and milkshakes whilst we wait for your Da' to come and fetch you home."

The older girl began to wail again, squirming around to get away.

"Mam, Mam!" she shrieked.

The two smaller girls joined in. Emma's heart broke as she hugged the trio. The nurses unhooked the children's fingers from Emma's skirts. Sister Kate smiled encouragingly at the children and Emma, before the two nurses led the sobbing children towards a waiting police vehicle. Emma's heart ached for the little girls.

One of the constables crossed the lawn and introduced himself to Emma and Jacob.

"Now then; as Sergeant O'Connor mentioned to Mr Miller here, I must take your names and details, a brief statement and then the lady can leave. You can probably go, too, Sir, when cleared to do so, by the Sergeant."

"I am not sure I can tell you anything important, Constable. I didn't see much. I was in the fernery," Emma said in a tight voice and gestured towards the shade house screened by shrubbery.

"Tell me what you can, Miss, starting with your name," said the constable.

He carefully asked questions and took notes. Emma's face was pale, and shock was now making her quiver. The policeman's questions petered out, and the young constable looked at Emma kindly and said, "I think that will do Miss, from what you and Mr Miller have said, I'm sure the Sergeant will excuse you and you can make your way home. Perhaps, with the Sergeant's permission, you could escort Miss Payne to the tram stop, Mr Miller?"

Jacob nodded and gazed gravely at Emma, saying, "Would you care to sit down for a minute?"

"No, I'll be alright, I just want to get out of this place!" Emma gasped.

The constable hurried off to speak to the Sergeant. After a few minutes he returned and advised, "Be aware that you may well be called upon again to assist with our investigation, so please don't leave the district for the next three days. Other than that, the two of you are free to leave the Gardens and be on your way. Thank you."

Emma glanced up at the constable, and asked, "What will happen to the children?"

The constable shrugged sadly, before saying, "The nurses will look after them until a relative is contacted and comes by to collect them…. I think they have some details and the identity of their mother from papers in her purse."

The constable hooked a thumb in the direction of the forlorn body of the children's mother.

Emma nodded and sniffed. Jacob put an arm around her shoulders to comfort her. His grey eyes were so sad, so worried, she noticed.

"Come on," he said quietly, "do you need to catch a tram? Taxi?"

Emma nodded and answered in a broken voice, "The number 96 tram," and then with bravado, "I'll be OK!"

The two moved off towards Domain Road. Emma kept her eyes averted from the huddle of police and the sad, crumpled figure sprawled on the grass. She was spared noticing the other victims of the gunman.

Chapter 2

A search for a lunatic and an invitation

Emma had a disturbed weekend. She couldn't stop thinking about the little girls, the children of the first victim of the *Botanic Gardens Sniper*, as the newspapers now dubbed the mad man who had stalked five victims on that awful Thursday evening. She had been unproductive at work on Friday, and the supervisor had sent her home early – she was clearly traumatised by the incident in the Gardens. She had made multiple errors and was distracted.

Emma had left her small bedsit in Caulfield and travelled to her parents' home in St Kilda for the weekend. Her mother's fussing and her father's sensible conversation stopped her thoughts from pursuing and dissecting the little girls' trauma and overthinking her own. A walk on the beach and along the windswept St Kilda pier which extended out into Port Phillip Bay, blew the cobwebs from her mind and refreshed her attitude.

On Monday, Emma was back at work, feeling more resolute and ready to do battle for the *Repats* with her typewriter. She concentrated in a determined fashion and her fingers flew over the keys. By 10 o'clock she was looking forward to a good strong cup of tea and made her way to the staff tearoom.

The newspapers sprawled across the tearoom table, the headlines screamed all the details of the Botanic Gardens Tragedy: *Killer Breaks Loose, Botanical Gardens Converted into Slaughter Yards, Horrible Butchery by Maniacal Gunman, Melbourne Aghast in Horror.*

Although she was reluctant to revisit the trauma, Emma felt compelled to read the articles; she was desperate to learn what had become of the children. Sifting through the columns of close print, she discovered that the gunman, whose motive was still unknown, had entered the Botanic Gardens on that 'fateful evening', Thursday, 24 January 1924. He had calmly unwrapped a recently purchased .44 calibre Marlin repeating rifle, leaving the wrappings and a sales docket fluttering on the Eastern Lawns. These items later provided an excellent source of information and evidence for the investigating police officers. The docket led police to the gunsmith who had supplied the rifle and ultimately to the identity of the gunman, Norman Alfred List.

List had loaded the rifle with 'dum-dum' or soft nosed bullets before calmly wandering through the gardens, traversing three hundred yards in four minutes, and discharging his rifle over a dozen times. He had randomly shot and killed two people, and seriously wounded another three, one of whom subsequently died. After the shootings, the gunman had dumped the rifle near the reservoir, scaled the wrought iron railings and disappeared into the throngs of commuters on Domain Road.

The newspapers described the victims:

Mrs Eugenie Strobhaker (39), the mother of the three children, was killed outright. She died with her crochet work still in her lap, stained with her own blood.

Mrs Marie Parry (42) was shot in the back and head and fell, not far from Mrs Strobhaker. She had crawled a short distance towards the Strobhaker children as if trying to protect them. Mrs Parry survived, although badly injured.

Mr Frederick William McIlwaine (65), a tourist from Ireland, was fatally shot in the chest. The man was found, still sitting on the bench on the Eastern Lawn. His death was instantaneous.

Mr John Moxham (37) was shot in the hand and abdomen and lingered for a day before dying of his wounds. He had been picnicking with his young family on the Eastern Lawn.

Miss Mabel Podbury (42) was shot in the chest and seriously wounded. According to the hospital reports, she was making a slow recovery.

In one article, the police rebuked members of the public who, after the shooting, had rushed into the Gardens to gawk and had potentially provided the gunman with an opportunity to escape into the crowds. Immediately afterwards, the staff gardeners had been armed with tools and sticks and scoured the grounds but failed to find the suspect. Wild rumours circulated as to the gunman's motive and identity.

A homeless man stepped forward a few hours after the shootings and, as it turned out, falsely confessed to the crimes. His motive may have been that gaol was a better option than the struggle of homelessness on the streets of Melbourne in a period when the post-war economic collapse was starting to bite hard.

"He too, was probably another war veteran, unhinged by the horror of European battlefields!" thought Emma, relating the circumstances of the confessor to one of her cases which she had been typing up that morning.

Emma continued to read and discovered that the detectives heading up the case were Detective Sergeant Piggott and detectives Davy and McKerral. They had moved swiftly, following leads provided by the gunsmith to discover the suspect's family home in Richmond. They searched his bedroom and found pictures of rifles of a similar model to the one he had selected in the gun shop. The suspect, Norman List, had apparently been conducting thorough market research into an appropriate rifle with which to inflict maximum impact on his victims.

The detectives interviewed List's family: his sisters and father, with whom he had been living. The family told detectives that List was nomadic; before the war, he had travelled extensively in the USA and Mexico, fossicking for gold, and working on farms. He may have been a mercenary in the Mexican Border War and then, with the outbreak of war in Europe in 1914, he had boarded a ship and travelled to Britain to serve with the Territorial Force in the British Army. (Scottish Rifles #54140) After the war, he worked his passage home to Australia as a steward on a passenger liner. List then returned to Victoria in 1923. He had worked at a timber mill in Koetong, near Tallangatta and more recently, he had been employed on a farm in Laverton. The family described List as being of a very studious nature, keen on mathematics and astronomy. The detectives drew a very long bow and suggested that such serious studies must have scrambled his mind. They ignored the more obvious scenario of a disgruntled returned soldier, suffering from the trauma of war, perhaps unable to hold down a job and reaching crisis point. A recent photograph was provided of the suspect, which was printed in the newspaper and the public was encouraged to be on the lookout for the fugitive. Emma studied the grainy image.

"Yes," she whispered, "that's him!"

He was described as 31 years of age, but of a younger appearance. Height: 5'2, medium build, good shoulders, small waist. He was clean shaven, dark complexion, black, untidy hair. He had high cheek bones, prominent gold teeth in upper and lower arcades, a large mouth which moved in an odd fashion when he spoke and a large nose with a distinctive bump on the bridge. He spoke with a slight American accent. He was last seen in a dark grey suit, grey felt hat, stiff collar and bow tie.

Emma nodded to herself, agreeing with all aspects of the description, except, since she had not heard him speak, she was unable to corroborate his accent.

The newspaper reported that the police had mustered a huge "army" of detectives and constables who were scouring the city for the suspect, Norman List, who was now a declared fugitive. The police had retrieved List's service records from the authorities and noted he had been diagnosed with syphilis and would require ongoing treatment.

"Well, that would explain his erratic behaviour!" thought Emma, again referring to cases she had dealt with at the *Repat* Department.

The detectives urged that pharmacists and medical facilities be on alert for a man fitting the description, seeking necessary medication.

The gunsmith, Donald McIntosh of Bourke Street, reported that List "had wanted to purchase a rifle to go big-game hunting".

"He had an excellent knowledge of rifles and knew his brands and was very particular, although he did purchase lower velocity cartridges than was recommended for the model, because they were cheaper," commented the sales assistant.

"I did suggest to the fellow that the cartridges he had selected were unsuitable for kangaroo hunting because they would result in too much hide damage," added the salesman.

A grim mental image skittered across Emma's mind.

List purchased the rifle for £7/10 using an endorsed cheque, hence revealing his name, and the name of a contact who had originally written the cheque out in his favour. The contact was List's most recent employer at a Laverton farm. The details provided for the gunsmith's records included an address, care of the Seaman's Institute, Victoria Road, Melbourne. These details led the detectives to List's service records and actual address.

One newspaper article declared that Dr Jones, Inspector General of the Insane, was interviewed and expressed the following opinion:

"At the time of the shootings, List was suffering from paranoia, a chronic or systemic form of delusional insanity."

Dr Jones went on to boldly state that, "List is not a violent maniac that has run amok."

Despite Jones' assertions, the journalist stubbornly created a headline which declared, "*Search for Lunatic*".

Detective Piggott suspected that List had committed suicide after the shooting by throwing himself into the reservoir. He grimly stated to journalists: "The body should float after four days."

In a later edition, it was reported that the police planned to drag the reservoir since there had been no sightings of a *floater*.

After searching the newspaper articles, Emma felt lightheaded and anxious. She was disappointed that there was no word on the fate of the Strobhaker children, and she desperately hoped that they were loved and comforted. She returned to the typing pool and fiercely concentrated on her rattling typewriter keys, trying to rid her head of Norman List.

At lunchtime, the supervisor called Emma to the front desk.

"There is a gentleman here to see you!" he called, staring curiously at Emma as she swept out of the typing pool room.

Emma was worried. She expected that it would be a police officer wanting to interview her, but at the front desk, a tall wiry figure was casually leaning against the counter.

"Oh, Mr Miller!" Emma exclaimed.

Jacob looked a little shy, which Emma found endearing.

"Um, I wondered how you were faring after the drama of last week. I remembered that you had said you worked here... I just thought I would drop by and check up on you."

He smiled, apologetically, his cheeks were flushed.

"That is very kind of you! Thank you!" said Emma quietly.

She smiled in return, it was a quick burst of sunshine across her pretty face before continuing, "I am doing OK, but I am desperate for news of the children."

"I think they will be traumatised for a long time," said Jacob sorrowfully, "I read in one of the broadsheets that Mrs Strobhaker had invited her neighbour along to the picnic with her children, but the neighbour had a dream that something bad would happen and refused to go!"

"Oh, that is spooky!" said Emma with a chill tingling up her spine.

"The Strobhaker children are *in the care of their father with extended family helping* – that's all that is reported anyway," continued Jacob,

"Oh, and of course they still haven't found the shooter, although they have a suspect in their sights: Norman List."

Emma nodded sadly.

After a pause, during which Jacob's eyes earnestly searched Emma's face, he said, "Umm, would you like to have lunch or maybe dinner, some time? It may have to be later in the week, though I am afraid, I have some meetings and a project to complete at the office."

He faltered, worried that he may have sabotaged his chances by not offering a more immediate date. Maybe she might consider it crass to talk about a date on the tail of such a tragedy. He smiled, shyly, anxiously.

"Those deep grey eyes," thought Emma as she felt her emotions swirl.

"That is kind! How could I refuse?" she said brightly, before adding boldly, "Dinner, it is, on Friday!"

Relieved, Jacob quickly arranged to collect Emma after work on Friday. He left with a jaunty swing in his step and turned and waved before disappearing down the stairwell. Emma sighed and smiled to herself.

"Everything alright?" called her supervisor.

"Yes... All good!" said Emma, blushing, before quickly returning to her desk.

*An image of Norman List published
in the Victorian Police Gazette and
newspapers, January 1924*

CHAPTER 3

Dinner with a side of List

The week whirled by for Emma. She was on an emotional high and felt her heart skip and butterfly wings brushed the inside of her diaphragm whenever she thought of Jacob. For the first time in her life, she felt she was clutching boldly at an opportunity and snatching control of her own destiny. The excitement of it all was delicious. She knew next to nothing about the man she now considered to have been her *protector* in the Botanic Gardens, but the experience, the adrenaline rush of being close to death, caused her to ignore her usual caution.

"Carpe diem" she thought to herself, and then, with a much more risqué attitude, she thought, "Seize the man!"

On Friday evening, after she had rattled her way through the last sheaf of documents in her in-tray, she slipped into the cloakroom to change. She was just applying her lipstick when her friend, Julie, popped her head around the door frame. Julie whistled lewdly, admiring Emma's choice of outfit.

"Oooh, you look very swish! Knock him dead, girl!" said Julie.

Emma beamed.

"Not too much?" she asked.

"Never! You are beautiful! Oh, *He* is here, by the way! At the front desk. A very handsome fellow! 'Never know what you might find in the shrubbery of the Botanic Gardens!" Julie laughed, blew Emma a kiss, and disappeared.

Emma rechecked her makeup in the grimy mirror, patted down her dress, and straightened her stocking seams before she scooped up her purse and small bag of work clothes and left the cloakroom.

Jacob stood tall and smiled appreciatively when he saw Emma.

"Hello, Miss Payne. You look lovely!"

Emma blushed.

"Thank you!" was all she could manage.

Emma was flustered and unsure what she should say, so she added lamely, "'Ready to go?"

"Certainly! Your carriage awaits, Fair Maiden!" said Jacob with a flourish.

The restaurant was far more up-market than those which Emma usually frequented. Crisp white starched linen, the full quota of cutlery for dinner service, attentive waiters, a subdued tinkle of a piano from a distant corner, gentle lighting and a *ladies' menu* – with prices of the various dishes hidden from the view of the gentleman's guest. Emma felt slightly giddy. Jacob was charming and although initially, their conversation was a little stilted as they searched for topics and explored one another's intellect, they soon slipped into an easy conversation sprinkled with banter.

"That glass of a crisp white wine probably helped," thought Emma wryly as she considered how comfortable she felt with Jacob.

It wasn't long before the subject of the Botanic Gardens' atrocity flitted into their conversation. A slight chill descended but Jacob felt the need to press on and deliver the information.

"I suppose you know that Norman List is gone?" he asked quietly.

Emma looked up at him sharply, "Gone? Gone where?" she asked.

"The newspapers this evening reported that they had found his body, in Packenham, a possible suicide," said Jacob.

Emma paled.

"Oh, that's terrible! Well, I suppose, it is, ... although, I guess he has paid his dues, now," she said quietly.

"I'm not sure I agree, Emma. I think he has escaped justice and there will be little comfort for the families of the victims," said Jacob stiffly.

"Yes, you are probably right, Jacob," said Emma seriously before asking, "What happened to List? Where did they find him?"

"Oh, some of the details are a bit sketchy and others are a bit graphic," said Jacob carefully.

Emma was hooked.

"Go on," she said, inclining her head inquisitively.

"Well, the police had a tip off that he was in the area from an ex-merchant seaman at Kensington. The fellow informed them that he had come across a *swaggy*[1] that fitted List's description who was camped up in a bush block on the fringe of the suburb. The swaggy had been asking about the possibility of getting passage on a livestock ship going to Adelaide. Then, just this morning, another fellow who was out collecting ferns in the paddocks near Deep Creek, Packenham, found a body in the creek. 'Probably been dead a couple of days," said Jacob.

"How did they confirm the body to be that of List?" asked Emma curiously.

"His poor sister had to go to the morgue for a look. Apparently, his gold teeth and a tattoo on his arm was what they based the identification on," said Jacob.

"Oh, that would have been ghastly for the poor woman!" sighed Emma.

"Dr Henry Mollinson, the Police medical examiner, was to examine the body later and I guess the papers will have all the gory details next week!" exclaimed Jacob.

"Yes, journalists are like a dog with a bone on the subject. The newspapers are filled with details about List and the dreadful massacre. 'Not sure now, how much is fact or very embellished rumour!" said Emma sadly.

"Hmm, I know what you mean: yesterday, there was a report, purported to be quoting List's last employer, a farmer in Laverton... according to the man, List was victim of a 'disease that was driving him off his head' and he and List's sisters stated that he kept saying he was hearing voices and thought people had control of his mind. He was off his rocker!" exclaimed Jacob.

"Probably the final deterioration caused by syphilis" murmured Emma, before covering her mouth with a hand as she considered her statement stretched the limits of polite conversation.

She hurried on,

"With all this gossip and talk, the jury would surely have been swayed to convict him before his case even went to trial."

Jacob nodded in agreement before adding,

"He was heading for the noose, no matter what! Another of the victims, John Moxham died on Monday. List was ultimately responsible for the loss of four innocent lives, injuries to the other victims and utter disruption to the lives of countless others including those three little girls!"

The waiter excused himself and set food ladened plates before the pair. The aroma of rich gravy which spilled across a perfectly cooked cut of beef, crispy baked potatoes and steamed greens made Emma's mouth water. She smiled at the waiter and thanked him before turning her gaze on Jacob.

"Thank you for bringing me here tonight! I feel really spoilt!" she enthused.

"My pleasure, but let's talk about more cheerful subjects!" said Jacob and then smiled, delighted that he had impressed Emma.

She nodded in happy agreement and savoured her first mouthful.

Over dessert, the conversation settled on their work lives. Emma spoke gravely about how important her job was in relation to helping returned ex-service personnel and their immediate families to achieve deserved compensation for their sacrifice during the war, and assistance to start new lives. She intimated to Jacob that she was becoming quite distressed by the trauma and stories which she had to record and was thinking about a holiday or, in fact, moving to the country for a new start.

"Oh, where were you thinking of going to?" Jacob enquired looking alarmed.

"I have family in Walwa. It is a beautiful little village on the edge of the Murray River in the North of Victoria. My aunt is quite fragile, carrying another child, I could go and help with her other little ones or perhaps find work in Albury, which is not far away. I would just like to get back to nature, to sit on the bank of the river under a towering Red Gum and watch the water swirl by, listen to birds calling and cicadas singing."

"That sounds dreamy and romantic!" laughed Jacob, "Off to bury yourself in a quiet back water?"

Emma smiled again.

"That burst of sunshine!" thought Jacob as he admired her across the table.

"Well, I have news in a similar vein," he announced, "My manager wants me to transfer to Albury to set up our new office."

Emma smiled encouragingly, "A fresh start for both of us! Away from the drama and dreariness of Melbourne!"

After a little more discussion, Emma was convinced that they had been thrown together by fate and she was determined to hitch her wagon to Jacob's star. Impulsively she leapt to a decision.

"I will contact my aunt tomorrow and arrange to go and stay with her in Walwa. Once you are settled in Albury, you could come and visit! I can show you around *God's Own Country*!" she enthused.

Jacob cocked his head and looked at Emma thoughtfully.

"Yes, I would like that! I would like it a lot!" he said.

PROCEEDINGS BEFORE CORONERS.

INQUISITION.

VICTORIA }
TO WIT. }

AN INQUISITION for our Sovereign Lord King George V., taken at the Morgue, Melbourne, in the State of Victoria, the 26th. day of February A.D. 1924 in the fourteenth year of the reign of our said Lord the King, by me, Alexander Phillips gentleman, a deputy Coroner of our Lord the King for the said State, upon the view of the body of Norman Alfred List then and there lying dead.

Having inquired upon the part of our Lord the King, when, where, how, and by what means the said Norman Alfred List came by his death, I say that on the 1st. day of February 19 24 at Pakenham in the said State the said Norman Alfred List was found dead having died from haemorrhage from a wound in the arm, I am of opinion such wound was self inflicted. There is no evidence to determine the state of his mind at the time

First page of the Inquest record relating to Norman List - Public Records Office Victoria

Notes: An inquest was held on 26 February 1924 which found that Norman Alfred List had died of self-inflicted wounds on 3 February 1924. Norman Alfred List, (30 years), was the son of Charles Ward List and Adelaide Emma List, and had recently returned from a job in country Victoria to live in his family's home in Charles St, Richmond, Melbourne, the house in which he was born.

[1]*Swaggy or swagman – a term applied to an itinerant person, most often male, who walked from place to place seeking work. A swag or "Matilda" was the swaggy's bedding roll. Inside the roll was the swaggy's meagre possessions and the bundle was usually secured with a leather strap and carried over the shoulder.*

CHAPTER 4

Escape to the country.

Emma's aunt, Minnie Drummond, was overjoyed to hear from her niece. Emma was one of her favourites and with a new baby about to make its appearance any day, she would welcome any assistance that the young lass was willing to offer.

"I shall catch the Red Rattler up to Albury this Thursday, the seventh, and stay for a fortnight. A bit of a holiday and, of course, to help you, and then I will have to return to Melbourne to finish up with the Repat Department. I can come back again in a few weeks and find work and make the move a little more permanent."

"Watch out! Women are in short supply in the Upper Murray. You might find yourself a husband and become a very permanent feature of the Upper Murray!" teased her aunt.

Emma laughed cheerfully and thought to herself, "I might have already found one!"

She put the telephone receiver back on its cradle and daydreamed about her aunt's farm and its idyllic location. She was buoyed by her decision and looked forward to a break from the Repatriation Department and the inescapable stress of her job. Coincidentally, Jacob was scheduled to move to Albury on the same day, and they had arranged to share a carriage on the express train from the new Flinders Street Station to Albury. Emma's imagination ran riot conjuring a variety of potential romantic scenarios to be enjoyed on a day trip to Albury when confined to a carriage with Jacob as her only companion.

Emma's supervisor had been short with her when she had filed her request for leave, but in the end, he had reluctantly granted permission. She had been a conscientious employee, and the supervisor was aware how draining the task had been for the young woman. He had a certain fondness for Emma and thought a holiday would be refreshing after the trauma of witnessing the Botanic Gardens Tragedy.

A busy week at work and packing for her holiday caused the time to pass in a whirl. All too soon, it was Thursday morning, and Emma found herself standing under the array of clocks at Flinders Street station. It was 6:30am precisely, her ticket was in her hand, bags at her feet. She scanned the faces of commuters surging towards her, looking for Jacob. He was late. She was anxious. Had she been too forward, too rash?

She was startled by a voice calling her name from behind her. Emma spun around and found a smiling Jacob striding towards her.

"'Morning! I am so sorry I am a little late, I was just loading my trunk on the train with the porter! Are you ready to go?" said Jacob.

"Yes! Off on an adventure!" Emma said, bravely optimistic.

"Absolutely! A change is as good as a holiday, and you are getting both!" Jacob said as he bent down and gave Emma a demure but warm kiss on the cheek. His eyes raked her face and she knew instantly that he was holding back, being polite, but the chemistry between them was intense. Her stomach flip flopped, and her cheeks burnt. She smiled up at Jacob happily.

Jacob picked up the heavier of Emma's suitcases and juggled his hand luggage to accommodate the extra load. Emma scooped up her small second bag and almost skipped alongside Jacob. She was excited at the prospect of travelling to Albury with this handsome man with whom she felt such a deep connection.

Emma and Jacob boarded the train, found the compartment to which they had been allocated and slid into their seats. When another young couple and an elderly woman entered the compartment, Emma felt a surge of disappointment. Her dream of being alone with Jacob was dashed and the steamy scenarios she had conjured dissolved instantly, but she was comforted when Jacob slid his hand over hers and squeezed gently. Their eyes met, and they smiled conspiratorially. Soon the steam whistle blew, conductors yelled out instructions, doors were slammed shut and, with a shudder, the train gathered speed and lumbered out of the station.

The travelling companions introduced themselves and a friendly conversation, was initiated. After a while, Jacob produced a pack of playing cards from his pocket and the two young couples played gin rummy whilst the elderly lady read a book and contributed to their animated conversation about current events, and aspects of the countryside and the small villages that flashed passed the windows. Later, they purchased sandwiches, biscuits, and tea from the refreshment trolley which was propelled down the corridor by a porter.

"Train picnic!" quipped Emma as she tucked into her sandwich happily.

It was late afternoon by the time the train drew into the Albury Railway Station. Emma felt crumpled and hot. Her heart sank as she realised that she would have to part from Jacob's company. She had known all along that he would be staying on in Albury to take up his post, and she would be collected from the station by her uncle and whisked off to the Upper Murray, but she was still saddened that the time had come to part ways. As hand luggage was retrieved from the overhead racks, the group bade fond farewells to one another and then exited the train. Jacob helped Emma to assemble her luggage on a bench near the ticket office. He took Emma's hand and gazed into her eyes gravely, as he said, "Well, Emma this is it, for the present. I will have to go and retrieve my trunk from the porter... do you think you will be right here, until your uncle finds you? Or would you like me to come back and wait with you...?"

Emma smiled wistfully before saying, "No, I will be fine! He should be here momentarily, I expect. Once I'm settled in, in Walwa I will make contact, perhaps a telephone call or a letter to your office? Perhaps you might like to visit? A picnic on the Murray River?"

Emma bit her lip and silently berated herself for prattling on.

Jacob grinned, "I am a bit jumpy about picnics after what happened! But yes, I would love to see you again! I'll send a message care of the Walwa post office and provide my telephone number and address. We can then plan to see one another!"

Emma smiled with a sense of relief and something else, a warm sensation around her heart.

A middle-aged man bustled up to the pair.

"Emma! So lovely to see you again, my dear!" he cried and hugged her affectionately.

He stepped back from Emma and looked with open curiosity at her companion. She hastened to introduce the men and provided a summary as to their connection.

"Good Heavens, Emma! What a terrible experience! I read all the newspaper reports but had no idea you were so close to the tragedy! No wonder you need a holiday!"

Albert Drummond clasped Jacob's hand in his own.

"Thank you so much for looking after my niece, Mr Miller! Where are you staying, can we give you a lift to your accommodation?"

"That would be very helpful, Mr Drummond, Thank you! I just need to get my trunk. I have a room booked at Sodens Hotel."

"Albert, please, Jacob! What a coincidence! I have booked rooms for Emma and myself at Sodens, too! We will have to overnight and get an early start to travel home tomorrow."

Emma smiled gratefully, pleased that her time with Jacob was to be extended.

Whilst waiting for Jacob to gather his luggage, Emma and her uncle chatted. She caught up with a summary of her Walwa relatives' summer activities and their bush Christmas. Jacob returned after a few minutes with a porter close on his heels, pushing a trolley bearing his luggage. Albert led the way through the rather grand station building and out to his vehicle, a dusty farm truck. The tray was loaded with supplies ready to be taken up to the farm. The men added Emma and Jacob's luggage to the load in the tray and then Jacob helped Emma clamber up into the cab alongside her uncle. He followed and soon Emma was firmly sandwiched between the men. She felt a tingle at the sensation of Jacob's thigh firmly pressed against hers. She blushed and smiled secretively up at Jacob.

On the short trip to the hotel, Albert arranged to meet up with Jacob in the hotel dining room to share an evening meal.

"I will just get Emma settled into her room - I expect she would like to freshen up!" said Albert, glancing at Emma with concern.

Emma nodded happily in agreement and was ecstatic at the thought of dining with Jacob.

Dinner was an animated affair. Jacob and Albert found they had common interests in cricket and fishing and the conversation flowed freely. They briefly touched on the Botanic Gardens Tragedy and Albert pondered what might have caused a man to go on a shooting spree and to kill innocent picnickers.

"The man must have been a monster!" exclaimed Albert.

"Syphilis, apparently!" stated Jacob, before apologising to Emma and Albert for being somewhat impolite.

Emma smiled reassuringly.

"Oh, it's nothing, don't worry! My mind has been broadened with all the cases I have been dealing with and typing up at the Repat Department! I am not a fragile petal!"

Albert noticed Emma was looking weary after her long journey.

"Come along, my dear, we mustn't keep Jacob from his rest and we too, will need to leave at the crack o' dawn tomorrow! Thank you again, for escorting my niece on the train and keeping her safe during that terrible event in Melbourne, Jacob. We will, no doubt, see you again soon! Good night, Sir!"

Albert smiled knowingly at Jacob and both men rose and shook hands. Jacob helped Emma to her feet and said goodnight to her with his gentle grey eyes stroking her face. Emma lingered but her uncle stepped up to chaperone mode and slipped his arm through Emma's and led her firmly from the dining room. After opening the bedroom door for Emma, he wished her goodnight and retired to his own room. Emma shut the door and threw herself on the bed and lay looking up at the ceiling rose, smiling to herself. Jacob had captured her heart, and she fervently hoped that he would be firmly entrenched in her future.

Sodens' Australia Hotel c1930 - State Library NSW

CHAPTER 5

Up the Murray River

Emma was roused by gentle knocking on her door and her uncle's anxious voice: "Emma, Emma, come along sleepy head! We need to make some dust and head to Walwa!"

"Yes, thank you Uncle Albert, I won't be long!" she called softly.

"I'll meet you in the dining room when you're ready. A quick breakfast and then we'll be off! Leave your luggage, I'll get the porter to pop up and fetch it down," directed Albert.

"I shall be quick!" assured Emma and leapt out of bed.

Drawing the curtains, she gazed out across the dark street. There was no one about. A subtle pink flush in the sky to the East announced the dawn.

She lit the small lamp on the dresser and gazed at her reflection in the mirror. Her hair was tousled, strands escaped from the thick auburn plait which lay over her shoulder. Emma sighed, disappointed that her nose was cursed with freckles but content with her overall appearance.

She poured water from the jug into the bowl and washed her face and hands. Stripping off her night gown and, standing naked in front of the mirror, she examined her body critically before soaping and rinsing quickly. Afterwards she dried herself, chafing at her skin, feeling a little chilled. She dressed swiftly, choosing practical clothes for the journey to the farm. She undid the plait and raked a brush through her hair. She captured the tendrils and smoothed her hair before recreating the plait and adding a pale blue ribbon to match her blouse.

Finally, she repacked her suitcase, checked the room to ensure she had not missed anything and hurried off to meet her uncle in the dining room. Other guests were yet to rouse, and Emma and her uncle Albert, had the undivided attention of the waiter. He brought a pot of tea and poured for the two guests. He slipped away and returned with a dish of creamy yellow butter and a small silver toast rack laden with hot toast. He took their order for bacon and poached eggs and disappeared through the clacking swing doors to the kitchen.

Albert smiled benignly at Emma: "Did you sleep well, My Dear?"

"Dreamless sleep…I think I was gone before my head hit the pillow, thank you Uncle Albert! And you?"

"I was awake for a while, checking the list of stores and chores to make sure I had everything ticked off before we left this morning, but then, yes, I slept well, thank you!" murmured Albert.

He attended to buttering his toast before saying carefully, "You seem quite taken with young Jacob. Do your parents approve?"

Emma blushed and giggled with embarrassment.

"Oh, Ma and Pa haven't met Jacob… it has been a bit of a whirlwind! The nasty incident in the Botanic Gardens tipped me towards a impetuous decision to have a break from the city. Jacob asked me out to dinner and, as it turned out, he was assigned a transfer to his employer's office in Albury. I certainly like Jacob; he is kind and amusing…."

She looked away to hide the longing in her eyes before finishing awkwardly, "We are just friends!"

The waiter saved her from further interrogation as he returned with fragrant plates of food. Breakfast was comprised of crispy slabs of bacon, thick slices of fried tomatoes and perfectly poached eggs.

It was just on 7am when Albert set the last piece of luggage in the tray of the truck and helped Emma up the step into the cabin. He closed the door carefully and strode around to the driver's door.

"Here we go then!" he called out with genuine pleasure at the thought of going home.

He started the engine, allowed it to splutter, settle and warm up, before pulling away from the kerb and they commenced their journey to Walwa.

As they crossed the Hawksview bridge over the Murray River, the cloudless sky was bright with morning sun, the temperature was rising, and the scenery was stunning. Albert provided a running commentary on the scenery, the weather over the preceding few weeks, the prospects for crops and livestock and a general catch up on the Drummond clan. He enthused about the works at the Hume Dam wall site and described what an engineering feat it was to be, how it would change the landscape and the approach to Albury. He swung his arm indicating the river flats and farmland which edged down to the snaking width of the Murray River.

"All will be gone! All under water!"

"Were the farmers compensated for the land? Are any homes going to be lost?" asked Emma, wondering if the government had got this form of compensation right after her experience with the Repat Department.

"I understand the rate was between £10 and £12 per acre depending on quality of land. Many buildings in the village of Bowna will be literally raised off their stumps and moved. I am not sure of compensation for homes that cannot be moved," said Albert thoughtfully.

He frowned as he considered the complexities of moving an entire house. Emma settled back in the seat with a sense of genuine contentment. She loved the bucolic scenery and was touched by her uncle's clear affection for herself and his family. She listened eagerly to his bubbly conversation and rarely had need to contribute.

The road hugged the riverbank on the Victorian side of the Murray. It was sinuous and bumpy. There were frequent creek crossings and some savage wash-aways. Emma was thankful that the weather was clear as she imagined that the road would become treacherous in winter. The country was superb, stands of graceful, but massive eucalypts dotted the paddocks and lined the riverbanks. The number of ringbarked stumps provided a graphic indication of the demand for timber by colonists and their impact of the natural environment as they converted grassy woodlands to almost clear-felled paddocks. The grass was summer bronzed and the livestock, the heavy horned Herefords, roan Shorthorns, and dusty sheep, grazed in a determined fashion across the clearings. Sheets of reedbeds swept to the water's edge. The rocky slopes were softened by clumps of shrubs and bracken fern. Birds flitted across their path, and Emma could see a variety of waterbirds feeding on the edge of the Murray. The river sparkled as it slid passed the banks and crept amongst the reedbeds. Mobs of kangaroos were startled as the truck rattled and thundered past. Youngsters scattered, but the older does and huge bucks just stood and gazed solemnly at the intruders. The grey kangaroos stood tall and alert, ears flicking, balanced on toes and tail, ready to flee but conserving energy, assessing the threat.

Over the preceding millennia, the Murray River had carved a passage between the hillsides creating a wide valley. At times, the steep embankments rose sharply from the road where gangers had hewn the roadway from the shoulders of the hills, on the high ground away from flood ways and swamps. The sight of tumbled rock strewn across some paddocks as if thrown by a great force from the hillsides, caused Emma to wonder about the possibility of ancient volcanoes. A few homesteads appeared: They were set back from the road and were simple structures of slab construction with shingle or brush rooves and rock chimneys. The homes were few and far between and Emma pondered the lonely lifestyle of the settlers. Her contemplations were interrupted as Albert drew up at the driveway of a property, seemingly in the middle of nowhere.

"I just have a parcel to drop off here, Emma. The old fella who lives over yonder doesn't travel to town much. I usually pick up some goods for him and drop them off when I pass," said Albert cheerfully.

Emma smiled and gazed around the landscape. The fences looked to be in disrepair and the cattle standing in the shade of a couple of Grey box trees looked pinched and sad. Albert hopped out of the cab before swinging himself up to the tray of the truck. He manoeuvred an awkward looking bundle to the edge of the tray before swinging it down as he stepped back. He placed the bundle just behind the gate post, a post so large that it looked like it was simply a decapitated tree with gate fittings attached.

As Albert settled himself behind the wheel, he blasted the horn twice. Emma flinched at the discordant blaring and then chuckled at her over-reaction.

"Sorry, Lass, that is just to let him know his parcel has arrived!" said Albert with a grin.

"Maybe we should have dropped it at his home," Emma suggested gazing up the driveway towards a small house slumped near a rock formation.

"Oh, it's alright... he is a bit of recluse... has been since the troubles..." said Albert enigmatically.

Emma cocked an eyebrow at Albert curiously. He grinned and explained:

"Old Andy was brought to Thollogolong district as a young lad, son to one of James Redhall's party, the manager of Thollogolong Station at the time. He was brought up on stories of the first selectors, the Spaldings. The Spalding party arrived in the 1830's, marked out boundaries, built a couple of dwellings, brought in some livestock and stuck it out for a few years. They cleared the land as was required by Government decree. The blacks were none too keen about their hunting grounds being fenced, their scar trees being felled and white fellas taking over, so they started hunting sheep and cattle – livestock proved more accommodating targets than kangaroos! There were reprisals from the Spaldings, but they were soon forced off by marauding blacks, after two white fellows were speared. By the time Old Andy's family came along, there was still an uneasy relationship with the Aboriginals. His old man came up with some sort of truce with the head man of the tribe. The agreement may have been weighted with lead. Even today, Andy has a shotgun mounted above the door lintel!" said Albert lightly.

"Do you mean that he would have shot the Aboriginal people?" asked Emma incredulously.

"The Aborigines don't understand land ownership – this misunderstanding creates tensions… the better armed you are, the more chance you have of hanging on to your land," said Albert simply.

"*Their* land," thought Emma.

"Nowadays, Andy is an old man, and since his son was a casualty of the war, and his wife died of a broken heart, he is a bitter and dour old man. He has had a tough life and now he just marks time, waiting for the pearly gates to open," said Albert sombrely.

They rumbled over a bridge spanning a meagre creek.

"This is Flaggy Creek," announced Albert.

"What an odd name for the little creek!" chirped Emma, happy to have changed topic.

"It is not always so restrained," laughed Albert, "just a few years back, it provided a cause for concern for Allan Withers, the Crawford and Company mail contractor. It had belted down over a hundred points of rain one night in mid-1916. The creek was running a banker, but Mr Withers was determined to get his load of mail and a couple of passengers through to Corryong in accordance with a tight schedule. Withers and his vehicle plunged into the torrent and soon the engine was flooded and stopped."

"Oh heavens!" gasped Emma, "Were they swept away?"

She was dreading another dark story.

Albert laughed, "Nope, Withers got wet feet wading and walking to get old Peter Sutherland and his trusty draughthorse. The pair had the technique down pat for extricating travellers from that creek! They hauled out the vehicle, but Withers had learnt his lesson and concluded that the weather was against them, so he and his passengers spent the weekend at the Sutherlands'!"

"So, the mail doesn't always get through!" laughed Emma.

"The downfalls of country living!" said Albert with a regretful grin.

A few miles further along the road, Albert pulled up so that they could stretch their legs. He parked under a gracefully drooping eucalypt. When he cut the engine, Emma was overcome by the silence of the bush. They stepped away from the truck and strolled down to the edge of the Murray which was broad but shallow at this point. Clear tannin-stained water rushed over a tumble of rocks. Emma's eyes drank in the sights; she revelled in the astounding beauty of nature. A massive tree trunk which had run aground during the winter floods, was adorned by a cormorant. It perched on a fractured branch with its wings hung out to dry. Its keen beady eyes were fixed on the humans, alert for danger. A mob of galahs squabbled in the tree above Emma. She stood and watched as the birds played and foraged, hanging upside down, pecking at one another, whilst others edged up and down the branches, pecking at the flowers and gumnuts. Every now and then, the mob would squark and take flight before wheeling around and once more alighting in the trees. There were other birds, more than Emma could identify and the incessant high-pitched racket of cicadas assaulted her ears. She laughed when she remembered that she had earlier thought the place quiet.

"Thirsty?" inquired Albert.

Emma spun around to see her uncle was filling a waterbag from the river. He was balanced on some rocks, leaning out into the cool depths to capture the fresh water in his waterbag. She discovered that she was indeed thirsty and went towards the riverbank to meet him. He passed the waterbag up to her and she awkwardly manoeuvred the heavy wet hessian clad bag to angle the spout into her mouth. She spilled some down her chin, soaking her shirt, but she appreciated the fact that the damp cloth was cooling.

"We had better get on or we won't be home before dark!" called Albert cheerfully as he cranked the engine to life.

As they approached a tight corner a few minutes later, Albert noticed a dust cloud drifting toward the river. He intuitively pulled to the left and, as they rounded the corner, they found themselves confronted by an oncoming bullock team. Emma was fascinated as she had never before seen such a thing. The bullocks were enormous, heavy horned beasts of multiple colours. The team was comprised of sixteen animals harnessed in pairs to draw a long, narrow dray with huge bales of wool packed on tight and high. The bullocky walked next to his team. He was a wiry, short man with a low-slung hat, dusty pants and sweat stained shirt. He wielded a long whip set on a shaft. He stopped, pushed back his hat, and then grinned broadly when he recognised Albert.

"Albert!" he roared, "Fancy meeting you here! These are your bales... off to the wool stores in Albury!"

"I thought we might meet you along here somewhere! How goes the toil?" asked Albert.

The bullocky called to his leaders who were continuing around the cutting without him, "Ho Johnny, Ho Baz!"

The team slowed and halted, blowing quietly. The bullocks' tails switched flies, and the harness jingled as they shifted. A dark coloured, lean dog slipped under the dray. He lay in the shade, panting and watching the man and bullocks with bright, tawny eyes. The man coiled his whip and stepped up to the truck. He swung himself up onto the running board to lean in the window for a chat. He looked curiously at Emma, his eyes twinkling. A rich aroma of sweat, tobacco and campfire smoke swirled into the cabin. Emma didn't find it offensive, just earthy and natural. His face was leathery, weathered by years of sun exposure, but his eyes were bright blue, piercing and alive. His smile was warm and genuine; his voice had a sing-song intonation. Emma could imagine him calling to his bullocks to guide and urge them on. Albert introduced the pair, and they exchanged pleasantries before they said their farewells and moved off into each other's dust.

"His must be a lonely life!" said Emma pensively.

"Oh, when he is amongst people, he is the life of the party! He has yarns and jokes... although some of them are quite unsuitable for polite company! He loves his boys, the bullocks! He's happy with his lot!"

"Where is his home?" asked Emma.

"He works for the Gadds, at The Glen. He has a humpy near the shearing shed."

"Humpy?" frowned Emma with mild confusion.

"A fairly rustic hut!" explained Albert, grinning.

"Does he have family?" asked Emma.

"I guess he must ... somewhere, but no wife that I know of."

Emma pondered the bullocky's lot: absolute freedom, outdoors, energetic but lonely.

The truck laboured up a steep incline. Albert had crunched the gear box to select the lowest gear and was leaning forward over the steering wheel as if to urge the machine up the hill. He looked concerned and Emma glanced at his sweating face with some anxiety. He caught her eye and grinned ruefully,

"She's getting on a bit, the old girl, and I might have loaded her a bit heavy! No worries, though, if she cracks it, we can always go up in reverse!"

Emma looked shocked.

"Oh, it's all good, lass. The reverse gear has greater torque!" said Albert confidently.

Emma wasn't sure what he meant but gazed determinedly out of the windscreen, also willing the vehicle onwards.

They eventually crested the hill, and a magnificent vista opened before them. Albert halted the truck. He put the hand brake on firmly and left the vehicle in gear before swinging himself from the cab. He stepped round the front of the truck and helped Emma to the ground, before walking a short distance to a cluster of rocks beneath a massive, contorted red gum. From this vantage point they could view the Murray River as it swung around Abraham's Bosum, a broad-based peninsula which projected towards the Northwest, forcing the river to swing around and almost back on itself before continuing its journey of thousands of miles, downstream towards the South Australian coast. It was a fabulous view and below them they could see the fertile silt flats, currently sown down to tobacco. Over the razor back, on the Eastern approach, Jersey and Shorthorn cattle grazed contentedly.

"Jack Cook's Dairy," murmured Albert, "Not far, now, to home!"

As they meandered back to the truck, they flushed a pair of rabbits from the grass.

"Bloody vermin!" huffed Albert, "Rabbits are beyond control! They eat everything!"

He helped Emma back into the truck before returning to the driver's seat, starting the vehicle, and continuing his dissertation on the topic of rabbits.

"Some idiot thought to bring them in from the Old Country, to make colonists feel more at home or to provide some familiar tucker. Six rabbits became thousands in a few years. 'Fed up with eating rabbit now! I suppose they do provide work for some – and the pelts are worth a bit. Young Claude Batson has it down pat... he works for several of the neighbours as a rabbit trapper. He had a real crack at Alf Lawrence's place last year. The tenant had let the place go. It became a court case in the middle of the year when the Lawrences sued the tenant, William Rae, for breach of lease contract. Batson gave evidence in court that he had killed four thousand rabbits and dug out eight hundred burrows within a week or so."

Emma gasped, "Four thousand rabbits!"

"Yes! He reckons that on one night he trapped and shot a thousand of the buggers, and at a shilling a pair, he made a tidy sum from the harvest!"

After a moment of thought, Albert added, "Some say that Batson is a bit simple, but he did give the rabbit plague some careful thought. He and Alf Lawrence put in a patent application for some cunning poison and delivery method which Batson had invented, assured, they said, of wiping out the rabbits! Last year, there was a bit of a hoo-ha - the Agriculture Department officials and local landowners gathered to watch Batson give a demonstration of the poison and technique.... Not sure what went wrong, but it failed. Happy rabbits gambolled from the warrens, and the gathering gave Batson a rough time. Laughed at him by all accounts. Batson went to ground and was furious!"

Albert looked thoughtful for a while contemplating rabbits and the local lad.

"He must have had some confidence in the poison that he had invented, if he was prepared to demonstrate to the Department and a group of farmers," said Emma thoughtfully.

"Not sure that Batson would have had the nouse to set up the demonstration, maybe Lawrence hung him out to dry. I haven't seen "Dilly" and "Ding" about for a while."

Emma shot a questioning look at Albert. He laughed.

"Batson was nicknamed "Dilly" by the young blokes at the Butter Factory when he worked there. I am not sure whether it was a dig at his competence or rather, lack thereof. You know, 'Silly Dilly' or 'a bit of a dill" or the fact he often carries his belongings in a dilly bag, like the aborigines. Either way, he didn't last long in the employment of the Butter factory. The new manager, David Sheppard, let him go, soon after he arrived to take over the management of the factory. Oh, and Batson called his dog "Ding". It's a rangy looking yellow mongrel, probably bred from a dingo. He and the dog are often seen stalking the hills, hunting. He is a sure-fire shot; he wins all the rifle club competitions. Ding, the dog, flushes game and retrieves the shot rabbits."

"Where does he live?" asked Emma, more to keep the conversation going, than out of curiosity. She was getting weary after a long trip.

"He lives up on Lawrences' hill in a hut – a loner he is. He used to board with the Barbers when he was working for them.... Barber is a dairyman, near the Butter Factory. Oh, and in recent times, he has become a tobacco farmer! Barber and a share farmer, Richard King, grow tobacco on contract for the British Australasian Tobacco Company... worth three shillings per pound, I hear! Might be a better option than milking cows! Well, Batson often goes to the Barbers' home for a meal. Mrs Barber has a soft spot for the fellow, gives him odd jobs around their homestead."

The vehicle rounded the final corner, and another magnificent vista was revealed. Emma eagerly peered from the window casting her gaze across the undulating paddocks dotted with sheep. On the rise, commanding a fabulous view of the Murray River, was a magnificent homestead. It was constructed of whitewashed weatherboards, encircled by a wide verandah and topped with an iron roof. Productive fruit trees dotted the garden.

"Well, here we are!" called out Albert as he swung the truck into the broad driveway. The avenue of poplars was lush and green, casting deep shade on the drive. Dogs and children rushed out to meet the truck with great excitement. Albert pulled up in the drive and hopped down from the truck, sweeping the youngest child up into his arms, laughing. The children were chattering ten to the dozen.

"Hold on, troops! You are deafening! You remember your cousin? This is Emma!" announced Albert.

Emma had climbed down from the truck and was standing on the edge of the group looking amused. Albert rattled off the children's names as they jostled for position. Emma looked up as a woman appeared on the verandah. She leant on the rail looking tired and heavily pregnant. She smiled gently at Albert as he called to her: "Minnie, me darlin'!"

It was said with a great deal of softness and love in his tone. He put the small child back down on the ground alongside his scampering siblings and a tribe of dogs, and hurried to his wife, taking her gently in his arms. He kissed her warmly and enquired as to her wellbeing.

Minnie shrugged him off with mild embarrassment, "Oh, I'm all good, been here before!" she laughed, wafting her hand towards the rabble of children and the swell of her belly.

"Come on in, Emma, let's have tea!" she said invitingly to her weary young guest.

A bullocky and his team - from the collection of Jim Harvey, Walwa Station

CHAPTER 6

Drummond family fun in the sun

The Drummonds were extraordinarily hospitable to Emma. She felt so blessed. The children were ecstatic to have their attractive young cousin come to visit; she provided a fresh audience for their antics and a guest with whom to explore the paddocks and riverbank. Emma was woken early on Friday morning with two of the youngsters bouncing on her bed.

"C'mon Emma! Wake up! Mam says we can show you the swimming hole. It's hot outside!"

She sat up in bed and laughed at the pair.

"Heavens, no rest for the wicked here! Give me a tick to get dressed and I will be along."

The children bolted out of the room, crashing the door shut as they fled.

Emma ran her hands through her tousled hair and then swung her legs out of bed. She went to the window and gazed out across the orchard. It was bright and sunny; cicadas were singing in the grass, and she could see a multitude of brightly coloured parrots flitting amongst the trees. Emma felt a surge of joy; she loved this branch of her family tree and the beautiful Upper Murray environment. She splashed her face with water from the pretty China bowl, which was upon the dresser. The home-made soap set on the crisp white washcloth, was coarse and heavily scented with lavender; fragments of the dried flowers dotted the surface.

Dressing quickly in a gaberdine skirt and a light blouse, Emma luxuriated in the freedom of not wearing stockings and instead, pulled on a pair of socks and her ankle boots. She had been on jaunts across the paddocks before and knew to dress in a practical, rather than fashionable mode.

Emma entered the kitchen, and her aunt directed her to join the rowdy group of children at the long dining room table. There were plates of toast, rich home churned butter and a bowl of boiled eggs.

"Help yourself," called Minnie, "I'll just bring in a pot of tea!"

"Oh, I feel bad! I came to help you, Aunt Minnie!" Emma protested.

"You can be a guest this morning, I will put you to work this afternoon! A slave will be wonderful!" laughed Minnie delightedly.

After breakfast, the children were impatient to start the excursion. They helped to clear the table under sufferance, whilst Minnie packed a basket with biscuits wrapped in a tea towel, two bottles of homemade lemon cordial, some enamel cups and two towels. She handed a broad brimmed hat to Emma and said with a smile, "Pop this on, Love, the sun is savage! Your freckles are charming, but we don't want to ruin your complexion!"

"You aren't coming, Aunt Minnie?" asked Emma.

"No, I am really looking forward to a couple of hours of peace!" said Minnie.

With that, they heard whistling from the verandah and Albert popped his head around the door jamb.

"Are the explorers ready?" he called out with a grin.

The children hurtled out of the door giggling and chattering.

Minnie escorted the crew to the gate and, as Emma ducked under the weeping eucalypt that stood on the boundary, Minnie broke off a switch of leaves which she handed to her niece.

"Here, you might need this! The little black flies are determined to crawl on your face at this time of the year. I find flicking a switch of leaves as you walk is better than swallowing a fly!"

Emma laughed and took the switch, flicking it in a few practice sweeps.

Albert carried the basket and walked alongside Emma, the children trotted ahead, occasionally returning to bring "treasures" for Emma to see: Cicada shells, shards of quartz, and particularly long eucalypt leaves. She murmured appreciative comments to the bearer of the treasure and firmly returned them to the finder, raising her hands apologetically and laughing, "No pockets!"

The walk to the river followed a well-worn path through a couple of paddocks and associated gates. A flock of sheep watched the group solemnly before dropping their heads to continue to graze the sun-dried stubble. A small mob of steers in the paddock alongside the river were more curious and cantered boisterously towards the group.

Emma anxiously called out, "Ooooh, will they charge us, Uncle Albert?"

"Nah, they are just curious! They'll pull up!" Albert assured her.

The children were bunched together in formation ahead of the adults. Suddenly they simultaneously shot off, squealing and racing to the huge gum that marked the position of the swimming hole. The steers were startled and skidded to a halt before galloping off with their tails held high, in the opposite direction.

Emma laughed happily.

The riverbank formed a natural crescent with a silty beach stretching to the water. The gum tree cast an impressive shadow. The children stripped off, dumping their clothes in piles on the riverbank. The boys entered the water in their underwear, the girls modestly remained in slips and bloomers. Emma sat on the bank and stripped off her boots and socks before hitching up her skirt and wading into the deliciously cool water. Albert set down the basket and spread the two towels on the grass. He sat on one of the towels and carefully watched the children, calling them to come closer to the bank if they strayed out towards the current. He was not a skilled swimmer and took his job very seriously to monitor the children. The Murray River was notorious for being a surreptitious killer.

"Even the strongest of swimmers can be caught in the current and swept under the snags," he advised loudly as he considered the list of local drowning victims who were now all resident in the Walwa cemetery or lost for good.

Soon, Emma returned to the bank and stretched out on the grass alongside her uncle.

"They are like fish!" she laughed, watching the children splash and play in the shallows.

"Can they swim?" she added.

"They can probably keep themselves afloat but no, not able to swim. It would be good to have baths like at St Kilda, so the children can have swimming lessons," he mused before adding, "Can you swim, Emma?"

"Yes, we had swimming lessons at school. The boys were better at swimming than the girls … less fettered by their outfits, I think!" she said with a rueful grin as she thought about the drag of fabric around her limbs during swimming lessons.

Their conversation ranged across several subjects. Emma appreciated how congenial her uncle was. He was easy to talk to and had detailed knowledge across a broad range of subjects and current events. He studiously avoided mentioning the Botanic Gardens shootings as Minnie had impressed upon him not to upset Emma by stirring up uncomfortable memories. He did, however, drill her on her work in the Repatriation Department and they discussed the devastating impact of the war on returned service men and the prospects of the Soldier-Settler Scheme to bolster the populations of the bush communities.

"The scheme includes ex-Navy types, but what would a seaman know about farming?" asked Albert scornfully.

"Many of the fellows across all the services of the AIF, came from farms, and those that didn't, have benefitted from the education provided as part of the demobilisation process. On board the troop ships coming back from Europe, they ran courses in everything from typing and shorthand to farm animal management and crop production."

Albert looked impressed.

"Afterall, they had anything up to five hundred men and of course, the nurses, on board for six weeks or so, so there was plenty of time to kill. They had to keep them occupied or boredom created issues!" said Emma thoughtfully.

Albert nodded sagely, thinking to himself that confinement on a ship with nothing to do, would have driven him mad.

Soon the children tired of water activities and came up the bank from the "beach", their bodies were dripping, and their long brown limbs glistened. They stretched out on the grass in the sun to dry. Emma noticed their nut-brown skin, tanned by the sun and she surmised that trips to the river were frequent occurrences.

Albert delved into the basket and produced the cups and cordial. He poured two cups and offered one to Emma, she took it gratefully. The other cup was passed to the eldest child.

"Now you lot, share... no guzzling!" he admonished with a grin.

He unwrapped the biscuits and handed a crisp golden oat biscuit to each child and one to Emma.

"Delicious!" she exclaimed.

"Minnie is a pretty good cook!" said Albert proudly.

The children told Emma all about school and their friends, and how they rode their ponies over the hill to the Mt Alfred school. Emma thought they were amazingly capable for such small persons.

"And what has happened to lessons today?" asked Emma as it occurred to her that it was Friday.

Albert grinned and said, "Special occasion.... a visitor from a distant realm! It's not often we have a young cousin visit, and the children were keen to introduce you to their world!"

Emma grinned at each child in turn and hugged the small boy next to her making him squirm and giggle.

After a drowsy period of reflection, whilst listening to the chatter of the children and calls of birds; watching the wide brown river as it swirled passed the bank, and savouring the last morsels of the golden syrup-sweet biscuits, Albert announced:

"C'mon you lot, we had better get on back home and make sure Mam is alright. You girls carry the towels; I will take the basket."

They set off up the track. The children were a little more subdued on the way home, dawdling along in file. Just as they approached the first gate, the two children in the lead froze and hissed: "Snake!"

The party froze. Emma paled; she felt her stomach do flip flops...she had a mortal dread of snakes. Albert shot out a hand and grasped Emma by the elbow.

"It's alright, Em! Just stand quiet and still like the children. Snakes aren't keen to have people for lunch; they only strike if startled or stepped on. If we all just stand still, the snake will go about its business and move off."

Albert was so calm and controlled that Emma felt immediately relieved.

"She's gone now! 'Under that log on the fence line," called Kate who was heading up the party.

"What type of snake was it, Kate?" asked Albert.

"Red Belly!" Kate replied.

"Are they poisonous?" asked Emma fearfully.

"Yes, but they aren't as aggressive as the brown buggers. Red Bellies are more inclined to slither off, rather than come after you!" stated Albert.

Emma looked horrified.

"Do you kill them?" she asked.

"They're terrific at keeping mice and rats down! I guess they have a right to live, too, so in general, we let them alone. However, if they take up residence in the garden or close to the house, I usually dispatch them, just because it is a bit awkward if they find their way into the dunny or choose to sun themselves in amongst the vegetables in the veggie patch," said Albert with a grin.

Emma made a mental note to be cautious on her approach to the *dunny*, the outside privy.

Albert called to the children as they approached the gate to the house yard:

"Go play in the garden for a while, don't come in and disturb your Mam, in case she is having a nap!"

As they stepped up onto the verandah, Emma and Albert noticed Minnie sitting in the big old rocking chair, her feet were perched up on a cushion on top of a footstool. She smiled as they approached.

"No, not sleeping, just resting! This bairn is intent on kicking its way out!" said Minnie with a grimmace.

Emma was concerned and hurried to her aunt.

"Don't worry, lass... it's all normal - better to feel them moving, than a still baby!" said Minnie soothingly.

"Would you like a cup of tea, Aunt Minnie?" asked Emma solicitously.

"That would be lovely, I told you I would put you to work this afternoon!" Minnie grinned.

Emma hastened to the kitchen. The aroma of fresh bread baking in the oven and the sight of flour dusted all over the kitchen table revealed that Minnie had not been idle in their absence. Emma busied herself making tea, humming happily. Other than potential encounters with snakes and other disconcerting forms of wildlife, she was happy to be in her relatives' home and was looking forward to her holiday in the peaceful agricultural hamlet of Walwa.

A selection of Arnold Playle images combined into a postcard - State Library of Victoria

Chapter 7

Sunday service

Going to 'Church' on a Sunday in Walwa was more than a spiritual opportunity; it was a social event. Before and after devotions there was ample opportunity to catch up with friends and to hear all the local news and share delicious gossip. In the absence of a church building, the community would gather at the Walwa Hall to hear a sermon delivered by whichever denomination of clergyman was visiting the town. The Presbyterian priest, Reverend A D Brodie, was scheduled to be the conduit to God for the community on Sunday, 10 February 1924.

As usual, Main Street was lined by horse drawn vehicles and a few motor vehicles. Children chased and played in the street as their parents took the opportunity to catch up with distant neighbours and relatives. The summer sun was harsh, causing the ladies to stand in the generous shade of the elm trees. They fanned their faces with prayer books and chatted quietly. The men stood in groups, swapping anecdotes and advice and swatting flies.

The Drummonds and their guest, Emma, arrived in their sulky, the two older children trotting along behind on their ponies. They pulled up near the Walwa Store and Albert swung down from the sulky and tethered the horse to a rail before helping the children to tether their ponies. He then stepped up to the sulky and helped Minnie to alight, steadying her carefully. Albert was concerned that she was looking a bit pale and tired and he was torn between wishing she had stayed home to rest and a reluctance to have her out of sight in case she went into labour. Emma hopped down with the agility of youth and mustered the children, shepherding them in the direction of the hall.

Curious eyes appraised the newcomer to town and Albert and Minnie proudly introduced Emma to friends and neighbours as they made their way toward the doors of the hall. By the time they entered the hall, Emma had begun to feel quite overwhelmed and fervently hoped that she could remember at least a few names of the people she had just met.

Reverend Brodie, arrived in a cloud of dust, looking a little flustered. He stepped out of his Model T Ford smiling gamely at the scattered congregation. He was met by Hugh Hanna, unofficial mayor of Walwa, and was heard to apologise for his tardiness:

"A bit of engine trouble... Mr Whitehead assisted and got me going, but I lost half an hour...I am so sorry!" said the priest.

"No trouble, Reverend, you are here now, and no one is worried! I'll muster the congregation whilst you slip into vestments," said Hugh affably.

The community trooped into the hall in the wake of the priest. There was clattering and scraping as chairs were arranged in rows and the assembly took their seats. The chatter hushed when the priest reappeared. Reverand Brodie stepped up to the lectern and laid a huge ornate bible on the surface.

"Welcome, Welcome!" he announced joyously.

Brodie smiled and gazed benevolently around the congregation before finally allowing his eyes to rest on a large bunch of young eucalypt leaves and arum lilies arranged carefully in a cream can to one side of the lectern. His smile broadened.

"Thank you for bringing some of nature's gifts into the hall to brighten up our place of worship!" Brodie said and smiled towards Elizabeth Brennan, one of the dedicated community volunteers and the most likely candidate for providing the floral tribute.

Reverend Brodie had an easy attitude and cheerfully engaged with the congregation. He led them in prayer and hymns and rounded off with a hopeful sermon. The sermon was angled to encourage a trust in God for an early Autumn break as Brodie knew the small agricultural community was getting nervous as the late summer grass dried and fodder diminished daily. The ambient temperature was rising in the confined space of the hall, and the congregation began to shift and rustle with discomfort. Noticing that he was rapidly losing his audience's attention, Reverend Brodie concluded the service with an enthusiastic rendering of The Lord's Prayer.

The congregation left the hall with relief. Small groups gathered in the street having a final conversation before setting off toward their homes in order to tackle a list of chores or to attend family gatherings.

Emma waited with the Drummond children on the perimeter of a group which included some friends of the Drummonds: Charles and Ruth Barber and the manager of the Jingellic Butter Factory, David Sheppard, together with William and Lizzie McGrath. The group was talking animatedly about a planned picnic on the river. The men were excited about a new fishing lure which McGrath had designed, and they were swapping tall tales of magnificent Murray cod caught during past fishing excursions. The ladies were planning the catering and if all the promised goodies eventuated, there was to be a truly magnificent feast at the picnic. Emma shuddered involuntarily at the mention of the word "picnic" and distracted herself by playing a clapping game with the Drummond girls. Albert thanked the group for their kind invitation for his family and Emma to attend the picnic but declined. He slid a protective arm under Minnie's elbow and said, "I think Minnie will benefit from putting her feet up for the afternoon! I think this baby is planning a grand entrance sooner than expected!"

Minnie smiled gratefully up at Albert, "Yes, I think we need to be off, dear! Sister Martin says she will drop by later for tea and a chat."

She noticed that Emma was determinedly absenting herself from the conversation and added quietly, "Anyway, I am not sure Emma is ready for a picnic!"

Albert looked across at Emma and nodded in agreement. They said their farewells, gathered up the children and set off home.

Walwa Hall c1925 - Jim Harvey collection, Walwa Station

Agnes "Lizzie" Johnson and her husband, John, perhaps off to Church. - Source: Bernadette Cheshire's collection.

CHAPTER 8

A picnic is planned, and an arsenal assembled

The Barbers arrived home from church. Charles helped his wife, Ruth, down from the trap at the house yard gate, before walking the pony and trap down the fence line to the water trough at the yards. He swapped the bridle for a headcollar and tethered the pony to a rail within easy reach of the trough. He hooked the bridle to the shaft of the trap, secured the reins and patted the patient pony. He then went off to the shed to collect his fishing creel and rods. He was whistling happily to himself, looking forward to a pleasant afternoon in the company of good friends.

Ruth, too, was enthused about the prospect of an excursion and had been chattering all the way home about what they needed to pack and the food she would take. She pushed through the door of their home, removing her bonnet and gloves as she entered the kitchen. She was startled when she noticed Claude Batson sitting at the kitchen table.

The lad was a frequent visitor to their home but was not expected on a Sunday. Batson had worked for the Barbers as a dairyman for a short time, just a few years earlier but had proved unreliable, so Charles had been forced to let him go. Ruth had a soft spot for the lad, she had been moved by his sad personal history: he had been an unwanted child in a large, poor family. When very young, he had been farmed out to be raised by relatives and Ruth recognised that he had never felt truly loved or valued. Whilst in their employ, Batson had boarded with the Barbers and even after his dismissal, Ruth continued to extend charity to the lad, often inviting him for a meal and, if the weather was rough, or if she had chores or odd jobs for him to do, he would occupy his old room for a day or two. Batson had become reliant on the emotional support provided by Ruth. He had hungered for a mother figure in his life since his own mother had abandoned him. Ruth filled the crevices in his soul.

"Oh, hello Claude!" said Ruth.

The young man pushed his chair back and stood politely, pulling at his forelock.

"Morning, Missus!"

"What are you doing here? I wasn't expecting you!" said Ruth with a smile.

"Ohh, I was wondering if you wanted any jobs done... I could split some wood for the stove... or som'at?" said Batson hesitantly.

Ruth busied herself stirring up the coals in the stove and putting the kettle on the hob.

"Thank you, Claude, but I think we are right today: Mr King split wood for me on Friday and helped me knock over a few odd jobs, so no, nothing for you to do today, but thank you, again!" said Ruth.

There was no response. Ruth paused from her task and turned to the young man who was seated again.

"Would you like a cup of tea before you go?" she added pointedly, watching Batson closely.

Batson was glowering and staring at his hands on the table. They were balled into tight fists, his knuckles stark white through tanned skin. Ruth watched him pensively, recognising that the mention of Richard King had touched a nerve.

"The lad is so jealous of King! What on earth is going on in his head?" she thought to herself.

Richard King was a 60-year-old bachelor who cultivated tobacco on the river flats towards Jingellic in a share farm arrangement with the Barbers. Charles had offered him lodgings after Batson had left their employ, and he often helped Charles with other farm work when he wasn't tending the tobacco.

Ruth knew that Batson was a little sweet on her.

"Nothing in it," she thought, "just a lonely lad who longs for a mother figure."

Recently however, she had noticed that Batson seemed offended and jealous if he found out that King had completed "his" odd jobs for the Barbers. The memory of the pair engaged in a petty tug of war for possession of a tea towel with which to help with the dishes after dinner on Wednesday night, flitted through Ruth's head. In the moment, she had laughed and mildly admonished the two men for being "silly", but she remembered the chilling expression on Batson's face when he gathered up his belongings and stalked out, slamming the door to the house. King had said something dismissive of Batson whilst he was still within ear shot and she heard a thud as Batson kicked King's boots off the verandah.

Ruth's reverie was interrupted as Charles, came in through the door. He, too, was surprised to see Batson.

"Hello, Claude! What brings you here this morning?"

Batson looked up at Charles, smiled grimly and said, "Ohh, 'just dropped by. I am going away for a bit. Won't be back for a while."

Charles regarded the lad solemnly, considering his announcement.

"Mr Murray was saying at church today that you had mentioned to him that you were heading to Melbourne... he said you had been dropping by most days to say "Goodbye"! Do you really intend to leave the district, Claude?" asked Charles.

Batson shrugged, again looking at his hands.

"Now he looks a bit sulky!" thought Ruth, curious about the young man's attitude.

Charles cocked his head and looked at Ruth, his eyes questioned her, she shrugged.

"Tea, Charles?" she asked, hoping to relieve the tension in the room.

Whilst the kettle was boiling, Ruth assembled the cups and teapot on the table and then took a loaf of bread from the crock and sliced it on the bread board.

"We are going to a picnic with some friends, Claude, so will not be here for lunch. Would you like me to make you a sandwich?"

"No, thank you, I'll be right" said Batson, although his eyes were looking longingly at the bread.

"No trouble! Here, I'll just pop some butter and jam on the crust to keep you going until you have your lunch," said Ruth warmly.

Ruth collected the butter dish from the Coolgardie and a jar of homemade blackberry jam. She smeared lashings of butter and a generous dollop of jam on the crust, slid it on to a plate and pushed it across the table to Batson. He smiled brightly.

"Thanks, Missus!" said Batson, before wolfing down the offering.

He mopped up crumbs and spilled jam from the plate with his grubby forefinger.

Batson's eyes followed Ruth closely as she moved around the kitchen. He watched with interest as she made sandwiches for the picnic. She loaded slices of homemade bread with cheese and sliced tomato. Finally, she wrapped them in a clean tea towel and packed them in an old biscuit tin. She popped the tin into a large wicker picnic basket. She added some fruit and flasks of her signature lemon and ginger cordial before going to the Coolgardie again to retrieve a pound cake she had made the day before. The kettle started to whistle, and Ruth clattered about making tea and pouring it into the teacups. She passed the cups to Charles and Batson. Charles picked up the newspaper from the dresser and sat at the kitchen table next to Batson to drink his tea. The headlines detailed the latest reports on the recuperation of the surviving victims of the Botanic Gardens Sniper attack, but Charles was more interested in the cricket scores and flipped the paper to the back page.

After a minute, accompanied by loud slurping, Batson put down his cup and he looked at Ruth with an appraising eye.

"Who is going to the picnic?" asked Batson quietly.

Ruth looked at him, trying to decipher his interest, before saying lightly, "Oh just some friends. We are going to sit under the willows near the McGrath's farm. The creek bank is always so nice and cool on warm days like today. I think Lizzie has relatives visiting, the Gainers."

"Is Mr Sheppard going to be there?" asked Batson.

"Yes, it was Mrs Sheppard's idea!" said Ruth brightly.

"...and King?"

Ruth nodded but a cloud scudded across her features. Charles looked up from his newspaper, a frown creased his forehead.

"You are curious, Claude!" said Charles.

Batson grinned broadly and shrugged before saying with resolve, "I might go rabbiting. Maybe shoot some foxes, too!"

He got to his feet and went to the small room in which he kept a few possessions and where he periodically spent the night. When he returned, he had changed into a tidy set of clothes, and he carried two rifles. At his hip was a leather holster containing a handgun. Charles assessed him with a degree of concern.

"Heavens Claude! You are a walking arsenal! What are you up to?" said Charles.

"I said... I am off hunting. Might go and get some fox pelts and rabbits," said Batson tersely.

Batson leant the rifles up against the wall and went out to the cupboard on the verandah. He returned with rags and kit to clean his rifles. He sat back down in the kitchen and concentrated on the job. Ruth had finished packing the picnic and slipped off to the bedroom to change.

"That rifle isn't yours, is it?" Charles asked, indicating one of the .303 rifles.

Batson looked up with narrowed eyes.

"I borrowed it from the rifle club," he said shortly, "Coysh gave it to me."

Batson was a member of the local gun club and a champion marksman but even so, Charles thought it unusual that the club would let a rifle go out on loan. He frowned as he weighed Batson's statement, then shrugged and left it. He noticed that Batson's hands were shaking.

"The lad is a bit jittery; I wonder what is niggling him?" thought Charles to himself.

Charles went to the bedroom to check on Ruth and by the time the pair returned to the kitchen, Batson was outside on the verandah. He was sitting on the step and hammering strips of rawhide to the soles of his boots.

"Now what are you up to Claude?" asked Ruth looking down on him with a broad, curious smile.

"It's for grip... I might go up the hillside a bit... the hide gives me a better grip on the rocks."

Charles came out onto the verandah and placed the picnic gear on a chair near the door.

"We are going now, Claude, we are expected by one. I am locking up. Have you got all you need from the house?" he called as he was shutting the front door.

Batson glanced over his shoulder. He frowned and muttered something which neither of the Barbers caught. Ruth was already strolling down the path towards the pony trap. She had her broad-brimmed straw hat on her head and was dressed in a light floral dress. She had a picnic rug under her arm. Charles followed with the picnic basket in one hand, a fishing rod in the other and his fishing creel slung over his shoulder.

"Ta-ta, Claude!" sang out Ruth as she turned and waved cheerfully.

Batson waved in return, but his face was still.

As the Barbers took off down the road in the pony trap, Batson was sauntering off towards Walwa. Charles noticed with deepening concern that Batson now had a couple of bandoliers criss-crossing his chest.

Not far down the road, on the way to Walwa, was a small cottage belonging to the Spicer family. Batson made his way around to the back of the cottage moving silently and peering in the windows cautiously as he passed. He paused at the back corner of the cottage and surveyed the yard. There was just a young lad, Henry Spicer, sitting on the back step, whittling. He was making a decoy duck from a lump of softwood. Batson watched for a while, assuring himself that the boy was alone before he stepped boldly around the corner. The boy looked up and jumped at the sight of Batson. Spicer was intimidated by Batson's odd behaviour under usual circumstances, so his unannounced appearance, bristling with arms, induced a deep sense of foreboding in the young lad. He got to his feet cautiously.

"S'awright Spicer! I am just here to collect some ammunition. I know your old man has some of the rifle club supplies here," said Batson evenly.

The boy's eyes widened, and he shook his head, denying Batson's claim.

"He does ... I know!" spat Batson harshly.

Batson stooped and leant the rifles against the wall of the house whilst he slid the bandoliers over his head, off his shoulders.

"Here, take these and fill 'em up with the bullets," demanded Batson.

He swung the bandoliers through the air and they landed with a thud at the boy's feet. Batson glared at the boy threateningly and picked up his rifles again. He then motioned with the rifle in his right hand indicating that the boy should pick up the bandoliers and follow his instructions. Spicer felt that he had little choice. He grabbed the bandoliers and hurried inside the cottage. Batson followed him. He stood in the doorway and watched the boy open the dresser, select a box of cartridges to match the .303 in Batson's hand and slide the cartridges into the loops.

"What are you doin' Claude? Why do you need so much ammo?" asked Spicer carefully.

Batson gazed at the boy grimly, his eyes were narrowed to slits, and he hesitated for a beat as he considered whether he should reveal the truth.

"Just going to pop some foxes and rabbits," he said simply.

The boy's eyes widened as he imagined that the calibre of rifle Batson was wielding would literally pop a rabbit. He chose to complete the task rather than argue with Batson, whose presence was making him increasingly nervous. When done, Spicer put the bandoliers on the kitchen table and stepped back. Batson put his rifles down again, leaning them against a chair. He picked up the bandoliers and slipped them over his head and shoulders, so that they were again criss-crossing his chest. He smiled raggedly at Spicer, retrieved his rifles and thanked him for the ammunition before backing out of the door and hurrying off, out of the garden. Batson doubled back once he was out of view of the cottage and set off at a brisk pace back towards the Barbers' home.

Batson was inflamed with a passion he didn't really comprehend. It was a mixture of jealousy, frustration, and mortification. Primarily, he felt peeved that Richard King was inveigling his way into the position in the Barber household that Batson had previously enjoyed. Batson was possessive of Mrs Barber, he felt validated by her kindness and concern for him – she had become a mother figure to him. King had snared the attention which Ruth had previously lavished on Batson. The older man stepped in and performed the odd jobs which Batson considered his domain, and for which Mrs Barber was always so prettily grateful. Batson was distraught and envious. In addition, since October, when the demonstration of the Batson-Lawrence patent-pending rabbit extermination technique had gone so horribly wrong in front of an assembly of government officials and eminent local farmers, he had been mortified and, in his overactive imagination, he relived that humiliation daily. The whole uncomfortable scene ran on a never-ending loop in his head. Batson felt that people sniggered behind his back and often in his actual presence. He had become a laughingstock, and this impression had eroded his fragile ego and worn down his self-control.

Batson's level of social incompetence isolated him from his peers, and he felt there was scant compassion for his situation from community members. He spent long periods in his own company, during which his inner voice wasn't kind, and he had plenty of opportunity to dissect all the wrongs, perceived or otherwise, inflicted against him. He hadn't woken up that morning with a plan but as he tramped back towards the Barbers' home his thoughts coalesced and the idea that popped into his head became a crusade or more accurately, a pogrom.

Batson arrived back at the Barbers' home and made his way around the side of the house to the window of the bedroom... "his" bedroom. He leant his rifles against the wall and unhooked the bandoliers. He then unsheathed the large blade knife strapped to his thigh and used it to lever the window open. He had done this before; Batson would often visit the home in the absence of the Barbers and without their knowledge. He would stalk around the house touching photographs in frames on the mantlepiece, fondling items belonging to Mrs Barber and maliciously hiding King's possessions or placing spiders and crickets in his boots. Today, his sour attitude pushed him towards a need to inflict a much greater level of disruption on the Barber household.

Batson trashed King's room, scattering possessions across the floor as he opened and emptied cupboards and drawers. He then went to the Barbers' bedroom and searched ... he didn't know what he was looking for, but he souvenired a wristwatch which he knew Mrs Barber was fond of ... he thought it may have been her mother's.

"She had a mother!" Batson muttered to himself sourly.

His thoughts picked at the wound on his soul: He was abandoned by his mother when she took up with a new partner and had a new family. He had been sent to Germanton, now called Holbrook, to be raised by an aunt. He had a childhood that was unstructured - he had plenty of freedom, but no love, not a soul cared about him.

He stole some more ammunition from Charles Barber's gun cabinet - another 250 rounds. In the kitchen, he packed some food: biscuits, apples, a hunk of cheese and a heel of bread, into a canvas bag and slung it over his shoulder. He looked around the kitchen and bitter-sweet memories sprang to mind: the kindness that he had been shown by the Barbers, the cosy meals he had shared with the couple, Mrs Barber's endeavours to teach him to read and write. Suddenly the image of Ruth Barber smiling and joking with King scrolled across his vision, but it imploded in an angry red haze as frustration and jealousy, once more, consumed him. He struck out, overturning kitchen chairs and upending the fruit bowl, smashing it to the ground. He unlocked the door and slammed out on to the verandah. He was seething with a bizarre rage. He stood and drew breath and came to a final decision. He collected his kit, ammunition and rifles and set off toward the Jingellic Bridge.

It was a brilliantly sunny day; the temperature was already oppressive but a breeze off the Murray River provided some cooling relief. Batson didn't notice conditions, he was fit and driven. He marched across the bridge with his characteristic long stride, the rhythm of kit and rifles thumping on his back provided a metronome for his march. His thoughts whirled as he teased and plucked at memories and situations which prickled his temper and angst.

A couple approached Batson, crossing from the northern side of the Murray. Batson eyed them suspiciously, recognising Charles Coysh and his wife. They greeted Batson cheerily:

"What ho, Claude! Where are you off to? Has war been declared?" joked Coysh.

Batson doffed his hat to Mrs Coysh and answered sullenly, "Just hunting - rabbits and foxes!"

The man frowned, sensing that Batson was in no mood for small talk. He reached a hand to his wife and protectively steered her onwards without offering further comment. Coysh looked back over his shoulder when they were out of earshot and whispered:

"He is an odd one, that Batson! A sandwich short of a picnic, I fear!"

Bridge over the Murray River at Jingellic c1925 - Arnold Playle collection, Man from Snowy River Museum

CHAPTER 9

Picnic site in his sights

The picnic party gathered in the paddock south of the McGrath's home, in the shadow of the Jingellic Creek bridge. They were about two miles west of the small village of Jingellic. McGrath's cowshed was on the opposite side of the gently roiling waters of the creek. William and Lizzie McGrath introduced Lizzie's brother, Charles Gainer, and his wife, Gwendoline, to the other members of the party, which was comprised of Charles and Ruth Barber, Richard King, and David Sheppard and his wife, Alice. The Gainers were visiting from Broken Hill, and they revelled in the verdant scenery - a dramatic contrast to their usual outlook across the raw, rocky outback vistas, dotted with the mine dumps of the "Silver City".

There were several children at the picnic, the offspring of the McGraths and Gainers and some friends. The children were excited and energetic. They scrambled down from ponies and traps and immediately started rough-housing and laughing, chasing one another about and chattering and squealing.

The men hobbled the horses in the shade of a coppice of trees and left them to doze and flick flies for the afternoon. The men shared the loads of picnic baskets, rugs and fishing gear amongst themselves, and set off upstream towards the selected picnic spot. The women carried parasols and mustered the smaller children. Lizzie McGrath held firmly to her toddler, Jean's hand, and watched as Bill, her near-teenage son, lead the charge of children to the picnic spot. They followed the creek bank as it snaked away towards the clump of willows which nestled along the riverbank opposite a tall, sharp embankment. It was a pretty spot. The trees provided dappled shade and just a little way upstream was a pebbled beach which jutted out into the creek. The current in the creek was gentle and provided a natural swimming hole for the children to enjoy.

The women selected a suitable spot to spread picnic rugs. The men set down the picnic baskets and then they retired to sit on some logs in a position where they could keep an eye on the children playing in the water, and at a suitable distance from the women so they could swap some bawdy jokes and discuss masculine topics without a concern for being overheard and upsetting the ladies. William McGrath was a decorated war hero, a former major in the 8th Light Horse. He had been part of the ANZAC troops who had campaigned in Gallipoli and Palestine. The men loved to hear stories of his war experience, and this was the most frequent topic of conversation. McGrath was a little cagey and would share only a carefully curated selection of war stories, as some of his experiences were still so raw and crippling that he could not bear to revisit the memories.

The children had already stripped off to shorts and shifts and were splashing and giggling in the shallows.

"Watch out for snakes!" called Lizzie with a shudder.

"No self-respecting reptile would remain in the vicinity of all that noise and activity!" said Ruth with a chuckle.

The women laid out containers of food and gingham napkins, enamel cups and flasks and bottles of ginger beer and cordial. Once they had the feast arranged just so, they called out for the party to come and eat.

The children rushed from the water and shook like puppies; a spray of droplets caught the sunlight. They shared the services of a couple of towels and sat down on the rugs, damp and happy. The men sauntered back to join the group. They stretched out on the grass and the women offered the food around. A delicious selection of picnic fare was on offer, and soon, everyone was munching happily.

Once appetites were sated, the conversation rattled along and topics ranged from local gossip - hatches, matches and dispatches, to current affairs, and the latest developments at the sites of local industry: the Jingellic Butter Factory, the Cheese Factories and the prospects for the tin mines at Mt Alwah and Jingellic.

Soon the children were agitating to get back in the water and the men were itching to try their luck with the fishing rods that they had brought with them. Gwen and Ruth volunteered to take up the Life-saver role, sitting on the logs to watch the children in the water, whilst Alice and Lizzie agreed to pack up the picnic baskets.

The men set off to catch "the big one" or really, any fish would do. They wandered down the creek bank in single file, following a track created by livestock and wildlife, chatting and laughing. Charles Barber was leading the way with Sheppard on his heels. Charles Gainer and King trailed along behind the leaders. McGrath was humming to him-self as he marched along at the tail in step with young Harry Poyntz, Ruth Barber's nephew, who was the oldest child present.

The cicadas were singing so loudly that the noise seemed to make the atmosphere throb. A fence line, which dipped down to the creek, intersected with the path that the men were following. As Sheppard was climbing through the fence he stopped suddenly as his pants were snagged by a barb. He bent to release the fabric just as a shot rang out. Barber, who was already on the other side of the fence turned to look behind him, whilst Gainer spun to look at King who had been in the act of lighting his pipe. Gainer assumed the noise was the matchbox exploding.

There was a second crack and King squawked, then grunted. Shep-pard spun in response to King's voice but he then crumpled as another shot found its mark. The men startled as they registered that they were under fire. McGrath, with the practised response of a war veteran, ducked for cover, taking Harry with him. Gainer stooped to assist King to his feet, but a bullet smashed through his knee, and he toppled forward, landing on top of King. Gainer panicked and scrambled over King's portly body. He slid down the creek bank, landing awkwardly in the water. Gainer struggled to right himself, pain shooting through his leg. He splashed and crawled across the creek until he found a spot under the overhang of the opposite bank where he was hidden from the gunman. Gainer slumped in the cool, shallow water, panting and mesmerised by the cloud of blood-stained water snaking away downstream from his leg. He felt sick and faint, the pain from the wound was unbearable.

Richard King wheezed as a blood stain bloomed across his shirt front. He crawled awkwardly towards David Sheppard. Sheppard's face was pale and haggard:

"I can't move!" groaned Sheppard, "Take cover - save yourself!" he grunted at King.

Barber knelt next to Sheppard and tried to assess the man's injury. Sheppard grasped Barber's hand and cried, "I am dying; don't leave me!"

There was panic and pain in his grey eyes. Barber was shocked when he saw blood seeping rapidly from a wound just under Sheppard's ribs. He hooked his handkerchief from his pocket, balled it up and pressed it firmly on Sheppard's wound.

"Hold it there, David...put your hand here," Barber directed.

He grasped Sheppard's hand and placed it over the compress.

"The women and children are in danger; I must go for help!" said Barber determinedly, snatching a glance over his shoulder towards the women.

"No! For God's sake, don't go! He'll shoot you!" pleaded Sheppard.

Barber looked towards the opposite bank, in the direction from which the shots had been fired. He frowned and considered the situation in haste.

"No, not him, he doesn't want me! I have been here all along and he hasn't turned the rifle on me!" declared Barber stoically.

McGrath rolled down the slope and took cover behind a willow. He considered that the gunman would have to reload the rifle clip imminently and hoped for a pause in the barrage of shots. He planned to risk all and run to his house for a rifle to return fire on the madman. He drew breath and steeled himself for the ordeal.

There was screaming from the women and children further down the creek. Barber could hear his wife's voice:

"You coward, you cur! Shooting at unarmed men!" screeched Ruth.

Gwendoline Gainer rushed towards her injured husband, splashing into the Jingellic Creek and screaming for the gunman to stop.

Barber looked up to the embankment again. For a moment, the marksman could be seen clearly as he stood and calmly wiped down his rifle muzzle with his hat.

"It's Batson!" Barber called to the women, "Take cover!"

A chill of fear clutched at Barber's innards as he recollected the accuracy of Batson's aim at rifle club competitions.

The women and children ran in terror before sheltering behind a dense clump of willows at the edge of the creek. The small children were wailing.

Barber was shocked. He knew he had to get help. He ploughed into the water and darted towards the shrubbery below the embankment from which Batson was shooting. Hoping he was hidden by the overhang; he crashed along in the creek before he ducked behind a coppice of trees and ran towards the cowshed. He paused behind the wall of the cowshed before chancing a course back across the creek, towards the horses. His goal was to get to a horse, then to ride for help, and a rifle.

McGrath had been counting the shots and when there was a pause, he considered that Batson would be reloading the clip for his rifle. He drew breathe and bolted out from behind his temporary cover, running in a zig zag fashion toward his home. He was completely exposed to the marksman but was spurred on by the gallant thought that he was taking the gunman's attention from his companions, particularly the women and children. Soon, bullets kicked up dust behind McGrath as he ran, ducking and weaving across the hundred and fifty yards to his house. A bullet grazed his thigh. The pain was intense, and he tumbled, rolling over onto his shoulder. He regained his feet and crabbed to the back door of his home. He put a hand up to the door handle and his wrist exploded in pain as a bullet smashed through the tissues. Bullets peppered the door and walls. Another bullet grazed his arm and McGrath rolled again and scrabbled across the verandah. He made it to the corner of the house and out of view of the sniper. He hoisted himself up and over the sill of the sitting room window and once inside his house, he staggered across to the cupboard where he kept his rifle. It was a familiar weapon; it was his service .303, the rifle which had been responsible for dispatching several Turkish would-be snipers during the conflict in Gallipoli.

"Here comes another bloody sniper," he vowed grimly.

Blood spurted from his wrist, and he took a moment to wrap a napkin, which he had retrieved from the dresser drawer, around the wound, securing it with a ribbon which was also in the drawer. With his left hand virtually incapacitated, he struggled to load the rifle. He completed the task awkwardly and thrust a handful of cartridges into his pocket. He set off once more; adrenaline was coursing through his veins, pushing him on. His only thought was to protect his companions, to revenge his injured friends.

McGrath crabbed across the room, smashed through the front door, and limped around the front of the house appearing at the opposite corner of the house. He scanned the scene, his eyes searching for the marksman.

"There!" he said to himself. It was a fair distance, but he was desperate to scare off the sniper. He rested the rifle in the fork of a tree, sighting with difficulty as sweat was running into his eyes. He cursed under his breath as he struggled to steady the rifle with one hand near useless. He pulled the trigger; the bullet spat dirt just below Batson's position.

McGrath could see Batson quite clearly, he came out of the shrubbery and appeared to stare down at the scene, and the carnage that he had inflicted. He looked across the creek towards McGrath before turning and running. He ducked behind trees and was heading towards a millet crop to the north of the picnic site. McGrath limped across the paddock, back to his companions. He waded across the creek, finding Mr and Mrs Gainer under the overhang supporting one another. Charles was in a deal of pain and was struggling to remain conscious. His left knee was shattered.

"Stay there in case he comes back!" hissed McGrath.

He considered that the Gainers were relatively safe in their current position.

McGrath hobbled off, finding the rest of the women and children in amongst the tangled roots of a clump of willows a bit further along the creek. They were unharmed, just terrified. Again, he thought they were in a safe position and commanded them to remain still and quiet.

He struggled up the bank and found his way back to where Sheppard and King were huddled in the grass. Both had suffered severe injuries and all he could advise was for the men to clamp their hands over their wounds. McGrath then hurried to the picnic site and collected tea towels and napkins. He returned to the men and created makeshift field dressings to bind Sheppard and King's wounds. King had suffered an abdominal wound, Sheppard had a through and through – a shot had smashed through his upper abdomen and exited next to his spine. Battlefield experience made McGrath aware that Sheppard had received a catastrophic injury. He spoke gently and encouragingly to the men and didn't reveal his fears for their lives.

Time had distilled during the terrifying incident, yet, when McGrath checked his pocket watch he discovered that ten minutes had elapsed since he had looked at the clock on the mantelpiece whilst he had been in his house retrieving his rifle. There had been no further gun shots and McGrath was relatively confident that Batson had scarpered.

He called quietly to the women and children, encouraging them to make their way to the shrubbery at the base of the embankment, near Sheppard and King.

Mrs Sheppard hurried to her husband's side, weeping. The children were pale and confused, numb with shock. Ruth Barber collected picnic rugs and tried to make the wounded men more comfortable. She covered David Sheppard with a rug. Shock had set in, he was alabaster-white and shivering.

After a nervous wait the group became aware of hoofbeats and shouts and then the rumble of a vehicle.

"Here comes the cavalry!" said McGrath with grim optimism.

Charles Barber, accompanied by his brother, Peter, and Charles Coysh galloped up the track from the bridge. Charles slid from his horse and hurried to the injured men.

"The doctor has been called: Dr England, was visiting up at Alf Lawrence's and will be along shortly and Henry is bringing the bush nursing sister, Sister Martin - she was up at Drummonds with Minnie. They are on their way; they won't be long!" Barber gabbled.

He was trying to provide encouraging information in a hurry. Barber was unable to hide his concern as he studied Sheppard's pale face. His eyes met with McGrath's who glanced about to make sure the women weren't looking at him and then shook his head gravely. Lizzie McGrath made her husband sit still and assessed his injuries, tears in her eyes. McGrath, was more relaxed now that there were armed men scanning the surrounds, protecting the party. He sat and allowed his wife to apply makeshift dressings to his injuries. He had four gunshot wounds, the most serious being a wound to his left wrist which had smashed the bones. In addition, he had flesh wounds to his right thigh and left upper arm. When he moved his injured arm, it revealed the blood on his shirt was from an abdominal wound. Lizzie examined it carefully and concluded that her husband had been fortunate, the bullet had grazed the flesh but had not penetrated the abdominal cavity.

"You are a dodgy character," she applauded her husband.

"Learnt a few tricks about ducking and weaving with the Turks in Gallipoli, my dear!" he said grimly.

"Constable Jolly has been alerted; he is mustering reinforcements from Holbrook and Tumbarumba. They will track down that mad man, that cur, Batson! I have no idea what has come over him!" said Barber with barely controlled fury.

Barber felt uncomfortable, somewhat guilty for harbouring a man who had wrought such destruction. He recognised that Batson had recently become surly and jealous of Richard King, and uncharacteristically sharp with Ruth, his wife, but he couldn't fathom what had triggered this malevolent madness.

"You had better get Gainer out of the creek. His leg is badly injured." said McGrath through gritted teeth. He was now sitting still and rigid, as the pain was starting to crank up in intensity as the adrenaline was ebbing.

Another party of men arrived; they were guiding in a truck which was backing up the rough and narrow track alongside the creek. The truck came to a halt as close as possible to the injured men. There was confusion and fussing as the injured were transferred to the tray of the truck. Picnic rugs were utilised as makeshift stretchers. Henry Barber and Sister Martin arrived. The horse drawing their gig was in a lather, evidence that they had come at a cracking pace. The nurse hopped down from the gig and hurried to attend the patients. She was helped up into the tray of the truck and immediately focussed on the task of triaging her patients. She congratulated McGrath on the quality of his field dressings. The children were put to work gathering up scattered belongings and picnic baskets and they loaded everything into the truck. The wives of the injured men climbed into the vehicle to accompany their husbands.

McGrath instructed the driver, Jackie Gale, to drive to Jingellic Butter Factory.

"We can meet the doctor there, halve his travel time and get away from this place in case the gun man returns!" he said with a shudder.

His words made those with rifles pay closer attention to their surroundings.

The group moved off towards the bridge, following the truck as it manoeuvred carefully up the track towards the road. The men organised the picnic party's horses and traps and moved off in convoy down the road towards Jingellic. The armed men positioned themselves as outriders around the convoy. They scanned the surrounding hills, alert for the gun man.

Each bump caused Sheppard and King to groan. Gwendoline and some of the small children were sobbing quietly, the nurse, Sister Martin, murmured encouraging words. It was going to be a long trip to cover the four miles to the Butter Factory that afternoon, and an even longer one to the hospital in Albury.

Picnic site on Jingellic Creek, south bank - Source author.

Picnic site, view of the embankment from which the shooter fired - photographer: author

CHAPTER 10

Flashbacks and fear

Sister Martin left the Drummond home after a quick, reassuring visit. The consultation had been arranged just after the Church service and Henry Barber had brought her out to the farm. Henry and Albert sat on the verandah discussing the cricket and local news whilst the ladies had retired to Minnie's bedroom for a quick prenatal examination.

"Everything is progressing well," announced Sister Martin as she packed her pinard stethoscope away in her gladstone bag, "His head is down and practically engaged. Not long to wait for his arrival!"

"His?" chuckled Minnie.

"Well, he seems big enough to be a bull calf!" laughed Sister Martin.

Soon after Henry Barber and Sister Martin had departed, Albert took the fractious children down to the river for a swim. The afternoon was warm, and Emma and Minnie were left to bask on the verandah in peace, admiring the splendid view across the river flats towards Jingellic.

Emma and Minnie relaxed in the shade, fanning themselves with elaborate Chinese fans. The fans had been wedding presents from one of Minnie's well-travelled relatives. Emma admired the richly ornate decorations on the fan she held and appreciated its cooling effect. They sat on slingback chairs; their feet propped up on cushioned footstools. On a small table between them, stood a jug with a decorative lace cover and two tall tumblers of homemade lemonade. The two women chatted like old friends.

"Here we are, solving the problems of the world!" laughed Emma.

After a pause and as she wafted her fan with vigour, Minnie, said in coquettish tones, "There is a *language* of fans, you know!"

Emma cocked her head, "What do you mean?"

"Think of crinolines, wide-hooped satin dresses, plunging nec klines... The elaborate dinner dances of the upper class. A small orchestra and the wide expanse of a ballroom. The intricate dance of the suitors and the suitable. The ladies would be on display, fanning themselves with deliberate movements. A flick like this would mean *take notice of me, I see you!*" said Minnie sotto voce.

Minnie demonstrated another attitude with the fan.

"This would mean *leave me alone!* and if all else failed, you could always smack an unwanted suitor with a really elaborate fan!" Minnie finished with a grin.

Emma laughed and practiced some fanning techniques before laying the fan across her face and leaning back in her chair:

"Would this be *it is past my bedtime, and I am asleep*?" said Emma and then snored in a very unladylike fashion.

Minnie giggled.

"I know the feeling; I could do with a nap, too!" Minnie agreed with Emma.

The sublime peace was shattered as a shot rang out in the distance and both women startled. It came from well beyond the Drummond farm boundaries, towards Jingellic. The sound was muffled by the intervening distance and vegetation, but it echoed from the rock faces across the valley. Emma sat upright, then froze and listened intently. The Botanic Gardens Shooting experience came rushing back and blood drained from her features.

Another shot, then several in quick succession. Emma looked at Minnie, her face pale and a frown creased her forehead. Minnie was also on alert but gamely tried to reassure Emma.

"Oh, it's probably just William McGrath practising for a gun club competition." she suggested but continued to listen, unconvinced by her own assertion.

There were more shots, then silence. Emma was restless. Minnie was concerned. She got to her feet and went to the edge of the verandah, leaning on the railing and peering towards the river, the direction towards which the rest of her family had headed on their way to the swimming hole. She watched for a while, straining to see down the track. After a few minutes, a smile broke across her face and she exclaimed, "Here they come! They must have been startled by the noise too!"

The children charged up the track, covering the distance in record time. Excited and puffing, they jabbered at their mother and Emma.

"Did you hear it?"

"Gun fire!"

"A bigger rifle than Da's rabbit rifle!" announced Ron confidently.

Albert caught up with the children and ran his eyes over the women with concern.

"Are you two ladies all right?" he asked with an anxious smile.

He noted that Emma was pale and rattled.

"Come on, we'll go inside and have a cup of tea, and lemonade for the tribe!" suggested Minnie meeting Albert's eyes and acknowledging his concern.

The children clamoured for a cooldrink and added biscuits to the order.

Whilst Emma made tea, Albert stepped into the sitting room and quietly used the telephone to find out what was going on. He connected to the exchange and was shocked as the telephonist gabbled an announcement, revealing the source of the gun fire before he could even ask for a connection.

"There has been a mad man shooting at a picnic party in Jingellic. He is on the loose. Stay with your family, lock the doors, arm yourself!"

"Who is the shooter? For whom are we to look out for?" asked Albert, shocked.

"By all accounts, Batson... Claude Batson.... He has gone mad!"

Albert disconnected, feeling shocked. He leaned against the wall and considered all that he knew of the suspect.

"Batson is a bit simple, a bit eccentric but I wouldn't have thought him a murderer!" he thought and then reconsidered the term as he didn't know if anyone had been killed... yet.

"Maybe it was an accident - could he have mistaken people for game?"

As soon as the idea came into his head, he dismissed it. Batson was an excellent marksman; he would only pull the trigger once confident of his target.

Albert went to the cabinet where he kept his rifle locked away from curious children. He checked there was nothing in the breech and slipped a half dozen shells into his pocket. He leaned the rifle against the wall near the door to the verandah. He locked the door. He checked the other doors and locked them too. When he re-entered the kitchen, he crossed the room quickly and locked the back door. He was feverishly thinking how best to tell the family the news; how best to tell Emma without terrifying her. After an internal debate, he opted for the truth and a head-on approach.

The family was looking at him with solemn curiosity. Emma was pouring tea. Albert sat down at his usual position, head of the table. Minnie looked at him, and channelled his concern:

"What's amiss, Albert?" she asked quietly.

"I was just talking to May Griffiths at the exchange," said Albert and paused.

Emma felt breathless, a pall of anxiety clouded her vision, there was an odd singing in her ears. She sat down quickly.

"There seems to have been a serious accident... well, maybe not an accident."

Albert paused again and thought. The room was quiet; everyone held their breath.

"A shooting, a man on the run. We need to remain calm but cautious. We shall all remain in the house. Lock the doors!" Albert's voice was staccato, his expression grim.

"Who is on the run?" breathed Minnie.

"It would appear to be Batson," said Albert and then added for Emma's benefit, "Claude, the rabbiter I was telling you about."

"Oh, my goodness!" said Emma.

Her world was spinning chaotically; lightening had struck twice.

"Is anyone hurt?" asked Minnie, tears welled, and she looked anxious.

"I don't know the details," said Albert sharply, "I anticipate that we will be informed soon enough!"

The children looked from one anxious adult to another. For a change, they were subdued and not squabbling, there was no chattering. The atmosphere was tense. Minnie gathered herself and said brightly:

"Oh well, we are safe, all together here, we shall have an afternoon of parlour games, or shall we get Emma to read to us?"

The children were galvanised to action. The older children were keen to take advantage of adult competition and wanted to play cards. The smallest child, Ron, fancied having Emma all to himself and shyly lisped, "Please can you read to me, Emma?"

Emma thought it would be an excellent distraction and sent the child to fetch a book whilst she made herself comfortable on the couch near the window.

Whilst the card game was being dealt, Albert stalked outside onto the verandah, gazing across the paddocks in the direction of Jingellic. There was no movement evident, other than disconsolate sheep picking across the scorched summer grass. Just an ordinary Sunday afternoon.

"Not very ordinary, now!" thought Albert before returning to the house and firmly locking the door.

Glenalva - The Drummond property - Source State Library Victoria

Chapter 11

Call the police!

Constable Rice had been horrified when the young Coysh boy roused him from his afternoon nap. He was yelling from the yard beyond Rice's door:

"Come quick! There has been a shooting - 'lots of people injured or dead!"

Rice's heart froze. His beat was rarely the scene of lawlessness. A few drunken scuffles at Smith's Jingellic Hotel, petty pilfering, infrequent cattle duffing, never a shooting. He bowled out of his small police station house, hastily hauling on his tunic and cap.

"What are you on about? What has happened," he shouted over the clatter of hooves on gravel.

The boy was excited and his gelding had caught the nervous energy and was spinning and snorting. Young Coysh struggled to settle the horse and convey the message.

"Mr Barber came hammering into Jingellic to get my father and rifles. They have gone back to save the picnic party. Claude, ... Claude Batson, he has gone mad and fired on the picnic party. He got four of them, I think! Maybe more!"

Rice wasted no time by asking further questions. He went to the yard, caught, and saddled his horse before returning to his office briefly. He put a quick telephone call through to Constable Jolly to alert his counterpart in Walwa to the action. He then collected his rifle and handgun. He checked that the handgun was loaded and slipped it into the holster on his belt and returned to his horse. He put the rifle into the boot suspended from his saddle. He cinched the girth up an additional hole and swung into the saddle.

"Alright then, young Coysh, where are we headed?"

The pair set off at a gallop. As they rode, Coysh breathlessly relayed all the information that he knew about the incident to Rice. They covered the few hundred yards from the Jingellic Police station, on the Victorian bank of the Murray River, to the bridge and clattered across the wooden deck to the northern side. At the top of the rise, Rice reined in momentarily, yelling instructions to young Coysh:

"Go to Mrs Griffiths at the Post Office, get her to place a telephone call to Holbrook and request that Sergeant Morris bring reinforcements to track Batson, give her as much information that you can, to pass on to the Sergeant. Oh, and get her to warn all on the exchange to be on the alert for a gunman!"

Coysh nodded and wheeled his horse. Rice jabbed his horse in the ribs and gave him his head. He galloped off towards Jingellic Creek.

Constable Rice met the party of riders and vehicles evacuating the picnic party when they were not far from the intersection with the Holbrook Road. He reined in adjacent to the truck and stood in his stirrups to view the occupants of the truck and address the witnesses. Rice surveyed the injured men lying in the tray of the truck, cushioned with picnic rugs, their heads cradled on the laps of their wives. He was shocked seeing the haggard faces, bloodstained clothing and dressings, the distressed children and womenfolk. He sucked the air in through his teeth, making a low whistle and asked, "What madness has occurred?"

Charles Barber edged his horse up alongside the constable. The men deferred to William McGrath, expecting him to answer, to take charge, but McGrath shook his head. He was pale and quivering with the shock of his injuries. Sister Martin rattled off a brief situation report in relation to injuries inflicted on her charges. Rice recognised that the patients needed to be transported to the Butter Factory with all haste, to meet the doctor and be provided with necessary medical care to prepare for transport to hospital, so he waved the truck and its escort onwards. As Rice and Charles Barber fell into step with one another, their horses cantering along easily, the police constable asked Barber:

"What on earth happened, Charles?"

"He just appeared on the embankment overlooking our picnic spot, about a quarter mile upstream on the Jingellic Creek. The women were on the grass under the willows and the children were playing in the shallows of the creek, not far away. The men, McGrath, Gainer, King, Sheppard, and I together with the older Poyntz lad - we were just making our way upstream, towards the fishing hole. Out of the blue, there were rifle shots. King fell, then Sheppard and Gainer. I looked up to where the shots were coming from. It was then I saw Batson."

"Batson? Are you certain?" Rice looked sharply at Barber.

"Yes! I had a clear view of him."

"Where is he now?" said Rice.

"When Lachie, came back with his rifle ... he had run the gauntlet of Batson's rifle shots to get his rifle from his house, ... he was wounded, but managed to get a shot away...Anyway, Batson thought better of taking on Lachie McGrath in a duel. He backed off and scarpered," said Barber breathlessly.

"Where to?" the constable asked, scanning the surrounding hillside.

"I didn't see... I had already gone – 'made a dash to get a horse and ride for help... McGrath thought he had headed north, through the Marchant's millet crop." said Barber.

"Was he on foot?" said Rice.

"Seemed to be .... And anyway, he doesn't own a horse," said Barber.

"Can you organise the group at the Butter Factory, ensure their safety until ready to transport the wounded? Post some sentries, send messages to locals to be on the alert for- and not to shelter Batson. I will report to the Murray District Superintendent, organise reinforcements and a search party, we will snare this cowardly cur!" said Rice.

Rice was fired up with loathing for the fiendish sniper. Barber nodded his agreement and hurried his horse to catch up to the convoy, Rice peeled off from the cavalcade and reined in at the telephone exchange and post office next door to the Jingellic Hotel.

William "Lachie" McGrath with the 8th Light Horse AIF 1915 - Australian War Memorial

CHAPTER 12

Call in the troops and triage the wounded

The news of the *Sniper at the Picnic* spread quickly across the district via the traditional bush telegraph and the more modern telecommunications. Those who had been following the dramatic newspaper stories relating to the Botanic Gardens Shooting were appalled that there was potential for a similar crime in their district. All community members were shocked about the violent nature of the incident and the identity of the suspect. Those in possession of a firearm, which was the majority, cleaned and oiled their guns, filled their pockets with shells and checked their outbuildings and locked their doors. The community was unnerved and angry.

On hearing Constable Rice's message, the Walwa Police Constable, Jolly, telephoned Benalla Police station and spoke to Senior Constable Gerecke. Gerecke assured him that he would relay the details of the horrific incident to the Murray District Police Superintendent and muster reinforcements from Albury, Holbrook, Tumbarumba, and Corryong. They would be dispatched immediately.

"We will mount a man hunt!" declared Gerecke, "I will dispatch black trackers, reinforcements, and an Officer in Charge. I would expect the first of them to be arrive by nightfall. Keep me informed!"

He hung up without waiting for Jolly's response.

Jolly immediately considered the logistics of accommodating an influx of police, the inevitable cavalcade of journalists and the prospect of an armed, energised, and panic-stricken community.

Already there were reports of sightings: Percy Emerson and Mrs Unger called the switchboard operator, Mrs Griffiths, to have her relay the message to Constable Rice and Jolly that an armed man had been seen crossing the face of the hill to the west of the Holbrook Road.

"He is heading to Lankeys Creek!" muttered Jolly to himself as Mrs Griffith's excited voice chattered in his ear.

He hung up and immediately called Holbrook Police Station. He was able to intercept Mounted Constable Tom Morris and Constable Rowlings before they set off from Holbrook.

"Keep a close watch on the farms through Lankeys Creek, we expect the fugitive, Batson, to be heading in that direction. The course he has embarked upon is rough going: steep, treacherous, …. he may be heading for the railway. Rumour has it he was keen to journey to Melbourne, but who knows… he is probably just getting away from his victims and the law!" declared Jolly.

Mounted Constable Morris was keen for the task. He was a decorated Boer War hero and a fine marksman. Jolly was confident that Batson would be intercepted.

Constable Jolly called the postmistress and exchange operator at Walwa Post Office, Mrs Amy Hughes, and asked her to send a message via the telephone system to request volunteer assistance from experienced bushmen – he was raising a large civilian party to strengthen the manhunt for the suspect, Claude Batson.

"Oh, and you had better call Dr Bowman in Holbrook and have him come along sharpish and attend the injured, please Mrs Hughes!" added Rice.

Constable Rice and Constable Jolly had arranged to meet at the Butter Factory to review the situation and check up on the status of the victims of the shooting. Ruth Barber watched them as they dismounted in the factory yard. She was sitting on the edge of the factory's loading dock trying to gather her wits and get some fresh air.

She called out to the constables:

"Good afternoon, officers.... well, not really a such a good one..." she added forlornly.

Recognising the shock and distress in her voice, Rice spoke gently but firmly.

"Hello Mrs Barber. I trust that the victims are being provided with necessary care?"

Ruth was close to tears but valiantly attempted a business-like voice and tried to make a comprehensive report.

"We were fortunate that Dr England was visiting up at the Lawrences... he came as soon as he heard, to render assistance. Of course, Sister Martin is still here. They have staunched the bleed-ing..."

Ruth gulped and hesitated, before continuing: "David, David Sheppard is in a bad way, but fortunately ...."

Ruth hiccupped a sob and hesitated before saying, "He seems un-able to feel pain at the wound or his legs. Richard King is labouring with his breathing and moaning..."

Her voice cracked and she continued quietly, "Mr Gainer is in so much pain with his knee, the morphine seems to be only partly effective. Lachie McGrath is stoic but clearly in a world of pain, too. He has had some medication but has gallantly refused a repeat dose, advising that since the supply is limited, it should be retained for King and Sheppard. The men's wounds have been dressed and splinted, and we are preparing them for transport. They'll need to go to Albury Hospital for surgery.... It will be such a difficult journey... seventy miles in an open tray, a rough trip, hours of travel, in the dark ...." Ruth burst into tears.

Rice sighed, glanced at Constable Jolly and the two policemen tried to reassure the woman, but the situation did indeed seem bleak.

"The patients are in good hands; the doctor and Sister Martin will keep them comfortable. Will Mrs Gainer and Mrs McGrath be accompanying the men?"

"Ye-es," hiccupped Ruth, "Charles and I will be going home after the truck moves out. The children have been taken to Henry Barber's home over in Jingellic, to be cared for .... Oh, except for my nephews, the young Poyntz brothers, they have gone home."

"We will have police, black trackers and civilians scouring the bush, Mrs Barber, they will arrive in a matter of hours. Batson will be found. He will be brought to justice," said Constable Jolly with quiet, reassuring confidence.

"I hope so..." said Ruth sorrowfully.

"Just one thing before I let you get back to it.... Please be aware, and we will tell the other members of the party, we will have to obtain statements from all of you. Please be available and try to capture all the facts in your memory."

Ruth nodded and muttered goodbye. She got to her feet, and hurried back inside the Butter Factory Office to see if she could help in any way.

The constables determined that the priority was to launch a manhunt for Batson, and they agreed that the best muster point for searchers would be the Jingellic Hotel. They remounted and hastened across the river to plan and launch the search.

Inside the Butter Factory, Dr England sighed and announced, "We have done all we can for these men. We just need to get them to Albury now."

Soon the truck was reloaded. The patients and Sister Martin were accompanied by the Jingellic publican, John (Finlay) Smith and his brothers; James and Darcy. They were armed and were prepared to defend the party from a potential attack from Batson. The victims' wives were to follow the truck in a motor car driven by Mr Fred Dopper. All were made as comfortable as possible. They were supplied with torches, flasks of tea, bottles of water and some left-over picnic food. The ladies refused the offer of food, saying they had no appetite in such a dire situation. Mr Coysh hopped into the cab of the truck to accompany the driver, Albert Ashcroft, - to keep a look out and be a secondary driver if Albert tired. He, too, was armed with a rifle, just in case Batson tried to hold them up.

The truck revved and moved off with some grinding of gears.

Ruth looked at her husband and asked hesitantly, "Do you think they will be alright?"

Charles Barber stared after the vehicles and shrugged wearily.

"I fear for King and Sheppard. McGrath is tough as old boots... he will be all right. And Gainer, despite being in so much pain, I think he will just be left with a bad limp, a souvenir of this frightful business," Barber's voice trailed off.

"I think we will all be scarred by the experience! What possessed Claude to do such a thing? Why?" wailed Ruth.

Ruth broke down and sobbed uncontrollably. Charles wrapped his arms around his wife and just held her. His mind was racing with images and thoughts.

"Come on Ruthie, we will go home, have a cup of tea..." suggested Barber.

"And lock the doors!" sniffled Ruth.

They walked over to where their pony was tethered in the shade of a wattle tree in the Butter Factory yard. The patient gelding whickered when he heard Barber's voice.

"Hungry, Old Lad?" said Barber patting the pony's neck and untying him. He helped Ruth up into the trap before mounting himself. Once settled, Barber clucked to pony, and they set off at a smart trot. The pony was determined to get home - his afternoon feed was late!

Ruth was reluctant to enter their home on her own and waited whilst Barber unharnessed the pony, rubbed him down and groomed him before turning him out in the paddock with a bucket of chaff and grain. Barber then hefted the picnic basket on one arm and took his wife's hand, and they strolled up the fence line to the house. In the late afternoon sunshine, they could see that the door to their home stood ajar. Barber hesitated, Ruth gasped and shrank away from the house, alarmed that Batson may be lying in wait for them.

"Quick," hissed Barber, "hurry back to the shed and hide behind the trap, I will call you if it's safe!"

Ruth didn't need any encouragement, she just bolted.

Barber put down the picnic basket and armed himself with a hoe which he found leaning against the fence near the garden bed that Ruth had been weeding earlier in the week. He stealthily approached the house and slipped into the kitchen, noticing the chaos and disturbance. His hackles rose, and he braced himself for a fight. He quietly moved through the small house reassuring himself that there wasn't a fugitive lying in wait.

"It's all right, Ruth!" Barber called from the verandah, "No one is in the house... well, not anymore! But he has trashed everything!"

Ruth's face was drawn and ashen when she stepped up on the verandah and peered into the kitchen.

"No! No! Oh God, it must have been Claude! What has he done? Why us?" Ruth wailed as she stared at her now chaotic kitchen.

"We can't stay here tonight!" she declared with a shudder.

Barber shook his head gravely and put an arm around his wife's shoulders.

"We'll have to report the break-in and damage to Constable Jolly. We can go and stay in Walwa with the Hanna's tonight. Joseph will accommodate us. Pack an overnight bag, I'll go and catch the pony again."

Barber set off back to the yards with a determined stride, his mind in turmoil.

CHAPTER 13

Batson bolts from the Bryants

It was a hard slog up the face of the hill, even for someone as fit and bush hardened as Batson. The heat radiated off the rocky slope sapping his energy. The loose shale skittered from under his boots and the extra grip provided by the leather strips affixed to the soles was the only thing that prevented him from following the dislodged shale and pebbles down the slope.

Nearing the crest, he reached out and grasped a sapling and hauled himself up onto a rocky outcrop. Breathing hard, he turned and stood for a moment, looking back down into the valley. The harsh contrast between the green of the millet crop in Marchant's paddock and the adjacent sun-bleached, heavily grazed paddocks was stark. Cattle, dotted across the paddocks were reduced to ant-like shapes by the distance. Verdant willows and tea tree described the sinuous course of Jingellic Creek. The water glittered in the harsh sunlight as the creek flowed inexorably towards the Murray River. Batson looked for the site of the Jingellic picnic, of the chaos he had created, but it was obscured from view by the bulge of the hillside below him.

Anxiety fluttered against his ribs and his conscience prickled for a moment before his inner voice snarled, "They deserved it! 'Had it coming...''

His conscience struggled to be heard, "Maybe King, maybe Sheppard but the other fellows?"

"Should've taken out that bitch, too," continued the persuasive inner voice.

Batson snorted, shook his head, and spun on his heel, before marching determinedly up the final slope. The bandoliers and rifles lay heavy against his back and shoulders, rubbing against the sweat-soaked fabric of his shirt, chafing his skin. His dilly bag and bed roll added to the discomfort.

Wending his way through strewn rocks, thickets of tea tree and towering eucalypts, he made his way to the crest of the hill before walking the razorback trail in a north westerly direction. The country was familiar; it was territory he had traversed many times when out hunting and fossicking. A small mob of grey kangaroos which had been dozing in the shade of an apple box, took fright at his sudden intrusion. They stood, ears alert and flicking, scenting the air. Youngsters in the mob shuffled nervously as they watched the approaching man. Batson eyed the mob disdainfully before raising his free hand and pointing a finger at the group:

"Bang!" he exclaimed sharply.

The kangaroos burst into motion, scattering, springing away across the clearing in an elastic gait. They disappeared into the shelter of the bush. A kookaburra laughed raucously, and a willy wagtail chided from the boughs above Batson's head. He smiled grimly to himself.

Batson reviewed his plan: he aimed to head to Holbrook and then beyond, to the railway station at Culcairn. His ultimate destination was unknown - just away from the Upper Murray, away from persecution. His mind filled with echoes of the voices, the snide remarks, scornful laughs, and his vision blurred as a red haze took hold of him again.

"Could bloody well go bushranging…. Teach them all a thing or two!" Batson growled.

He thought for a bit and then shouted, "Bad Dog Batson!"

He let out a strangled groan and shook his head vigorously, Conscience and Revenge were still battling in his head. Batson hauled the flask from his dilly bag. He uncorked it and took a long draught, concentrating on the cooling sensation of the water sliding between tongue and palate, before swirling down his throat. He forcibly ejected the disquiet from his mind and focused on his surroundings. He needed to concentrate to keep his footing and hold his course as he picked his way down through the dense vegetation towards Lankeys Creek.

The sun was dipping to the west, and the heat was dissipating from the close air amongst the dense bush as Batson neared the roadway leading to Lankeys Creek. The small locality was comprised of a handful of properties, a hall, a set of rudimentary tennis courts and a wine shanty. He had cut across the rough terrain following bridle tracks and wildlife trails, descending from the hills through the valley to the west of Jingellic Creek, before rounding the lower slopes of the next crop of hills to get to Water Creek. He was tired of pushing through scrub and thought he would take the easier route on the road. It was late and he assumed traffic would be negligible or absent on the quiet stretch of road. He stepped onto the well-worn track and marched along doggedly.

As Batson was rounding a cutting, he heard hoofbeats and his thoughts immediately anticipated a mounted constable. He slid a rifle off his shoulder and was hastily loading a cartridge when a pony and rider cantered around the corner. Batson dropped to a knee, and he squeezed the trigger, but the pony skittered sideways as Batson's form emerged from the gloom and the shot failed to find a mark. The rider, a boy, squawked, threw the tennis racquet he was carrying at Batson and turned his pony, before he spurred the animal back the way they had come. Batson let him go.

"Saturday… tennis at Lankeys Creek!" he muttered to himself.

His stomach growled and he remembered that he hadn't eaten since Ruth Barber had made him a jam sandwich just before noon. He grimaced thinking about Ruth and his fingers caressed the wristlet watch in his pocket; the watch he had taken from her dresser whilst venting his frustration in the Barber house earlier in the day.

Batson recalled that the Bryant girls were keen tennis players. He wondered if they had left the courts for home yet. Pretty girls, always friendly, and their mother was an excellent cook, he thought. Perhaps he could get a bed for the night and a feed. Spurred on by the thought of food, he cut across the hill and made his way to the Bryant's property, Bannockburn, on Parsons' Creek. He examined the dust of the driveway, and, despite the increasing gloom, he could see tracks of a jinker exiting the gateway, but no returning tracks.

"Should be home soon…" thought Batson.

He shut the gate across the driveway, barring traffic and forcing a confrontation. He lay down in the bracken near the gate post to wait for the Bryant lasses. The bracken was cool and collapsed under his weight to create a springy but stalky bed. Batson stretched out and relaxed. He closed his eyes and allowed his ears to roam, identifying bird calls, picking up the distant chuckle of the creek and soon, hoof beats. The Bryant girls came along the track at a smart pace, reining in the pony when they saw the gate was closed. They were confused and anxious, even more so when Batson rose from the ferns, and they saw he was prickling with arms and ammunition.

He smiled in a ragged fashion and held his hands away from his body in a placating gesture as he approached the jinker.

"S'awright girls, I am not here to harm you! I was just set to delay the coppers…. They might be looking for me!" he boasted.

The girls paled.

"What would the police be wanting with you, Claude?" asked Margaret carefully.

She was the elder of the two, and the one who gripped the reins and the whip. She considered flicking the whip across Batson's face and wheeling the pony, but the track was narrow, and she would be unlikely to get them beyond the range of the rifle in the short space of time a whip lash might buy them. She was very aware of Baton's reputation as a marksman.

Batson grinned wolfishly and said, "Oh, I might have got myself in a bit of trouble."

Neither girl said anything but watched Batson closely.

"Like rabbits in the sights" he thought to himself.

"Look, come on girls, let's go down and see your Mam and maybe she can give me a bite to eat and a cuppa tea. I am famished!"

He felt a thrill of power as he watched alarm skitter across their pallid features.

"Ohh, don't worry, you know me, I won't harm you!" he added placatingly.

Annie and Margaret were terrified but could see no escape. They waited whilst Batson swung the gate wide, before hopping up behind them in the jinker. He casually rested one of his rifles across his knees.

Margaret clucked to the pony and shook the reins gently. The roan pony struck out for home.

The Bryant girls were dumbstruck by fear and, since Batson was not much of a conversationalist, the drive to the Bryant cottage was accompanied only by the sounds of hoofbeats, jangling harness and the sounds of the bush. The track was narrow. The shrubbery clawed at the jinker as they passed. They clopped and rumbled across a narrow bridge and the noise alerted the farm dogs who rushed out to meet the jinker, barking and swirling around the pony and leaping up at Batson.

Batson eyed the dogs nervously. Mrs Bryant appeared on the verandah and called the dogs off. Initially, she smiled and called out to the girls asking about tennis but when she caught sight of Batson, her face clouded. One of the neighbours had ridden by earlier in the day and passed on the horrific news of the shooting at the Jingellic picnic. She froze as Batson approached. The girls dismounted from the jinker and stood, fidgeting whilst watching their mother solemnly.

"What are you doing here, Claude?" called Mrs Bryant calmly, whilst anxiously examining her daughters for signs of harm.

"Oh, I am just travelling by, I thought you might be willing to share dinner with me, perhaps give me shelter for the night?"

"I see," replied Mrs Bryant slowly but thinking quickly, "happy to give you a share of dinner if you give us no strife. You can roll your swag out in the hay shed."

She was reluctant to have Batson stay at the property, but she was also aware that she little choice and didn't want to anger the young man, whose reputation of eccentricity preceded him.

"Come on girls, get a wriggle on! Annie, can you get some kindling from the wood heap, and Margaret, attend to the pony. Come in Claude, I will make you a cup of tea."

The two cattle dogs had their hackles up and were sniffing at Batson's legs, their frames were tense and menacing. Mrs Bryant pushed the dogs away from Claude and gently admonished them, "Git away, boys!"

She led the way into their humble cottage and busied herself stirring up the coals under the hob and putting the kettle on.

Batson surreptitiously scanned the room and listened to the house, assuring himself that there was no one else in the home. He settled at the kitchen table after resting his rifles against the wall near the dresser, along with his bandoliers, swag, and dilly bag. The rifles were within arm's reach, and he had his back to the wall with a view of the back door and the door to the hallway.

As Mrs Bryant was setting cups on the table the girls slunk into the kitchen cautiously. They glanced at their mother before resting their eyes suspiciously on Batson. He looked up and smiled grimly.

"Teatime!" he announced, "sit down, girls!"

Mrs Bryant held her girls' eyes with her own, willing them to steady and not inflame the situation.

"It's Sunday, so we were just going to have leftovers for tea.... Roast lamb, bread, cheese and tomatoes and greens from the garden... will that suit you, Claude?" she asked pleasantly.

"That would be good!" said Batson, smiling encouragingly.

Margaret moved carefully to the Coolgardie and retrieved the jug of milk for their tea. Mrs Bryant tipped boiling water into the enamel teapot before placing it on the table and rotating it, twice to the east, thrice to the west, whilst gazing at Batson pensively.

"So, what has happened, Claude? Why are you armed like a trooper? Why so far from home?"

Batson shrugged and considered a response.

"I have had enough, Missus. It has all got too much for me," he said quietly.

He paused; the women waited.

"They are always on at me. Ribbing me. No friends."

His words spilled in a bleak staccato.

"I just need to make my mark. I have decided to go and do a bit of bushranging!" announced Batson with bravado.

The girls looked frightened, Mrs Bryant forced a calm expression onto her face and quietly poured tea. She pushed a cup toward Batson and followed with the milk jug and sugar bowl.

The girls' eyes watched the ants scatter across the rough wood of the tabletop as they were disturbed from their hiding spot, beneath the pottery sugar bowl.

"Is that a sensible path, Claude?" asked Mrs Bryant quietly.

Batson shot an annoyed frown at the older woman.

There was a tense silence for a minute before Batson offered, "I don't have anything else I can do. 'Thought about it a few years ago. Down river, I met up with a fellow. A mate. He and another fellow were camped on the Murray at Burrowye. He had been in the navy, in the war. He had a pistol, and we had a bit of a shooting competition. He won, but only because I have only ever used rifles before. We had a plan to go bushranging then, but he let me down and pulled out. He went on another path," the words spilled from Batson's mouth.

Memories scudded across Batson's features before he frowned again and then suddenly, his face broke into a wolfish grin, and he said, "When I was a kid at Auntie's in Germanton... Holbrook, now, you know, me and me mates used to ride out to Morgan's Lookout. Mad Dog Morgan! We would play at being bushrangers and act out shooting Constable Maginnity, robbing coaches... But never hurting women!" he added, as the girls were shifting anxiously and looking at their mother with panicked eyes.

"No, don't worry, you are safe with me!" Batson reassured the women vehemently.

Mrs Bryant stood, keen to move the conversation away from violence.

"I will just get the dinner together! Annie, Margaret go and pick some salad greens and tomatoes from the garden. Oh, and lock up the chickens!" said Mrs Bryant in a calm voice.

The girls bolted gratefully from the kitchen. Once in the cool gloom of the garden they whispered to one another. Annie suggested they get the pony and ride for help.

"No, that won't work, Mam would be left alone and in danger!" said Margaret urgently, "We will have to just play along, keep each other safe and when he goes tomorrow, we can alert the police and trackers."

The girls collected the vegetables and returned to the kitchen with brave faces and a resolve to be calm.

Dinner was a quiet, tense affair in the Bryant household that evening. Batson's noisy chewing and boastful commentary relating to his plans for his proposed bushranging career provided the only soundtrack to the meal. He assured the women that he had plans in place to be successful. He pointed out that he had planted caches of ammunition and food in the hills surrounding Walwa and Jingellic and explained that he knew the terrain of the Upper Murray like no other.

"I can live off the land. They'd never catch me!" Batson declared.

"Why don't you just go to another district, make a new life for yourself, Claude? Bushrangers always get caught!" suggested Mrs Bryant quietly.

Batson glared at the woman.

"I thought about going to Melbourne, but it would be the same... different place but people would treat me the same...I want to make my mark!" his voice broke with something akin to anguish as he spoke, and his face clouded.

Batson's inner voice was back, niggling at him.

"Make a mark to obliterate the white feather?" the voice chided.

A jumble of images and memories of snide remarks skittered across his mind: Richard King declaring pompously that "Batson was *only* the Walwa Rifle Club champion because all the genuine marksmen had enlisted and had done their duty.... they had fallen in service to King and Country or had no need to waste their time shooting at stupid targets!"

Batson remembered that Percy Barber had found King's comments hilarious. Batson felt the jibes burrowing through his soul.... The pain was reignited.

When dinner was done, and the dishes had been washed and put away in the dresser, Mrs Bryant announced that she and the girls were going to bed.

"You can roll out your swag in the hay shed; you should be comfortable. The dogs won't bother you," said Mrs Bryant with a confidence she didn't feel.

Batson looked at Mrs Bryant thoughtfully before saying, "I am comfortable here in the kitchen. I will just stay put."

Mrs Bryant tried to keep the alarm from her face and just turned on her heel, shepherding her two girls from the room. In the hall, she hissed at the girls: "We will all sleep in my room and barricade the door!"

Dawn broke and the raucous squabbling of magpies under the orange tree beside the back verandah roused Batson from his restless doze. He stretched, rolled from his bedding, and got up. He stood, listening to the household and beyond. All was quiet, no threats. He rolled up his swag and checked his kit. His thoughts ran with jumbled images of the picnic, the shooting, blood, the victims, his unintended victims, and those that he had failed to bring to account.

"I will get you, ... *The Prince*, and you, too, you two-faced witch, Mrs Ruth Barber!" Batson snarled the names of his targets, louder than he intended.

He moved to the backdoor, cracked it open and listened, reassuring himself that the cottage was not being watched. He stepped out onto the verandah and urinated noisily into the flowers just off the steps. Batson returned to the kitchen. From deeper within the house, came sounds of stirring: The Bryants were moving about.

"Would you muster some breakfast for me, please, before I am off, Missus?" Batson called out hopefully.

He could hear the women whispering to one another.

"Missus!" he called with menace.

"I am coming!" called Mrs Bryant sharply.

She emerged from the depths of the hallway catching up whisps of greying hair and creating a loose bun behind her head as she moved. She was dressed as she was the previous evening. Her clothing was rumpled and creased. She and the girls had slept in their clothes in case they had needed to run, or worse, fight.

She glared at Batson and said with exaggerating politeness, "What can I get for you, Sir?"

Batson ignored her tone and responded, "A cuppa would be nice, maybe some toast and eggs?"

He could hear the chickens in their coop in the garden heralding their egg production efforts and a rooster crowed lustily, welcoming the new day. Mrs Bryant huffed and silently went about gathering breakfast supplies and setting the table. The girls emerged with equally creased and crumpled clothes. They helped their mother to prepare breakfast in a surly silence. Batson sat near the stove with a rifle between his knees, his dilly bag on the table and the rest of his kit on the floor at his feet.

The eggs were sizzling in the pan and toast was browning in the oven as Mrs Bryant poured tea. Batson watched the activity a little wistfully; it reminded him of the happier times he had spent in Ruth Barber's kitchen, "Before King came along!" he thought with malice.

Annie crossed the kitchen floor and stooped to open the door of the Coolgardie to get the butter for the toast. As she reached inside, something caught her eye through the window. She started as she observed a pair of horses and riders on the approach. Before she could say or do anything, the dogs started baying and barrelled up the drive to announce the visitors.

Batson shot to his feet, ducked his head to the window to see what was up, before glaring around at the panic-stricken women.

"They have found me!" he shrilled, gathering his rifles and kit, "Stay here, don't scream!" he ordered, before crashing through the house, down the hallway, and out of the door at the back of the house. He jogged across the patch of thirsty grass which passed for a lawn and pushed through a wooden gate into the orchard. There were voices behind him: men shouting, dogs barking. As he ran, he stole a glance over his shoulder. He saw the two mounted constables, throw themselves from their horses. They ran after Batson ducking between the outhouse and the cottage. One had a clear view of Batson and dropped to a knee, raising a rifle to his shoulder.

"Stop! In the name of the law!"

Batson threw himself sideways behind a scrawny apple tree just as a gunshot echoed across the valley. The shot missed its target, but Batson's hat flew from his head. He lost no time retrieving it and scampered in a zig zag fashion through the orchard. Rifle fire followed him. He reached the back fence and threw himself over the obstacle.

There was another crack as he was mid-flight and a bullet grazed his arm, parting the fabric of his sleeve. Beyond the fence, Batson was immediately cloaked in the dense bush. He turned and loosed a volley of shots at his pursuers. He couldn't see a target through the cross hatchings of tree trunks and canopies of the orchard, but he hoped to put the officers to ground and provide himself with an opportunity to flee. He turned and fought through the tea-tree and wattles, holding onto his kit and rifles doggedly. He had recognised one of the police officers as Seargeant Tom Morris from Holbrook. A chill ran down his spine. Morris came with an enviable reputation: He was nominated for a Victoria Cross in the Boer War and, from the numerous rifle club competitions in which both had participated, Batson knew that Morris pipped him for the title of the best shot in the Riverina.

Batson pulled up behind the monstrous girth of an ancient Red Gum and took a bit of time to organise his kit. He swung the bandoliers across his chest, slung a rifle on each shoulder along with his swag. It was then he noticed the absence of his dilly bag. He sighed, re-membering he had left it on the table anticipating that he would be resupplied with food after breakfast. Batson listened to the approach of the officers; he could hear them crashing through the bush not far behind him. Ducking between the trunks and dense foliage of a tea-tree coppice, he headed off in a direction due west of his last position. Now running at right angles to his previous direction of travel, Batson hoped that the change of direction would throw the police off his heels. He dropped down a steep embankment and scrambled into a deep erosion channel. The going was rough, but there was plenty of cover as the channel switch-backed down to Parsons Creek. Batson paused again and listened. He was thrilled to hear that the police officers were still moving on the original course - they had anticipated that Batson would take the easier path.

Batson found a huge wombat cavern in the wall of the embankment; it was under the roots of a Kurrajong tree which was valiantly trying to maintain its grip on the steep bank. He stopped and checked his tracks. The shale in the base of the erosion channel was forgiving and there was no evidence of his approach. He hoisted himself up the bank and settled his kit and his body at the entrance to the cavern behind a shroud of tree roots. He sat still, listening. There was no noise, no approach. He held his position for half an hour. He sipped water from his flask and rested and thought about the breakfast he had almost eaten and his dilly bag on the Bryant's table. His stomach rumbled.

Sergeant Morris and Constable O'Connor were frustrated and snapped at one another as they gave up the chase and trudged back down the hill towards the Bryant home.

"We had him in our sights! He shouldn't have got away!" growled Morris.

"We should have come down from the gate on foot, under cover!" said O'Connor.

"We didn't know he was in there!" said Morris pointedly.

"Bloody dogs!" spat O'Connor.

Morris stooped and picked up Batson's hat from where it had landed after spinning from his head in the orchard.

"That was a bit close!" said Morris, as he pointed out a fresh nick in the crown of the sweat-stained hat.

"Not close enough!" said O'Connor sorrowfully.

The Bryants were standing on the back verandah when the police officers appeared from the orchard. Their expressions were anxiously curious. Morris removed his hat and addressed the women.

"Lost him in the bush!" he said, his tone flat and laced with frustration, "May have winged him but couldn't find any tracks. We will continue down to Jingellic and report to the Officer in Charge of the investigation. We will get some trackers back here a bit later."

"Will Claude come back?" asked Annie tremulously.

Morris shook his head, "I doubt it, but perhaps consider going to stay with friends or relatives until we have him cornered."

Mrs Bryant sighed and shrugged, "We have stock to look after! We won't be ejected from our home by Claude! I will just clean and check the rabbit gun." she said bravely.

"Well, lock the doors and don't go out after dark!" advised O'Connor.

Mrs Bryant relayed the comments made by Batson in relation to his proposed bushranger activities and caches of supplies.

Morris nodded sagely and said confidently, "Well, that's a good sign that he intends to stay in the locality! He will show up somewhere and we will snare him!"

The policemen said their goodbyes to the women, swung up on to their horses, and cantered off towards Jingellic.

Germanton (Holbrook) Police station, c1915 vs c2015 - Albury and District Historical Society

CHAPTER 14

Call in the cavalry

Albury police station was humming with activity as police officers were mustered and ammunition and arms were distributed from the munitions store and assigned to officers. Kit bags lined the corridors awaiting loading into the vehicles. Telephones trilled and multiple conversations and shouted instructions assaulted the ears. There was a thrill of excitement and eager anticipation emanating from the assembled men.

At 10am Superintendent Cook, of Murray Police District, swept through the corridors summoning the officers as he went. He entered the incident room followed by his men and *The Blowfly,* as Cook liked to call the persistent journalist who hovered around the Albury police station collecting snippets of information to be printed in the columns of the Albury Banner. Cook glared at the journalist and was about to order him off premises but then thought better of it, as he considered that publicity would be good for his reputation, perhaps lead to a promotion. He settled for a baleful stare and then turned his attention to his officers.

"Settle down, gents!" he ordered and referred to his notes whilst the police officers drew up chairs and focused their attention on *The Chief.*

"This is Detective Cleaver," said Cook, indicating the wiry man in a dark suit who stood quietly alongside, "he will be Officer in Charge on scene in Walwa and Jingellic. I will remain here in Albury and manage communications, resources, and press releases."

He glared meaningfully at Phillip Hardwick, *The Blowfly*, who merely raised his eyebrows and smiled benignly at his nemesis.

"This is what we know about this Batson case – *The Picnic Sniper,*" Cook paused, admiring his turn of phrase before continuing, "The fugitive is a 24-year-old male, identified by witnesses as Claude Valentine Batson. He has fired on a picnic party on the Jingellic Creek, one and a half miles from the village of Jingellic. He has gravely injured four male members of the party. The victims were admitted to Albury Hospital, this morning, just after 3am after an horrendous trip from Jingellic in the tray of a farm truck. Two victims are in a poor condition and, in consideration of this, officers have met with them this morning and obtained bedside depositions. Motive for the attack is unknown. Description of the offender is: 5'6, slim build, swarthy complexion, clean shaven, thin features, wavy black hair, last seen wearing black boots, blue suit, black hat. He walks with a distinctive long stride. He is heavily armed. Obviously, he is considered extremely dangerous."

Cook paused and let his gaze slide across the faces of his officers, allowing the gravity of the situation to sink in.

"We will move out at 11am and travel in convoy to Walwa. Please ensure you have adequate kit for three days, after which another group will relieve you, if necessary, although I anticipate a rapid conclusion of this case, as we have excellent cooperation from all districts. A contingent of mounted police and trackers have been despatched from Holbrook, Tumbarumba, Wagga Wagga, and Gundagai. In addition, Seargent O'Neil from St Kilda Road Police Department is arriving by train this afternoon, accompanied by some highly skilled officers, several of whom were resident in Walwa in their youth and are very familiar with the terrain. In addition, armed civilians have volunteered to comb the hills. We envisage that Batson will soon be flushed from cover and captured," announced Cook confidently.

The mention of armed civilians on the loose caused mild consternation. The journalist scribbled notes furiously. In capital letters he wrote a note to himself to raise the controversial issue of gun registration for community discussion. A brave constable asked boldly, "Will armed civilians present some risk to official searchers - will we be potentially caught in the crossfire?"

Cook frowned at the constable, noting his identity and temerity.

"No, Constable Peters, they will be under the direction of Detective Cleaver, who will ensure that there will be no vigilante, poorly considered actions ... from any party!" said Cook in a patronising tone.

The police officers glanced around and murmured to one another doubtfully.

Cook huffed and announced, "There will be a further briefing of any developments when you reach Walwa, and then you will be allocated to search parties. I remind you to keep your wits about you. Batson is reputed to be a champion marksman, a skilled and experienced bushman and knows the country like the back of his hand! Now, off you go, collect your kit, and assemble in the quadrangle to load up into vehicles. Good luck and good hunting, lads!"

As the constables jostled and pressed to leave the room and collect kit bags, Peters could be heard enquiring of his colleague in a puzzled tone:

"If Batson is such a champion shot, why didn't he kill anyone?"

"One victim is near dead! The Chief just said they conducted bedside depositions from the victims earlier this morning, maybe they anticipate more to follow!" said the younger officer, Constable MacDonald.

"Yes, but a sniper worth his weight, would dispatch a target instantly with no questions asked!" mused Peters reflecting on his own experience during his time with the AIF.

As a member of the ANZAC troops in 1914, Peters had spent hours hunkered down behind the sparse cover on the Gallipoli heights, waiting for an unsuspecting Turk to appear in his sights.

"Maybe this Batson character is a sandwich short of a picnic … maybe he wanted to wound and inflict pain and terror, not cause immediate death for his victims!" deduced Peters.

MacDonald paled and offered, "We had best watch each other's backs then, or hunters might become the hunted!"

"Enough yapping!" growled Superintendent Cook, "Pick up your kit and hop to it!"

—ele—

Constable Jolly from Walwa Police Station and Constable Rice, the Jingellic police officer, were conducting an informal community information session to a clamouring group of townsfolk from both sides of the Murray River at Smith's Jingellic Hotel. It had become the headquarters for the investigation. The police officers stood in the shade of the bullnose verandah of the hotel and called for order.

"Settle down! Settle!" called Jolly gruffly.

The group of, predominantly men, shuffled forward to listen.

"Aw'right now!" announced Constable Rice, "We have a difficult situation here.... We know that a man opened fire at a picnic party yesterday lunch time!"

"Batson!" growled Frank Hunt who was leaning casually against the verandah post.

"Innocent, until proven guilty!" offered the schoolteacher.

"Well, yes, Claude Batson is the alleged gunman. We must find him, and he must be brought to face justice. No shooting on sight!" warned Rice.

"What if he shoots first?" asked a shearer from the back of the crowd.

"If he shoots first, you probably won't be in a fit state to get a shot away!" suggested his companion, "Batson can shoot the buttons off a military tunic at a hundred yards!"

The crowd started to jostle and clamour again.

Jolly took control.

"Now see here! I want Batson apprehended, but we also want our people safe," stated Jolly firmly.

He glared sternly at the crowd before continuing, "We know that Batson will have the upper hand in the hills, so we will wait for reinforcements and trackers. In the meantime, providing you can be assured that your women folk are safe and protected, we will accept armed volunteers to set up roadblocks on all access tracks and roads, bridge crossings and fords within a five-mile radius of Walwa and Jingellic. We know he was last seen and came under fire from Seargent Tom Morris and Constable O'Connor at the Bryants' home at Parsons Creek just after eight this morning. He then headed East up into the hills. Our concern is that he has a vendetta on members of the picnic party and may well circle around to come back at them."

"So, he is still in the area? Not heading for Melbourne? He kept going on and on about going to Melbourne whenever he appeared at my house!" said Alf Lawrence.

"Yeah, he came to our camp yesterday morning," said John Kelly, "he was proper peculiar! All uptight and brandishing his rifle about. He boasted about what a crack shot he was and knocked a mistletoe knot out of a gum tree which was over 150 yards away."

"I was real' glad when he pushed off – he could have made us his next targets!" added his brother.

"Maybe he wants to go and buddy up with Squizzy Taylor?" called out one of the Wilsons' lads excitedly. He had been an avid follower of the frequent updates in the headlines of newspapers on the notorious Melbourne gangster. Squizzy was the lad's hero.

"Order, Order!" called out Constable Rice, feeling that they were losing control of their audience.

"Quite so, thank you, Constable Rice!" said Jolly, "As I was saying, if you wish to volunteer to the civilian brigade to protect our community and potentially apprehend our suspect, Claude Batson, then you will need to register with us here, and we will allocate you to strategic points across the district. Those who do not own a rifle, we can furnish you with a rifle and ammunition – for self-protection only! You cannot take the law into your own hands! We don't want posses taking off across the hills and shooting one another by accident!"

There were several chuckles and sarcastic comments from the crowd.

The constables stepped back and opened a freshly marked-up ledger in which the volunteers were to insert their details and sign a brief waiver. There was a rush of men to sign up.

Just then, Sergeant Morris and Constable O'Connor cantered around the cutting to the South of the hotel and pulled up near the crowd of men in a clatter of hooves. The officers slid from their horses and tethered them to a rail. The horses were blowing hard and were lathered with sweat.

Jolly and Rice grinned in greeting across the crowd. Constable Jolly pushed through the throng to meet his colleagues, leaving Rice to manage the registrations.

"Good morning, Sergeant, Constable! You had a bit of excitement this morning, I hear!" said Jolly.

Morris grinned ruefully as he smoothed his uniform, removed his cap, and mopped his brow.

"Had a shot but winged him at best! O'Connor has souvenired his hat though!" announced Morris.

O'Connor retrieved Batson's hat from his saddlebag and showed Jolly the bullet hole in the crown. Jolly whistled in appreciation of the near miss and continued:

"I have been advised to expect Detective Cleaver from Albury to take up the role of Officer in Charge of the search and investigation. He and a team will leave Albury at 11am. In the meantime, the publican has made the dining room available to us to set up the headquarters for coordinating the manhunt, and he has a telephone."

Morris nodded in agreement. Jolly deferred to Morris' superior rank and suggested,

"The volunteers are just registering. Perhaps you and Constable O'Connor could determine the appropriate locations for check points and allocate the volunteers?"

"Do you have a map?" asked Morris.

"Yes, we have combined the information from a couple of official maps and transcribed appropriate features to a large blackboard so that we can mark sectors and locations," said Jolly with some pride.

"Excellent!" said Morris appreciatively and allowed Jolly to lead the way to view the map and commence planning the campaign to capture the fugitive. Morris was looking forward to the hunt. It was reminiscent of his Boer War campaigns, and he was itching for action.

It was twilight by the time the convoy of officers arrived from Albury. They dismounted from the vehicles and stretched wearily. Kit bags and rifles were retrieved, and the constables assembled in formation to await directions from Detective Cleaver. Constable Rice hurried out of the Jingellic Hotel to meet them. He pulled up and saluted stiffly to Cleaver.

"Evening! Detective Cleaver, I believe!" said Rice.

"Quite so! Constable Rice, is it?" said Cleaver.

"Yes, Sir!" said Rice smartly.

"We shall welcome some refreshment and a briefing as to the developments to date. We were pleased to note the effective roadblocks and bridge checkpoint on the way in. Well done!" said Cleaver with a smile.

"The locals have been very keen to volunteer to catch the fugitive, Sir. Sergeant Morris from Holbrook, has taken charge of the operation on the north side of the river," said Rice.

"... and to the south?" asked Cleaver

"Constable Jolly, from Walwa police station is coordinating the Victorians and reporting to his superiors in Benalla and Wangaratta, he is expecting a party of mounted constables under Sergeant O'Neil from St Kilda Police Department at any tick, too." said Rice.

"A real federation of police assistance!" commented Cleaver and signalled to his officers to follow.

They pushed their way through the front bar, which was crowded with patrons, all curious to observe the police activity and keen to catch a snatch of information which could be turned to gossip.

"I would hope these fellows haven't left women and children at home to defend themselves from Batson!" growled Cleaver.

Rice glanced around and assured the Detective that the patrons were mostly single men.

"Best call time, so that we can discuss police business and partake of refreshments without unofficial ears," commented Cleaver brusquely.

Rice hurried away to talk to the barkeep, Finlay Smith.

The police officers clattered into the small dining room and settled into chairs. Soon waitresses delivered food to the tables, together with jugs of water. The men were famished and tucked in heartily.

Cleaver studied the map and asked questions of Constable Rice.

"What do we know of the fellow, Claude Batson? Is he likely to clear the area, or double back to his home.... Where is his home?" asked Cleaver.

Rice indicated the Bryants' property on the map.

"He was here at 8am, had a shootout with Sergeant Morris and Constable O'Connor, before ducking into the bush. Heading east, they thought, but at 5:30pm he was spotted by Mr Unger, here on the hills above Horse Creek, some three miles from Jingellic. My best bet is that he is doubling back ... he seems to have unfinished business," said Rice gravely.

Cleaver raised his eyebrows in a questioning manner.

Rice hurried on, "One of the picnic party, Charles Barber, who was very familiar with Batson, was concerned that Batson may have snapped and had his sights on his wife, Ruth Barber."

"Romantically?" asked Cleaver.

"No, no, he was jealous or angry and Barber feels that Batson wanted to do her harm. It would appear that Batson has gone to their home and ransacked it," said Rice.

"Before or after the shooting?" queried Cleaver.

"I understand it was before, because the time for him to get over the hill to Bryants' doesn't allow for him to have gone back to the Barbers' home after the shooting."

"So, if he was seen up here, north of Jingellic at 5:30pm, what is your projection as to his whereabouts?" asked Cleaver.

"I don't want to presume, but I would imagine he would be making to cross the Murray River in order to return to Victoria," suggested Rice.

"Can the man swim?" asked Cleaver.

"He is an experienced bushman, but I have no idea about his swimming abilities. He is heavily armed, so I would imagine he would cross at a ford or bridge to avoid getting his kit wet," answered Rice.

"These are the fords?" asked Cleaver pointing at the map.

"Yes, Sergeant Morris has armed civilians watching the crossing points."

"I think, once the men have eaten, we will dispatch an officer to each of these points to support the civilians. With a rotating watch arrangement, they can keep an eye on the crossings 'till daylight and then in the morning, we will sort search parties with trackers to scour the countryside and bring him to ground," said Cleaver confidently.

Jolly added to the conversation: "We were advised by Superintendent Cook, that adjacent districts have been notified, and squads have been dispatched from Wagga Wagga, Tumbarumba and Gundagai, in addition to parties already here, so the net is closing around him!"

Satisfied with the plan, Cleaver announced the arrangements to the assembled police officers and settled down to eat his meal.

View towards Walwa from hill above Jingellic - Arnold Playle Collection, Man from Snowy River Museum.

CHAPTER 15

Jacob

Minnie was sitting at the kitchen table with a large bowl of peas and a pot set in front of her. She was rhythmically shelling the peas, and dropping the fresh, bright green morsels directly into a saucepan, ready for dinner. Emma was tending the roast. The phone jangled, startling the women from their thoughts. Emma flinched and inadvertently splashed the juices from the pan onto the range. The fat sizzled and spat at her.

"Ouch," she said in frustration and manoeuvred the joint back into the depths of the hot oven. She closed the door, wiped her hands on her apron and enquired, "Would you like me to answer the telephone, Aunt Minnie?"

Minnie nodded and watched whilst Emma crossed to the door and slipped through into the dining room and picked up the receiver from the sideboard.

"Hello, Drummond residence," she said confidently.

The operator, May Griffith, hesitated as she tried to reconcile the unfamiliar voice with the telephone connection on the switchboard.

"Oh, I was expecting Minnie or Albert Drummond," she said quizzically.

"Yes, Minnie is here, she is a little indisposed at present, may I take a message, or can I help you?" said Emma.

Minnie was tired and was thankful that her niece had the initiative to field the call. She listened in on the conversation.

"I have a gentleman on the line who is requiring to speak to a guest of the Drummonds, Miss Emma Payne. I was wondering if Minnie and Albert had such a guest?" said the switchboard operator, who was barely able to contain her curiosity.

Emma's innards swooped against her ribs, as she was flooded with anxiety for her parents' welfare.

"This is she.... I am Emma Payne," she said with a slight catch in her voice.

"Very well," said the operator.

There was a click on the line and a hum.

"Putting you through now, Mr Miller!" announced the operator.

Emma's innards did a further flurry of gymnastics, and she couldn't help the big smile that broke across her face.

"Jacob! Jacob, it is so lovely that you have called!" cried Emma.

"I hope you don't think me presumptuous, but I had to make contact! There has been a confusion of talk in the office …. has there been a shooting up there, near you? Are you quite safe?" Jacob asked anxiously.

Emma was flattered that the young man was concerned for her wellbeing.

"Yes, quite well, quite safe! I understand from the information Uncle Albert has gleaned from the bush telegraph, that a rabbit trapper has snapped, gone mad and shot up a picnic party!" said Emma.

Jacob was shocked, "What! Like Norman List in the Botanic Gardens?"

"Yes! So strange - two similar tragedies in a month!" said Emma gravely.

Emma felt a new twinge of anxiety rising at her core.

"Copycat or coincidence?" pressed Jacob.

"No idea!" said Emma

"Have they caught the madman?" asked Jacob.

"Uncle Albert says there are troops of police and trackers flooding into the district and about seventy armed civilians have turned out to comb the hills to catch him! He says the fellow is in the hills on the north side of the Murray, he would have no reason to come back to the Victorian side," said Emma.

"Where is Albert now?" asked Jacob with concern.

"He has gone to fetch the children from school in the truck, just to be careful!" said Emma with a forced cheerful lilt.

"There is a company of ex-AIF fellows from Albury and Wodonga who are volunteering to the search parties up there, I feel I must come too. It must be so terrible for you! The incident must have stirred up so many appalling memories!" said Jacob.

Emma was immediately excited at the prospect of seeing Jacob again.

"I shall ask Uncle Albert and Aunt Minnie if you might have a bed and stay here on the farm!" she said with enthusiasm.

"No, I don't think that would be appropriate!" said Jacob a little stiffly, "I would certainly love to see you, but I hardly know your uncle, and we aren't stepping out!"

"Hmmm, we could change that!" said Emma boldly.

Jacob chuckled. A deep throaty, exciting sound, even with the distortion of the phone line. There was another tone on the line and Emma kicked herself for her naivety as she realised the operator was listening in on their conversation. She coughed and a flush of embarrassment glowed on her cheeks.

"I mean, this would be an opportunity for you to meet the Drummonds!" she said quickly.

Jacob caught the suggestion and said firmly, "No, the search parties will be very busy, and we are to bring swags – we have been told that we are to camp together in the hall whilst deputised, as it were... but I will make time for afternoon tea with yourself and the Drummonds, or perhaps lunch at the hotel or a café?"

"That would be lovely, I shall look forward to seeing you again! Call when you know when you will be available, and I will let Aunt Minnie and Uncle Albert know of the plans!" said Emma happily.

"Goodbye Emma!" said Jacob.

Jacob's voice was like syrup. Emma couldn't contain herself and sighed like a schoolgirl and whispered in a voice laced with excitement, "Goodbye, Jacob!"

Emma skipped back to the kitchen; she couldn't resist the urge. Minnie watched with amusement.

"Good news?" she asked with a glint in her eye.

Emma coloured again and replied awkwardly, "Umm, yes, that was Jacob... Jacob Miller, the fellow with whom I travelled on the train. He was the one who helped me in the Botanic Gardens..."

She faltered as her thoughts swirled back to the terrible day in Melbourne.

Minnie caught the drift and smiled encouragingly. "Oh, how lovely that he called you! Is he coming to visit?"

Emma was grateful for her aunt's understanding.

"Yes... indirectly. He is volunteering to the civilian search party for Claude Batson. He says there is a group of ex-AIF fellows coming up to help and he will find some time to catch up with me, well, us, whilst he is in town. He was worried about me!"

Minnie smiled at her flushed and excited niece.

"Young love!" she thought to herself, but aloud she said, "Come on Emma, best get to peeling potatoes! We can discuss Jacob at dinner; I am sure Albert will be thrilled to catch up with him again! We could have lunch together or afternoon tea!"

Emma nodded gratefully and ducked into the pantry to retrieve some potatoes and hide her flushed cheeks from her aunt.

CHAPTER 16

Day 1 of the search for Batson: Tuesday, 12 February 1924

Batson sat on the bank of the Murray River. He was tired. The sun was just starting to push at the base of some wispy clouds to the east, staining the clouds salmon pink. Birds were stirring and calling.

It had been a hard trudge down from the hills under the cover of darkness - there had been no moon to guide him, so Batson had been forced to stay on the wider trails, navigating by a memory map. He was familiar with the path but in poor light, he had been snared numerous times by blackberry thickets, slapped in the face by low-slung boughs and almost brought to grief by unstable rocks underfoot. He was scratched, sweaty and surly. Pulling off his boots and socks, Batson eyed the stretch of river he intended to cross. The water sidled by in inky blackness.

Coming to a decision, he rolled up his trouser legs and wrapped his rifles in his jacket and secured the bundle with his belt. He removed Ruth Barber's watch from his pocket and caressed the face of the watch with his thumb thoughtfully before pushing it into the folds of his swag for safe keeping. The fugitive stowed his swag and the two bandoliers in a disused wombat burrow between the roots of a willow and pulled some dry bracken fronds across the entrance to hide the cache. Finally, he stuffed his socks into his boots and, knotting the laces together, he draped the boots around his neck. Picking up the bundle of rifles, he made his way down the steep riverbank to the edge of the water. He paused, scanned his surroundings, and listened for a few minutes. He expected that the police would have set up lookouts along the river crossings. He had seen the roadblock on the bridge at 2am. The guards had been playing cards by the light of a hurricane lamp to keep themselves awake. They were talking quite enthusiastically - perhaps some liquor had been used as a stimulant. Their voices carried on the breeze, up the hill to where Batson had squatted for some time, resting and watching them.

Batson was satisfied that nobody was monitoring this stretch of the river. He sucked his breath in through his teeth and steeled himself for the embrace of cold water. Even at the height of summer, the Murray was chill at its depths. With an origin in the High Country and created from snow melt and deep underground springs, the river was always freezing. The sticky, warm conditions overnight made little difference to the Murray's cold currents.

Batson stepped into the river and flinched; the bone numbing cold was shocking. His feet sank into the silty mud, and he steadied himself by swinging his free hand wide whilst the other raised the bundle of rifles above his head. He had crossed at this spot numerous times in the past and knew that he would have to manage the swift water channel and cross to the shoal of river pebbles which created a wide, shallow approach to the island. It wasn't a big island, but it was a favourite haunt of Batson's. It was contoured, with mounds created by flood-borne silt deposits on top of aboriginal shell middens. These provided a quiet haven of grassy knolls between stands of tall river red gums. Willows had colonised the banks so there was always plenty of shade and camouflage from prying eyes. The rolling grassed expanses were perfect to roll out a swag and there was an abundance of fallen limbs and driftwood for campfires. The twisted tree roots and snags in the river provided an excellent habitat for fish and Murray Cray. Batson would often spend time on the island during summer for a change of scenery and diet.

He pushed on through the icy water, he knew that there would come a point where the current would snatch at him, and he would have to swim or float to cross the deepest portion of the channel. He had done it before and was confident that he could push off and let the current take him downstream a little and within a chain he would be back to a depth where he could wade.

He had made an error: he hadn't considered the recent rainstorm and subsequent torrent of minor flooding. The contours of the riverbed had changed, and he was indeed caught by the slick current, but it was not cooperating with his plans. He started to panic. He struggled to keep his bundle aloft, his rifles dry. His dense trousers were acting like a sea anchor, dragging him down in the water. With no belt, he felt his trousers slide down his hips, the fabric was interfering with his kicking, he was being dragged under. Water was not his friend. Batson clawed at the fabric of his trousers pulling off the restrictive garb. As he struggled, he felt his boots leave his neck. Water was in his mouth, his nose, there were spots before his eyes, panic was making him thrash. Finally, his trousers were gone, and he was able to get his head above water. He snorted and coughed, clearing his airways. He was thankful he had managed to keep the bundle above water, well, mostly above water. His arm was tiring, and it was awkward to propel himself with a one-handed stroke. He kicked out to steady himself and his foot struck a snag. Pain bloomed up his leg as his toes were smashed into a submerged tree. The current pinned him against the snag and his shirt was held fast by unseen branches. Using his feet against the tree trunk he levered himself up, keeping his head above water. The fabric of his shirt gave way, tearing down the seam, but it was still held fast. Batson shrugged off the shirt, swapping his bundle from one hand to the other to extricate himself from his shirt which was now tethering him to the tree trunk. He allowed the current to take his body over the submerged tree and suddenly he found himself in relatively still water in the lee of the tree. He was near done.

Batson's feet found the stony riverbed and he pushed off to the shallow water at the edge of the island. He waded and limped to the bank and pulled himself up onto a grassed hillock. He was exhausted and fell to the grass in a heap. Blood pounded in his ears, and his breathing was ragged. He coughed to clear some residual water from his airways and stretched out in the sun. The warmth eased his shivering.

After a few minutes of recovery, Batson sat up and reviewed the damage. Two toes on his right foot were a bloodied mess, he had scratches across his ribs and arms, and his clothing was reduced to underwear. He was exhausted. He lay back down and rolled over to warm his back in the sunshine. After a few minutes, he propped his head up on his forearm and listened. Satisfied that all he could hear were sounds of the environment, and no evidence of trackers, or troopers, he thought he could risk a nap. He shuffled over a little so that his form was obscured from the view of casual observers by a screen of shrubbery. Within a few minutes he was in a deep and dreamless sleep.

Batson was roused by insects. There were flies crawling on his face and into his wounds, a relentless buzz of activity and intrusion into his orifices and injuries. He sat up and swatted at the swarm. He had slept longer than he had anticipated, and anxiety swept over him. He searched the hills above him and his surrounds, listening for trackers. Satisfied that he was unobserved and alone, he made his way down to the edge of the river and washed the blood from his wounds. His skin felt prickly and tight with the beginnings of sunburn.

He regretted that he had not had the foresight to stash some clothes with his caches of ammunition on the island. He moved silently through the undergrowth and checked on the security of two of his caches. He uncovered the larger of the two and exchanged his two rifles for a Webley revolver and ammunition to suit. He rewrapped the rifles in a dry sheet of canvas which he had stashed in the cavity of his cache and slid them deep into the crevice. He hung his now soggy, jacket within the hollow of a tree, hoping it would dry without shrinking. He spun the chambers of the revolver and slid a bullet into each chamber. No pockets meant no spare ammunition, but he assumed six bullets would be sufficient for his purposes. His intention at this point was to check on the Barbers' whereabouts, potentially tick off at least one of the two remaining targets and to obtain clothes and food, since he had lost his clothes in the river and his dilly bag had been abandoned when he fled the Bryants' home. Batson's stomach cramped at the thought of food.

Satisfied with the revolver's action, he repackaged the remaining ammunition and slid it into the depths of the cavity alongside the rifles. As he withdrew his arm, he hooked his hand around to a secondary cavity and retrieved a tin of biscuits. Batson chuckled to himself and marvelled at the stroke of luck that caused the freight carter to lose several tins from the back of his dray earlier in the week. Batson had happened along just at the right moment and was fortunate to retrieve four tins which he had subsequently stashed in various caches across his "territory". He sat down in the grass and munched on several sweet shortbread biscuits, before returning the tin to his cache. The growls in his stomach were muffled by biscuits. Batson disguised the entrance to the cache with branches and fern fronds and set off across the island toward the Victorian side of the Murray.

It took some time to traverse the scant mile to the Barbers' dairy. Batson had worked his way through the paddocks sticking close to the cover of tree lines and shrubbery to avoid being spotted by searchers and lookouts on the surrounding hills. He was forced to hide in a gully at one point, as a commotion broke out. Two policemen swooped out of the tree line near the road and accosted a young lad pushing a small mob of heifers across a neighbouring paddock.

"Stand firm or we will shoot!" shouted one of the officers, the other loosed two warning shots regardless.

The lad either fainted or threw himself down in terror. The police officers dragged the lad to his feet, looked at his face and yelled at the unfortunate farm hand.

Batson found the scene hilarious and chuckled to himself.

"Not Claude Batson, you dogs! He is too smart to be caught in the open!" he muttered.

As a precaution, Batson held his position, hidden in the gully, just in case the gun shots brought in additional troops.

Thirst and hunger goaded him to move and once at the dairy, Batson crept around the perimeter peering in through the crude windows. The cows which were leaving the dairy yard, gazed at the stranger curiously, before moving off toward the paddock.

Percy Emerson was just finishing up after the afternoon milking – he was shovelling dung from the milking bales. He was whistling to himself and clanging the shovel on the packed gravel. He didn't hear Batson approach, but he was startled by movement at the edge of his vision.

"Claude! What are you doing here?" he stuttered.

Emerson was partly amused and partly fearful to see the practically naked form of Batson standing before him. He looked him up and down before freezing when he noticed the handgun which Batson had gripped in his right hand. Emerson dropped the shovel and slowly brought his hands up in surrender.

"Oh, it's aw'right.... I am not after shooting you!" scoffed Batson.

Emerson was slightly relieved but still wary with the pistol trained on his chest. He thought better of speaking and waited for Batson to continue.

"I was driven to it, you know..." said Batson quietly. His voice caught, and he dropped his eyes as disturbing memories flooded his head.

"Why?" ventured Emerson.

"Persecution!" hissed Batson. "If they ever get me, I hope they put me on trial, then I will tell them everything!"

Batson was agitated and jumpy. The revolver's muzzle was swinging from side to side. Emerson was increasingly nervous.

"You want some milk, Claude? You look like you could do with a feed!" Emmerson suggested.

Batson calmed a little and nodded.

The two young men moved into the cool storeroom and Batson drank the fresh milk from the milk can with a dipper. The milk ran down his chest from his lips and pooled in his chest hair. Emerson watched, his thoughts racing to determine how he could overcome the fugitive. Batson was more athletic than Emerson, and armed. Emerson gave up on the thought of being a hero.

"They are after you, you know, Claude.... Men have come from across the district. They are armed. There are black trackers!" announced Emerson.

Batson looked mildly alarmed but then his expression shifted, and he cocked his head and asked curiously, "Do they think me a Bushranger? 'Always fancied going bushranging!"

Batson laughed; the tone was harsh, slightly maniacal.

"Sheppard died last night," volunteered Emerson quietly.

Batson glowered but didn't reply. He looked around the room with sharp, darting eyes. An old military tunic was hung up on a nail near a small vent. It was dusty and had mud wasp nests clustered amongst the folds and buttons. Batson grabbed it and thrashed it against the wall to dislodge the mud wasps and most of the dust before shrugging into the coat.

"I'll just take your trousers from you, Emerson," said Batson, gesturing with the pistol.

It was Emerson's turn to glower, but he dropped his pants without comment.

Batson pulled on the lad's clothing awkwardly with one hand, the other occupied by the pistol. Emerson sat on a milk can with his hands on his bare knees to demonstrate he was no threat to the jittery, fledgeling bushranger in front of him.

After a moment Batson fixed his eyes back on the lad and asked bitterly, "What about that bastard, King?"

"Hanging on..." said Emerson before adding, "Lachie McGrath is pretty poorly and their visitor, don't know his name, he is recovering from a smashed-up leg."

"King and Sheppard had it coming... those other two, they just got in the way!" barked Batson.

Batson looked a little remorseful but then his mood shifted rapidly, and he said, "I will not rest until I get them... and "The Prince"

"The Prince?" asked Emerson curiously.

"Percy-bloody-Barber... I would give a tenner to get The Prince!"

Emerson was keen to know why Batson applied the moniker and wondered why the older Barber brother was a target, but Batson's ire had returned, and Emerson didn't want to risk enraging him further by enquiring.

"I took Mrs Barber's watch... it was her Mam's. Don't know why I took it," mused Batson with some regret.

Emerson didn't say anything.

"She can have it back. I left it with my swag. On the other side of the river, across from the island. You tell Mr Barber!" said Batson.

Emerson nodded.

After a pause, Batson said maliciously, "I could have popped off a lot of coppers by now... so careless, they are... are they even looking for me?"

"Oh yes," answered Emerson cautiously, "there are hundreds of searchers!"

"There were two gunshots this morning and yelling... *Stand firm, we have you covered,* these troopers yelled at a lad in the paddock! I had them covered, I could have easily shot them!" said Batson boastfully.

"That would have been young Clegg, was it? I hear he was pushing up some heifers and the outta-town coppers thought he was you. Fired warning shots!" said Emerson with a grin, "I bet he needed to change his underwear!"

Batson motioned with the revolver for Emerson to move off, outside the dairy building. They stood near the road behind the dairy and Batson swung his head from side to side, listening.

"There is a motor car coming!" Batson hissed, and he threw himself into the gutter at the side of the road, hiding amongst the sedges and weeds.

"I am watching you, Emerson! Do not give me up or you will be meeting Sheppard!"

Emerson froze and gazed as a vehicle rounded the cutting. It sped along the road, raising a boiling dust cloud from its tyres. Emerson noticed that Batson's eyes were on the vehicle, so he cautiously waved his hand to flag down the occupants. They failed to see his furtive wave as a signal.

"Police!" hissed Batson.

"In a hurry!" commented Emerson sadly as the vehicle flashed passed without checking.

"If I had my rifle, I could have had a crack at them!" said Batson savagely.

"They might come back!" suggested Emerson hopefully.

"Hmm, that they might!" answered Batson, his eyes appraising the dairyman as he scrambled to his feet.

"Now you get about your business, no need to follow me! I will shoot any that pursue me! I will not be caught alive!" snarled Batson as he levelled his revolver at Emerson's chest again, in a threatening manner. Without another word he spun and took off into the bush across the road.

Emerson breathed a sigh of relief. Aware that Batson might be watching him from the cover of the bush, he went back to finish his work in the dairy but was determined to leave as soon as he felt it safe, find some trousers and take his information to the police officers.

Batson cut through the bush and dropped down behind the Barbers' house. He sat, concealed amongst undergrowth in the tree line just beyond the homestead, watching and listening. After a few minutes he approached cautiously, continuing to listen for sounds of occupation or a trap. The house was deserted. The door was locked but he gained access through the window which was still ajar from his incursion the day before. Once inside, he relaxed in the cool interior. He was hungry and searched the kitchen for some food. The Coolgardie held butter, some soured milk, cheese wrapped in muslin and a big wedge of watermelon. He took the watermelon and devoured it before leaving the rind on the table in a smear of watermelon juice. There was a half bottle of whisky on the dresser. He was not usually a drinker, but he thought the alcohol might soothe the discomfort from his scratched and battered body. He opened the bottle and necked it. The whisky was harsh as it seared its way down his gullet.

He fell into a chair, placed the bottle on the table and held his head in his hands thinking about the last few days. He rationalised repetitively about how it was his right to inflict suffering on those who had made him suffer.

"An eye for an eye!" he murmured, reciting the only Bible quote that had lodged in his brain from his brief exposure to the Catholic education system.

"Long, painful deaths on you... suffer for how you made me suffer!" he growled.

Batson smashed his hands on the table causing the whisky bottle to topple. The liquor spilled across the surface and dripped off onto the floor. Batson watched the bottle roll, following the fluid, before smashing onto the floor.

A vision of the police vehicle flitted through Batson's head. He remembered the roadblock on the bridge. Emerson had mentioned that there were search parties...he roused himself.

"Need a plan," he muttered.

Batson's eyes skittered around the room. He saw a pen on an ornate stand with a cut glass inkwell on the dresser, alongside of which was a basket of papers. He rose and crossed to the dresser again. Pulling a document from the basket, he flipped it over to reveal a blank page. He took the pen and ink and the page back to the table.

"I will leave a note – spin them a tale, buy some time." he whispered to himself.

He dipped the pen and spent a moment searching for the words. When he put pen to paper his marks were clumsy and poorly formed and his spelling was in keeping with his limited schooling.

C Batson is taking a dose of cinide. It tastes luvley. I left my rifle and cartriges down near Drummonds on the other side of the river ireland. Good By mother dear. CVB

He admired his composition before taking the paper by the corner and wafting it about in the air to dry the ink. It amused him when he noticed that he had written on the back of Richard King's Commonwealth Tobacco Producers' Return. He put the page on the table and used the saltshaker as a paper weight.

Batson then went to his room and retrieved a pair of pants, belt and a khaki work shirt which he pulled onto his weary frame. The bed looked inviting, but he knew he couldn't stay, and risk being found in the house. He searched the house and out on the back verandah for footwear, but his large feet were a poor fit for King's or Barber's shoes and his damaged toes complained about confinement.

"Bugger it!" he snarled.

He went back into the house and rifled through the drawer where Barber kept his ammunition in the vain hope there might be some shells suitable for the revolver which was now firmly lodged in his belt.

But no, Barber didn't own a revolver. Next, he went out to the shed and found the container of cyanide which Barber used for lacing grain to control rabbits. Returning to the house he opened the container and spooned some cyanide into a glass. He mixed it with a little whisky which he scraped off the table. He upended the rest of the cyanide container, spilling most of the contents across the table. He reviewed the scene and considered that he had made a fair crack at providing investigators with the idea that he had poisoned himself.

"Suicide..." he muttered.

Batson considered the concept of suicide. He remembered that the Church thought it a sin, but he was conflicted.

"If it was Ok for Lachie McGrath to shoot men in another country..."

He thought for a moment and then clarified the thought: "The Turks in Gallipoli... Or for the police to hang Ned Kelly, why is it considered so wrong to kill yourself?"

Batson caught his own reflection in the mirror on the dresser. He regarded his dishevelled appearance, his gaunt face and wayward hair before declaring, "Surely it is a man's right to choose his own death... to be judge, jury, executioner. Or to choose an escape from a life not worth having..."

Batson's eyes prickled. He reached out and retrieved the cyanide container, sealed it and pushed it deep in his pocket.

Batson stepped outside and found his dog, "Ding" waiting patiently under the tree in the front yard.

"Where did you spring from, ya' ol' bugger!" said Batson with an affectionate chuckle.

He rubbed the wiry blonde ears and patted the dog's flank. Ding wagged his tail and panted happily, leaning on his master's legs with his tail sweeping side to side with enthusiasm.

"You will have to stay here, ol' fella. I can't feed you in the hills and you might give me away!" said Batson forlornly.

He led the dog down to Barber's yards and tethered him in the shade of a tree near the water trough. He patted Ding's head, "Goodbye, ol' mate!"

Ding whined and watched anxiously as Batson set out across the paddock, making for the hills which rose behind the Barbers' house.

Walwa, "The Point", looking westerly - Arnold Playle collection, Man from Snowy River Museum

CHAPTER 17

Barber interview

Detective Cleaver called into the Hannas' property, "Springfield" to interview the Barbers. He stepped through the small gate adjacent to the building that was formerly a post office and then morphed into the temporary home of the Bank of Australasia. Nowadays, the building had been relegated to a storage shed. He followed the path to the front door, noting the pretty cottage garden which was struggling to survive in the drought conditions of a harsh summer. Cleaver stepped up on the verandah and rapped at the door. He could hear footsteps on the approach and the door swung wide revealing Joseph Hanna. Cleaver introduced himself and stated his business, Hanna nodded and showed the police officer through to the sitting room. Charles Barber arose from his chair as the officer and Hanna entered the room. Hanna announced the guest.

"Good morning, Detective Cleaver, we have been expecting you. Allow me to introduce you to my wife, Ruth," said Barber.

Cleaver shook hands with the pair and was shown to an overstuffed lounge chair. Once everyone was seated, Cleaver produced a notepad and a pencil and looked seriously from one to the other.

"Now then, Mr and Mrs Barber, we have your statements as to the circumstances of the attack on the picnic party by the fugitive, Claude Batson but there are just a few aspects I would like clarified, please," said Cleaver.

The Barbers nodded in unison and Charles said, "Of course, ask away."

"To begin, I must extend my condolences on the passing of your friend, Mr Sheppard, I understand you were quite close," said Cleaver sincerely.

Mrs Barber frowned slightly, her eyes were fixed and moist, her high cheek bones were flushed. She held her hands in her lap firmly, as if to stop them flying away.

Barber just shook his head angrily and said, "It is just dreadful, ... madness!"

Cleaver cleared his throat and continued, "How can you be sure that the shooter was Claude Batson?"

"I had a clear view of him as he stood up and stepped around the tree at the top of the embankment. He was looking across the creek at us. It was just before Lachie McGrath took off to get his rifle. Batson had fired six shots, and he just stood and wiped the barrel of his rifle, looking down on his victims," said Charles grimly.

"Yes, I could see him too, as we gathered the children and hid in the willows. He stood clear of cover when he was trying to shoot Lachie McGrath who was dodging and weaving towards his house. Mrs Gainer called him a coward and risked her life as she charged across the creek to get to her husband," said Ruth, her voice catching with emotion.

Cleaver nodded gravely.

"Why is it, do you think, that he didn't shoot *you*, Mr Barber?"

"I am not sure," said Barber thoughtfully, "I suppose he had no quarrel with me; we had always been cordial... although he was a changed man when he came back into my employ in September... well, compared to when he was last with us in '21."

"In what way," asked Cleaver gently.

"He was tetchy and anxious. I think he may have been keeping bad company," said Barber.

"He was furiously jealous of Mr King, wasn't he, Dear?" offered Mrs Barber.

"Oh, why?" queried Cleaver.

"Oh, just little things made him so cross! It almost got nasty the other night when I asked Mr King to help with the dishes... the two of them practically had a tug o' war with the tea towel!" said Ruth with a perplexed expression.

"Yes," agreed Barber, "Ruth said the two of them were being childish and Batson lost his temper and stormed off into the night! He hated criticism – that was why he fell out at the Butter Factory; Sheppard pulled him up on his work and his attitude was intolerable, so Sheppard had to let him go. And that issue about the rabbit poison demonstration a few months ago..."

"Oh.... what was that about?" asked Cleaver.

"Batson is a rabbit trapper, he did a lot of work for Alf Lawrence, particularly when his tenant, Rae, let the pests and weeds get out of control. There was some talk about an easier way to exterminate the rabbits. Batson thought he had a magic new method... a gas or something. Something like mustard gas from the war in France... He thought he would make his fortune! 'Don't know what happened, but there was a demonstration for the department officials, local farmers, the press and such. It went wrong. Everyone thought it a bit of a joke. Batson was humiliated and criticised. He was furious. He seemed to think he was set up and somebody had stolen his idea of the poison," said Barber.

"There was that girl too..." added Ruth quietly.

Cleaver cocked an eyebrow and Ruth went on:

"There was a young lass Claude was keen on ... they fell out before Christmas. Claude was truly infatuated," she said thoughtfully.

"Another lad cut his grass..." added Charles Barber.

"Not sure Claude really had a foot in the door, Dear, he didn't have much to offer a lass as a future husband!" said Ruth sadly.

"I think he blamed, Percy for that one... sometimes Percy gets a little too interfering!" said Charles with a frown.

"Percy?" asked Cleaver.

"Percy Barber, my brother in Jingellic," said Barber.

After a pause, Barber blurted out, "It was a murderous and determined attack on King ... I am adamant that Batson's plan was to shoot Sheppard, King, my wife, and my brother Percy, had he been at the picnic!"

Ruth paled and shrank back into her chair covering her face with her hands.

"I am sorry, my dear, but we need to ensure that we are protected, and this murderer is captured!" said Barber sternly.

"I understand that Claude Batson is one of the champion marksmen of the district, Mr Barber," stated Cleaver thoughtfully.

Barber nodded and Cleaver continued, "Well, I wonder why he failed to land a kill shot."

Ruth flinched and her shoulders shook.

"I am sure he was worked up and his hands were shaking... it's not like he had been in a combat situation before," suggested Charles.

Cleaver gazed into the distance.

"Perhaps," he agreed quietly before continuing, "Do you have any idea as to the number of rifles or handguns Batson owned?"

"I know he had a rifle of his own. It was like an extension of his arm!" said Barber.

"He also had two handguns, didn't he, Dear? I confiscated them last year because he was too casual with them... he was wandering around like a gunslinger!" said Mrs Barber.

"So, you had some concerns about his respect for the handguns? Did he get them back?" asked Cleaver.

"I seem to think I reluctantly gave them back after Christmas... maybe in January, I forget. I told him not to be silly with the handguns... he could have hurt someone..." murmured Mrs Barber and again looked distraught.

"Well, I think that is all for now, thank you! I would recommend that you remain here with Mr Hanna until we have apprehended Batson.

In the meantime, we will put an armed guard on your home, in case Batson should return there," said Cleaver.

Cleaver thanked the couple and stood up to leave.

"We will capture him and bring him to justice!" he assured the Barbers.

Cleaver left the house and climbed behind the wheel of his vehicle. He sat for a moment considering the interview. He picked at the incongruity of a champion marksman missing targets.

"... they were literally sitting ducks!" he fretted to himself.

He shook his head and started the vehicle. He swung around and headed back to Jingellic to report to the officer who was due in from Wagga Wagga: Inspector OH Parker had been assigned to take command of the manhunt for the fugitive, so that Cleaver could concentrate on building a case and collecting evidence for the coronial inquest into the death of David Sheppard.

Wilsons' Walwa Creek Store c1915 - Image from Arnold Playle Collection, Man From Snowy River Museum.

CHAPTER 18

Briefing of troops

Constable Jolly was talking ten to the dozen, trying to provide comprehensive background information to Sergeant O'Neil and his officers, who had just arrived in Walwa. The team of seven officers had been dispatched from St Kilda Road Police Station in Melbourne, to assist in the capture of Claude Batson. The officer in charge was Sergeant O'Neil, and the team had been selected specifically, as three of the officers were particularly familiar with the Upper Murray district: Mounted constables Ellery and Stanley Murray were brothers who had been raised in Walwa and had been knockabout chums with Batson as youths. Senior Constable D Bunworth had been stationed at Jingellic Police station for a period of six years, just prior to Constable Rice's appointment and was also familiar with the fugitive and the Upper Murray. In addition, there were three other very experienced mounted constables, S. Foote, R.L. Johns and J.J. McCarthy. It was a formidable group of skilled bushmen who all possessed elite tracking skills.

Once O'Neil was satisfied that he was across all the facts, the senior officers and Jolly set off to the Jingellic Hotel, the designated search headquarters, to participate in the afternoon briefing and to be introduced to the NSW contingent. The tone of the investigation had changed somewhat now that the charges applicable to Batson had been upgraded because of Sheppard's demise. It was now a murder investigation.

The mounted constables were directed to take their kit to the Walwa Hall where they would be accommodated together with the other volunteers who were in town for the manhunt. Afterwards, they were to proceed to the stables at the rear of the Walwa Hotel. Horses had been requisitioned from local farmers for the officers to use whilst on assignment in Walwa. The constables were to familiarise themselves with their mounts and ensure they were suitable, before riding over to Jingellic to receive orders.

The police vehicle, driven by Senior Constable Bunworth, spun in the wide main street of Walwa and motored off to the west. They bumped over the rustic wooden bridges at the edge of the township, crossing first, the Sandy Creek and then the Walwa Creek. Bunworth was relaxed and enjoying the familiar scenery. They made their way up the hill and the vista of the river flats opened before them. They passed a small, sparsely marked cemetery on the south side of the road. An avenue of pine trees marked the boundary. Jolly provided a running commentary for the benefit of the Melbourne officers. He was pointing out the Barbers' property and was making a point about the vast rugged territory in which Batson was on the loose just as they rounded the corner on the approach to Barbers' dairy. Bunworth glanced at the lad standing idly on the edge of the road near the dairy but failed to notice Batson concealed in the gutter. He thought the fellow was waving in an odd, restrained fashion, but didn't pay much attention, as the vehicle barrelled by in a cloud of dust.

The Jingellic Hotel dining room was jammed to overflowing with police officers. Civilians, including several eager journalists, casually leaned on window ledges outside the building and there was a hush in the bar room as all were listening in on the police briefing.

Detective Cleaver introduced Inspector Parker to the gathering, announcing that he was to be the new NSW officer in charge of the man hunt. He had been dispatched from Wagga Wagga just that morning to relieve Cleaver, allowing Constable O'Connor from Tumbarumba, and Detective Cleaver time to concentrate on gathering evidence for the coronial inquest into the death of David Sheppard.

There were angry mutterings from the community members when they were reminded that one of their own was now dead.

Cleaver acknowledged the Melbourne contingent of officers and introduced O'Neil and Bunworth to the gathering before continuing:

"We now have a strength of twenty-seven police officers, six members from Melbourne, seventy civilians and several black trackers. All are committed to hunting down this mongrel, Claude Batson! The community is nervous and jumpy and when there are so many rifles at the ready, the entire situation is dangerous, no matter what Batson's mindset is! So, we need to keep the general community calm!"

One of the journalists, Hardwick, Superintendent Cook's *Blowfly*, made a note to himself, another reminder to explore the concept of gun registration and restrictions again, with reference to the current atmosphere of gangland anarchy in Melbourne and Sydney, with the likes of Squizzy Taylor rampaging across the city. The gun ownership situation was now firmly in the spotlight in the wake of two shocking picnic massacres.

"I wonder if Batson was a student of the Norman List attitude to picnics," he thought to himself.

He was pleased that a neat and intriguing copycat theme was emerging, a very newsworthy and reader-attracting trope.

"Do you think it likely Batson will suicide, just as Norman List did after his picnic killing spree?" interjected Hardwick from his position in the doorway between bar room and the dining room.

Cleaver's head jerked towards the source of the interruption. He glowered.

"I would remind you this is official police briefing and to keep your comments and opinions to yourself at this juncture!" rebuked Cleaver sternly.

The journalist shrugged, unperturbed, and scribbled on his note pad.

"We have received intelligence from a witness, Mr Unger, that Batson was sighted on the ridgeline, three miles north of Jingellic, just yesterday afternoon and that was where we concentrated our initial efforts. In addition, all roads, bridges, and fords have been watched by armed guards to prevent Batson's access. Railway Stations have also been advised to be on the alert for the fugitive. To date, there have been no further sightings, but we have two expert trackers who will pick up his trail and we can triangulate search parties to intercept him," said Cleaver confidently.

There was a commotion in the bar room as a person slammed through the front door and pushed through the crowd.

"I have news! I have seen Batson!" yelled Percy Emerson excitedly.

The young man was provided with free passage through the throngs, and he stepped through the door into the dining room with a confidence and pride born of one pleased to be delivering vital news.

All eyes swivelled to appraise the young man. Constable Jolly stepped forward and introduced Emerson to Detective Cleaver and Inspecter Parker, indicating that the young man was a dairyman employed by Charles Barber and Albert Drummond. Cleaver suppressed the frustration he felt, now that his briefing was being hijacked and nodded to the young man before saying in a resigned tone, "What can you tell us, Mr Emerson?"

"He appeared at the Barbers' dairy just before... he was practically naked, a bit battered and he held me up at gun point!" said Emerson enthusiastically.

The audience drew breath collectively and there were angry murmurings.

"Go on...," said Cleaver.

"He took some milk – he was starving!" stated Emerson.

"Did he harm you?" queried Parker, scanning the young man for injuries.

"Nah... put the wind up me! But I know Batson, we haven't fallen out," Emerson assured the assembly.

"Why naked? Is he deranged?" asked Parker, frowning.

"I suppose he swam the river... he pinched an old jacket from the dairy... and my trousers!" said Emerson ruefully.

There were some sniggers at the lad's predicament – being held up by a gunman for the prize of his pants.

"Did he have boots on?" asked Cleaver.

Emerson shook his head and Cleaver continued, "Well, that will slow him down! Which way did he head for after he left you?"

"He threatened me not to follow ... but I saw him head towards the lower slopes of the range behind Barbers'," said Emerson.

"He may well be heading to his hut," suggested Jolly, "Batson has a hut on Lawrences' Hill just above Walwa."

Jolly stepped up to the map which was pinned on the wall of the pub and indicated the positions of Batson's hut and Barbers' dairy for the benefit of the newcomers.

Cleaver felt control of his briefing ebbing away; the audience was restless and whispering and there was hubbub in the bar room at the revelation of Batson's proximity to the township of Walwa. Some of the civilian men downed their pints and left the hotel to, presumably, take up the hunt or to go and protect their homes and families. Cleaver rapped his baton on the table and called out, "Order, order!"

Inspector Parker arose and exerted his command, "Thank you, Detective Cleaver. Constable Jolly, can you please meet the Mounted Constables under Sergeant O'Neil's command, at the Barbers' Dairy. Take young Mr Emerson with you and pick up Batson's trail. Take the tracker, Gilbert, with you, too. We will have another squad, and a tracker approach the hut from the Walwa township perimeter. We should be able to trap the fugitive within a pincer movement up on Lawrences' Hill."

Parker turned to Cleaver and Constable Rice and advised them to bolster the roadblocks and lookouts on the river crossings to contain Batson in his presumed position.

There was excitement and movement as officers got to their feet and assembled outside to mount up on horses and load into vehicles. Emerson trotted along with Jolly, happy to be the centre of attention.

Cleaver remembered his promise to the Barbers and organised a detail of police officers to mount a look-out on the Barber homestead and he dispatched a constable to monitor the Hanna homestead where the Barbers were temporarily resident.

"Take cover in a shed or surrounding shrubbery and keep watch over the Barber homestead. I want to surprise the fugitive when, or if, he enters the home for refuge or supplies. Don't enter the building. A covert operation, mind!" Cleaver ordered sharply.

*The Bluff behind Walwa - Arnold Playle collection,
Man from Snowy River Museum*

CHAPTER 19

A journalist's view

Phil Hardwick watched as the police and most of the civilians left the Jingellic Hotel in a cloud of dust. He had arrived in the district the previous afternoon, and he was now berating himself that it was already Tuesday evening, and his punchy, fact filled article on Batson, *The Last of the Bushrangers*, was decidedly scant on necessary facts. He flicked through his notebook with its pages of cryptic Hardwick shorthand, but there was little that would snare his readers yet.

He pulled a stool up to the bar, contemplating his next move.

"Would you be having a pint, sir?" asked Finlay Smith, the publican.

Hardwick nodded in a distracted fashion and reached a hand into his pocket for necessary coin, slapping the change on to the bar. The publican slid the coins off the bar and punched a key on the till, the drawer slid out with a jangle of a bell and the coins rattled into the slot. The noise penetrated Hardwick's reverie. He fixed his gaze on Smith and introduced himself as a pint was poured and pushed across the bar with foam oozing down the side of the glass.

"I am Phillip Hardwick, journalist with the Banner. I need some background on Batson, to add some colour to my article, information for my readers. Who would be best to approach?" he asked.

Smith considered his response carefully, before saying:

"The Barbers are probably most familiar with him. Mrs Barber sort of took Batson under her wing. He would stay overnight in their home on occasion, even long after they gave him marching orders from their employ. They aren't home, of course.... Maybe try at "Springfield" on the western edge of Walwa: The Hannas' it is. Joseph and his son, Hugh, are the unofficial Mayors of the district. They know everyone and I think the Barbers are camping there for the while," said Smith.

"Did Batson drink here?" enquired Hardwick.

"No. Rarely saw the fellow. He was a teetotaller. Sometimes he would drop by with fellows from the rifle club or after cut-out from the shearing shed, but he only ever had a lemon squash. Most often he was a loner. Kept himself to himself," replied Smith.

Hardwick finished his beer and wiped the foam from his whiskers with the back of his hand. He gathered up his notebook and slid it inside his jacket pocket. He took his hat from the counter and called his farewells before pushing through the doors. It was still warm despite the sun sliding off, over the hills. As he got into his Ford, he shrugged out of his jacket and rolled up his sleeves. He cranked over the engine and set off for Walwa.

Joseph Hanna was dismounting in the yard next to the Springfield homestead as Hardwick rolled through the gateway. He tethered his horse and watched as the stranger came to a halt and stepped out of the vehicle.

"Good afternoon, Sir!" said Hardwick warmly, "Would you be Joseph Hanna, by any chance?"

"I would! Who might you be?" asked Hanna in return.

Hanna was a little disconcerted by the influx of strangers into "his" town. This fellow wasn't in uniform and didn't have the bearing of one of the plain clothed officers, so he was a little suspicious.

Hardwick hastened to introduce himself:

"I am Phillip Hardwick, senior crime writer for the Banner and syndicated nationally," he announced with a flourish.

Hanna failed to look appropriately impressed but offered his hand politely, noted Hardwick.

"What can I help you with?" Hanna asked as they shook hands.

"I am obviously recording the manhunt for- and investigation into the case against Claude Batson. I am keen to interview persons who are familiar with the fellow to provide my readers with some background, to add colour to my reporting," declared Hardwick.

"I see," said Hanna sternly whilst examining Hardwick, "You are probably aware that the Barbers are currently guests of my household. They would most likely have had the closest relationship with the fellow."

Hardwick nodded enthusiastically and smiled encouragingly.

Hanna came to a decision and waved to Hardwick, "Follow me. I will see if the Barbers are available."

He led the way through the gate and up the path to the back of the house. They passed extensive vegetable gardens and neat flower beds adjacent to the walls of the house. He swung around the northeastern corner of the building and stepped through the French doors leading directly into the kitchen. He pulled out a chair at the kitchen table and motioned for Hardwick to take a seat.

"I will just track down the Barbers... one moment please," Hanna declared as he swept through the door which he closed firmly behind him.

Hardwick gazed around the neat kitchen, noting the rows of bottled peaches sitting on the counter next to the sink and a huge preserving pan upside down, draining. The perfume of peaches hung in the air and Hardwick presumed that the annual bottling activity had been the project for the day for the women of the household.

He heard voices from within the house and a clatter of footsteps before the door swung open and Joseph Hanna, followed by a stocky neat man, entered the kitchen. Hardwick stood politely.

"Here we go: Phillip Hardwick, meet Charles Barber," said Hanna.

They shook hands before taking their seats at the table. Barber looked at Hardwick expectantly.

"Mrs Barber isn't joining us?" queried Hardwick with mild disappointment.

"Mrs Barber is indisposed," said Hanna as Barber merely shook his head.

Hardwick explained his intentions to the men before pulling his notebook and pencil from his pocket and laying it on the table in front of him.

"I shall make notes of our conversation, if you are comfortable with that?" said Hardwick carefully.

"Of course," said Barber, "anything to ensure the accuracy of reporting," he added pointedly.

Hardwick nodded and a wry smile slid across his features.

"The fugitive is reported to be Claude Valentine Batson, are you confident of his identity, Mr Barber?"

"Yes, yes, I had a clear view of him as he stood on the bank looking down on the scene after the initial barrage of shots," replied Barber curtly.

"I was provided with your statement to the police, Mr Barber, is there anything you wish to add or adjust?" asked Hardwick.

"No, my statement was comprehensive." said Barber firmly and thought to himself that this would be a very short interview if the journalist was to be reliant on the police statement.

"Very well, Mr Barber, my main interest today, is some background in relation to the fugitive. I need to fill in the gaps and paint a picture of the man for my readers. At this point, all I know is his name, a physical description as distributed by police and I have seen a photograph of the man. I would like to expand on this basic information...perhaps his employment history in the district. The most telling information I need though, is his character, his background, what would have made him commit such a heinous crime?" stated Hardwick.

Hanna nodded sagely.

Barber knitted his brows and thought carefully, before saying, "It is a mystery to me, I saw nothing to forewarn of this disaster."

"Yes, I always thought the lad peculiar, but not mad! Preferred his own company ... and that of his dog, Ding," agreed Hanna.

"From all accounts, he had a bad start to life: Batson's mother delivered him out of wedlock, down in Bowna, a small settlement further down river. His father shot through and later Florence, I seem to think that was her name, married another fellow. Young Batson was passed along to a spinster aunt in Holbrook to raise," offered Barber.

"Oh, yes? Whom might she have been, Mr Barber?" asked Hardwick.

Barber looked puzzled and then sighed.

"It's no good, the name escapes me... it wouldn't serve anyway, Batson wasn't long in her care - he went feral and practically raised himself in the bush. Picked up some work with drovers and trappers, laboured on farms, that sort of thing," said Barber.

"So, when did he come to your attention Mr Barber?" asked Hardwick.

"Several years ago. He came into the district and worked for some neighbours as a dairyman. Just a lad he was, then. My wife heard his story from Batson's grandmother, Bridget, before she passed, about a decade ago. Old Mrs Batson felt guilty, in the weeks before she went to meet her maker, that she hadn't helped her first grandson or her daughter... they had become estranged, you know. Ruth promised Bridget that she would do what she could for young Claude," said Barber.

Hanna picked up the story, "He was an independent lad. Alf Lawrence supplied him with a trapper's hut on the hill up there," Hanna gestured toward the range out the window towards the westerly aspect of Walwa, "free rent, as long as he kept the rabbits at bay."

"I gave him some consistent work for a few years, then he plucked up the courage to talk to me about a share farming arrangement last year, when I was slowing down... a bit of a gammy leg you know, but his work was inconsistent. Every now and then he would just take off and disappear. He would have been a very unreliable share farmer," said Barber with some sorrow.

"When was that, Mr Barber?" asked Hardwick.

"Oh, somewhere abouts October last year, I think. Anyway, I had already agreed to take on Richard King – he grew tobacco on the flats and helped me with other jobs on the farm," said Barber.

"He went to work for the butter factory after he left your employ, didn't he Charles?" asked Hanna.

"Yes, Barrow Brothers took him on under the new manager, David Sheppard. Sheppard was out to make an impression and was stirring up production... Batson didn't last long," said Barber.

"Did he leave with a gripe, then?" asked Hardwick eagerly.

"From what he said to Ruth, I think Sheppard got in first, but Batson was about to quit. The young fellas were giving him strife, teasing him when he got tasks muddled up,... there were a few scuffles, I was told," Barber said quietly and looked regretfully at Hardwick.

"I think the Barrow Brothers' workers started calling him "Dilly", or "Silly Dilly". He wasn't stupid, more naïve and... well, different. Also, small town gossip... the lads had heard that his father, Kennedy, had been in trouble... spent time in the Albury Gaol, he might be in an asylum now. Newspapers have a lot to answer for..." said Hanna glaring at Hardwick for a moment.

"Oh, it is a newspaper's role to report facts, to warn the community about issues and criminals and ensure bad eggs are aware of consequences before they embark on a life of crime. Information, education and advertising, you know!" said Hardwick brightly.

"Facts," emphasized Hanna, frowning, "not gossip!"

"Exactly!" agreed Hardwick with a serious nod, "That's exactly why the likes of me, interview a wide range of witnesses to ensure that all of the facts are revealed, accurately."

Hanna felt he had been outwitted and said nothing.

"There was the invention...." said Barber.

Hardwick's ears pricked, he said nothing but gazed at Barber with expectation and pencil poised. Barber filled the void in the conversation:

"Alf Lawrence had been overrun with rabbits. He had leased out his property to a fellow from Tumbarumba. Rae, I think his name was… it ended in an untidy fashion with a court case – breach of lease contract, expenses for repatriation of the property. Fences were dilapidated, rabbit warrens everywhere, the orchard untended. Lawrence sued Rae. Witnesses included Batson, me, umm… Jack Cook and John Johnson. I think that was all. Batson was employed by Alf Lawrence to eradicate the rabbits, and he presented the bill for his labours in court. He killed over four thousand rabbits and dug out over eight hundred warrens. In the process, he was thinking about a more efficient manner to exterminate the pests. He and Lawrence applied for a patent in August, last year, for a "Rabbit Exterminator" – it was the most enthusiastic and talkative I have ever seen Batson. He was bragging that he could exterminate rabbits effectively and efficiently at a cheaper rate than the current methods. He declared that he was going to clear the Upper Murray of rabbits! Alf organised a demonstration… just before Christmas. The papers, the Lands Department, Agricultural hierarchy, and the most respected, influential landowners gathered on Lawrences' Hill in amongst a city of rabbit warrens. He set up his contraption and the group watched and then laughed as rabbits gambolled away. Abject failure! Batson was humiliated and vowed that he had been sabotaged," Barber stated and looked regretful.

"Yes, he was black and irritable for weeks," agreed Hanna thinking about the scene on the hill.

"Were any of Batson's targets at the demonstration?" asked Hardwick.

Both men glanced at one another with a mildly surprised and anxious expression.

"Well, yes, now you come to mention it; my brother Percy, Richard King and David Sheppard were all there. Overall, there were a couple of dozen persons at the demonstration," said Barber.

"Was the patent approved?" asked Hardwick.

"After such a disastrous demonstration, I shouldn't imagine so," suggested Hanna.

"No, I think there was more to it... Batson told me that it was refused on the grounds that the invention was too much alike to a previously approved patent. Batson was adamant that someone had stolen his idea!" said Barber.

Hardwick scribbled furiously.

"So, Batson was a bit of a loner with a poor start to life and limited education," summarised Hardwick, "Would he have followed national news, read the broadsheets or listened to the radio?"

Both men looked puzzled at the direction the journalist's questioning had taken. They shook their heads in unison.

"Unlikely. He was practically illiterate – it was one of the reasons he lost his job at Barrow Brothers... he couldn't follow written instructions," said Barber.

Hardwick nodded and continued scribbling notes. After a long pause he looked up and, eyeing both men in front of him, he asked, "Have you heard of Norman List? The Botanic Gardens Picnic Massacre?"

The connection registered with both men immediately.

"Are you suggesting that Batson was inspired by the madman in Melbourne?" asked Hanna.

"Well, there are some similarities, and the two events are within a few weeks of each other."

"A copycat killing?" suggested Barber.

Hardwick loved the phrase and was pleased that Barber had made the connection and used the phrase.

"Unless someone else described the Melbourne event to Batson, I doubt he would have had the knowledge," said Hanna thoughtfully.

"Would you consider that Batson could have had such a conversation?" asked Hardwick.

"I can't think with whom he would have spoken, he was such a loner. I think it was only ourselves, grudging conversations with King in our home and perhaps some communication with Alf Lawrence. He was sullen and quiet most times. He didn't attend community events...dances or church or the like," said Barber carefully.

"What about the rifle club?" asked Hanna.

"Perhaps," agreed Barber, now looking alarmed at the thought.

"About the rifle club..." said Hardwick, "I have been told Batson was a champion shot..."

Hanna and Barber nodded their agreement in unison.

"Odd that his shots were not kill shots then, don't you think?" asked Hardwick.

After a moment's thought Barber suggested, "Yes, the detective made a similar observation, I can only imagine he was upset and highly strung, perhaps his hands shook, an episode of madness?"

"Maybe he wasn't actually intent on actually killing his targets?" offered Hanna.

That thought chilled the men as they considered the pain that Batson had inflicted on his victims.

"The lad that came into the hotel this afternoon, relaying his encounter with Batson at your dairy, Mr Barber, ...your dairyman, I believe," said Hardwick.

Barber's face paled and he looked shocked.

"Percy Emerson saw Batson?" he asked.

"Oh, did you not know? I presumed the police would have informed you...." said Hardwick.

Barber shook his head and his eyes flicked to Joseph Hanna.

"Where are the ladies, where is Ruth?" he beseeched.

"Oh, they will be fine! They took some bottled peaches to the hotel and then they were going to the store. They will be back soon. Probably just having a chat!" replied Hanna breezily.

"Are you worried that your wife is a target?" asked Hardwick of Barber.

"Perhaps," said Barber with grave concern, "I am now of the opinion that Batson could have had some fantasies about my wife, he was possessive, maybe he thought of her as a mother figure. I think Richard King may have unwittingly usurped Batson's position in the household... well, in Batson's view."

Barber's hands gripped one another on the tabletop. His knuckles were white.

"I am worried that Batson wanted to punish King and my wife," he said.

"Do you think he wanted to kill them?" asked Hardwick.

"Maybe. Yes, his aim wasn't true, but now that Sheppard has passed," Barber's voice cracked, "well, he is now up for murder, so his intentions may well have escalated. Look, please excuse me, Mr Hardwick, I am concerned for my wife. I will just go and collect the ladies from the store and escort them home!"

With that, his chair screeched across the floor as he stood quickly and strode from the kitchen. Hardwick gazed through the window, watching Barber trot off up the path, towards the road.

"Were there any further questions, Mr Hardwick?" asked Hanna.

"Is there anything you can add to the description that I have been given of Batson: twenty-four, dark unruly shoulder length hair, swarthy complexion, ..."

"That covers his description," said Hanna.

"Very well, thank you for your time and assistance!" smiled Hardwick.

The men shook hands again and Hardwick took his leave.

As Hardwick was drawing out of the Hanna's drive he was held up for a few minutes as a convoy of trucks and vehicles passed along the road. Curious, he followed them into Walwa.

*Walwa footpath scene. Walwa Store in the background -
Arnold Playle collection, Man from Snowy River Museum*

CHAPTER 20

Jacob in Walwa

Jacob unfolded himself from the back seat of the vehicle and stepped out stiffly. He adjusted his clothing which was glued fast to his skin with sweat. He was dying for a drink and desperately needed to stretch his legs. His companions, a group of ex-AIF volunteers, were rowdy; imbued with a renewed sense of comradery after being confined in the back of a truck, shoulder to shoulder on an interminable trip on rough roads to the Upper Murray township of Walwa. It had been several years since they were last together, embroiled in the horror of combat and the mud of the battlefields of Europe. They anticipated that the manhunt for Batson would be practically risk free - it couldn't be more hazardous than what they had faced at the Somme, Passchendaele, Gallipoli, or Beersheba. Overall, they considered it an excursion with *the boys* more akin to a hunting trip and they were excited by the prospect.

Hugh Hanna hurried across the road from the Police Station, where he had been awaiting the arrival of the group of AIF veterans. He, too, had been comrades-in-arms with some of the fellows during the war, and felt a rush of gratitude that they had rallied to assist *his* town in the search for Batson. Hugh took a position on the steps of the Memorial Hall and called for a bit of hush. Curious townsfolk drifted down the street, drawn by the noise of a convoy of vehicles and the hubbub the men had created.

"Attention! Attention, please!" called Hugh, "Welcome and thank you for coming! I am gratified that Stephen Brown here, was able to muster such a fine contingent of fellows! The Walwa and Jingellic communities are immensely grateful for your assistance!"

There was some disjointed and slightly puzzled clapping from the townsfolk at the perimeter of the group.

"Just this afternoon, we have had a sighting of the fugitive!" announced Hugh.

There was a buzz of excited chatter.

"A pincer operation is underway as we speak, just up in the hills to the west of Walwa.

Hugh swung his arm and gesticulated in the direction of Batson's hut.

"We anticipate capture, but if unsuccessful, the Officer in Charge will coordinate volunteers to scour the hills in a coordinated fashion at first light. It is suggested that you all roll out your swags in the hall, just here behind me, and join us in the dining room of the Walwa Hotel for refreshments and dinner, before an early night and a fresh start!"

Hugh grinned broadly and stepped down the stps to shake hands with former comrades.

There was jostling and excited chatter as the group gathered their kit and trotted into the hall. There was an air of anticipation and high spirits. Swags were rolled out and kit bags placed on top.

Hugh called out over the ruckus, "Those of you who have arms and ammunition, we will need to secure these in the storeroom to avoid any incidents or theft by Batson or others overnight. You can retrieve arms at daybreak!"

The gathering in the hotel was equally noisy: lots of back slapping, war stories and potted histories of activities since demobilisation. Most were intent on liquid refreshments, rather than dinner and they crowded into the small bar. Their primary aim was to get their money's worth before "time" was called at 6pm.

The atmosphere in the dining room was like a brigade reunion - a noisy mess-type meal. Jacob was a little reserved. He took note of the surroundings and kept an eye out for Albert or the real object of his desire, a sighting of Emma.

Hardwick slipped into the dining room and took a vacant chair at the back of the room. A waitress noted his arrival and, assuming he was one of the volunteers, hastily delivered a plate of food. Hardwick accepted it with a smile, but no confession, he was famished. He tucked into the meal and allowed his ears to roam, listening in on numerous conversations from the surrounding tables. He discovered that most were ex-AIF servicemen from Albury. He picked up on the excitement that the men held for the task ahead of them.

"At least the odds are more in our favour!" chuckled one of the older fellows as he stood to politely return his plate to the kitchen.

Hardwick noticed that the fellow walked with a marked limp, and he concluded that he had brought home a permanent souvenir from the battlefields.

Hardwick overheard a conversation about bushrangers. His curiosity was piqued, and he tuned in to that conversation. A local was scoffing at the suggestion that Batson might be termed *the Last Bushranger of the Riverina.*

"A lad that cracks it, shoots up a picnic party and then legs it for the hills is hardly in the league of the likes of Dan Morgan or the Kelly Gang! He didn't even commit robbery under arms!" said a desiccated grey-haired old man who was hunched over his plate of food.

"Did the bushrangers scour the Upper Murray, too?" asked a fresh-faced young fellow, part of the contingent from Albury.

The old man settled back into his chair drew his bushy brows together as he thought and then launched into a story. His listeners stopped eating and watched the old man, waiting in eager anticipation for what he had to impart.

"Dan Morgan was a pretty handy bushranger; he had the squatters on edge, that is for sure! There is a hill just outside of Germanton... Holbrook, it's called now... They had to change the name to avoid memories of the Kaiser! Anyway, that hill is called *Morgan's Lookout,* for good reason... he and his cronies would rest up amongst the boulders and from that vantage point, they could spy down on the surrounding countryside and see the coppers on the hunt or their victims scuttling by," said the storyteller.

"When was that?" interjected one of the newcomers.

"Dan Morgan was harassing the coaches in the sixties, he was a wrong 'un, that one," said the man, hissing through his teeth and shaking his head.

"Then, there was Ned and his gang ... locals had more sympathy for the Kellys. They came through in 1879, on their way to Jerilderie. Eliza Dunn was publican, then, at the original Jingellic Hotel, the Redbank Hotel. It was down near the customs house on the Victorian side of the Murray, near the ford. She cleared the bar one afternoon, sent everyone packing. Later that night, a party of horsemen came to the hotel for refreshments... their horses had hessian bags wrapped around their hooves, and rags around the harness to muffle the noise. Once rested, they disappeared into the night..."

"Were you there?" asked the young fellow eagerly.

The old man studied the young man, trying to determine if the veracity of his tale was in question. Once satisfied that the question was based on enthusiastic curiosity not derision, he continued.

"Agnes Eliza, *Lizzie,* Johnson, was one of Eliza Dunn's daughters, she watched the riders come and go from her bedroom window in the Hotel. The penalty for aiding and abetting bushrangers was steep, so Eliza was running a big risk but like I said, the Kellys had many sympathisers and after all, Eliza and the Kellys were Irish, from the same County."

"When was the last bushranger trouble in the area?" asked one of the other Albury fellows.

The old man scraped his hand through the grey stubble on his chin as he thought.

"That would have been in the nineties... the Dora Dora blacks were stirred up by a couple of runaway convict blacks. I s'pose you could call 'em bushrangers. I can still remember their names... I don't know why! They were Jacky and Willie!"[1]

The old man paused and considered why their names might have stuck in his memory and what made them become bushrangers.

"I s'pose it could have been due to the opium they used as tea!" he chuckled darkly before continuing.

"Two settlers were murdered; their property looted. One was a woman in Wangaratta, the other a Pole called Murszcavitch. They shot him in the back with an arrow... or speared him, I forget. Either way, the Mail coach found him on the side of the road near Basin Creek in Talmalmo. He was no good, a few days later he died. There were reparations metered out to the runaways and their conspirators," he said grimly.

His audience considered his words in silence, understanding the truly bloody implications of reparations on the indigenous population of the area. Aboriginal men, women and children would have paid for the runaways' crime.

"So, this Batson, what are we to expect from him?" asked one of the volunteers.

Another local chimed in on the conversation at this point, saying, "He is a champion marksman, so be warned! He has lived rough most of his life and is a true bushman... 'knows the hills like the back of his hand."

"Is he likely to hang around, then? If I were him, I would be off to the never-never, to disappear!" suggested the volunteer.

"Unger saw him crossing the face of the range, just north of Jingellic, above Horse Creek, yesterday afternoon. So, it would seem he is circling back." offered a farm hand from Jingellic.

"Maybe he has unfinished business?" stated Jacob Miller sombrely.

It was Jacob's first contribution to the conversation and eyes flicked to study the young man, aged and hardened by the experience of war. Hardwick scribbled some notes.

The conversation was interrupted by waitresses serving dessert, they moved between the tables with trays delivering small bowls of bottled peaches and lashings of cream. There was a clatter of cutlery as the men tucked into dessert with enthusiasm.

Constable Jolly halted. He pulled his cap from his head and ran his fingers through his thinning hair whilst glaring about in the deepening gloom at the surrounding scrub. The planned assault on Lawrences' Hill to snare Batson in the location of his hut had been a fiasco. Sergeant O'Neil's Melbourne squad together with Jolly and the tracker, Gilbert, had gathered at Barber's dairy after the briefing at Jingellic Hotel. The young Emerson lad was keen to show the troopers and tracker where Batson had hidden in the ditch adjacent to Barbers' dairy when the police vehicle had sailed by earlier in the afternoon. He pointed out the direction towards which Batson had headed away from the dairy.

The tracker picked up some dubious signs towards the tree line at the base of the hill but on the dry shale surface, the tracks soon disappeared. Extrapolating a route to reach Batson's hut, they crashed through thick undergrowth but soon had to abandon their mounts because the shrubbery was just too dense. They dismounted and left the horses in the charge of a very disappointed Emerson. The troop forged forward on foot until they hit Snake Gully and the tin mines precinct. The light was starting to fail, they had no tracks to follow, and Sergeant O'Neil declared that in poor light, Batson had all the advantages, and they would be foolish to continue to stalk a known sniper. Cloaked in a dejected silence, they trudged back to where the horses were tethered. Jolly felt the pangs of failure.[1]

---

1. *Jacky and Willie were Boolyal (29) and Thunimberi or Tinnamburra (23). They had been displaced from Fraser Island, Queensland. The police employed them as trackers, but they absconded from Benalla after allegedly assaulting a female settler. Later they came into contact with the Polish immigrant in Talmalmo and fatally wounded him. Dismal conditions, displacement from family and country, the stress of what they witnessed, and an opium habit contributed to their actions. After capture they were housed in Albury Gaol for a period before standing trial. There was community support for the men, recognising cultural differences and a fund to provide advocacy was established.*

CHAPTER 21

Day 2 : Wednesday 13 February 1924

At first light, Jolly's telephone rang, rousing him from a ragged sleep. He was flustered, aware that he had overslept and to compensate, he answered the telephone with a front of over enthusiastic cheer. It was Detective Cleaver.

"Batson has been in Barber's home again. Most likely after he spoke to the dairyman, Emerson, and before the men, who were posted to watch the house, arrived yesterday evening." said Cleaver.

"Was he trapped there?" asked Jolly hopefully.

"No. He has disappeared, but he left a note. It sounds like a suicide note but I don't believe it. A ruse, I suspect. I need you to muster a search party and scour the island and riverbank near Barbers' river flats. Batson told the Emerson lad that he had dumped some articles, possibly ammunition, down on an island. We need to collect what we can, to limit his supplies. In the meantime, we have found Batson's dog, and we are going to see if it can help track Batson," said Cleaver.

"Very well. I have some suitable men in mind. Have O'Neil's troopers been dispatched on a task, or do I need to provide them with orders?" asked Jolly.

"O'Neil has his orders to resume the search of the hill in the vicinity of Batson's hut, whilst the volunteers from Albury have been dispatched to comb the hill from the south side under the supervision of the two Constables called Murray. Former Walwa residents, I believe," said Cleaver.

"Very well, Sir. We will be off to search the island as soon as the men have mustered," said Jolly firmly.

"Constable O'Connor from Tumbarumba, will meet you at the island. Superintendent Cook insists that the New South Wales police be represented during the search," said Cleaver.

The click of the disconnected line was loud in Jolly's ear. He was now even more anxious that he was on a go-slow: everyone else was on the move, and he was still in his nightwear! He sighed and dressed quickly. He felt sticky and uncomfortable but there was no time for a wash, instead he merely poured a glass of water and rinsed his mouth out, before drinking the rest of the glass. He ran wet hands through his hair before stalking across the short gravel path from his residence to the police station to retrieve his tunic and cap. He picked up the telephone receiver in his office and asked Mrs Hughes on the exchange to connect him to the Hunt brothers' residence.

Paddy Hunt answered the call and Jolly arranged for him to muster four additional local men and to meet up outside the police station in forty minutes. He then hurried off to catch his horse from the paddock.

The morning sun was warm on Jolly's back as he tipped oats and chaff into the feed bin and hooked it on the rail in front of his horse. The tension eased in his shoulders as he curry combed and brushed the gelding to a sun-bleached shine. He picked its hooves and checked its shoes, before saddling up. He and the gelding were a team and grooming the animal always put Jolly in a good mood, but not so, today. His thoughts tumbled in his head as he worked. He picked through the facts of the case and considered what he knew of Batson and considered what his movements might be. He found that he was anxious. Not only because a deranged fugitive was on the rampage, but also, that there were so many strangers in *his* town. The presence of so many top-brass police officers was harrowing. He felt that he was under scrutiny, and he worried that his performance would be found wanting.

The gelding finished its feed, and Jolly swapped the feed bin for a bucket of water. He left the horse tethered as he hurried back to the station house to retrieve his pistol and rifle from the gun cabinet. He hesitated near his desk and wondered if he should put in a report to his superiors in Wangaratta. As he was dithering, the phone rang. Mrs Hughes' voice was simpering on the crackling connection, "I have Superintendent Cook on the line for Constable Jolly, please."

"Put him through, thank you Mrs Hughes." said Jolly curtly.

Whilst the connection was being made, Jolly wondered why Mrs Hughes couldn't have just made the connection directly, why she needed to announce the caller. He thought acidly that maybe it had something to do with ensuring that she could listen in on the conversation...

"Jolly, I have been consulting with Inspector Parker this morning. He has advised me as to the contents of Batson's supposed suicide note. You have heard of these findings, I take it?" said Cook.

"Yes, Sir. Detective Cleaver relayed the information...."

Cook cut Jolly off mid-sentence and continued: "Whilst it may be possible that he has metred out his own punishment, I doubt it. I am ordering you and all under my command to ignore the suicide note and work on the assumption that he is still alive, still armed and dangerous. Make no mistake, take no risk. We will not be fooled by this ruse."

"Yes, Sir, I will ensure everyone remains vigilant," replied Jolly earnestly.

"Anything to report from your side of the river, Jolly?" asked the Superintendent.

"Sir, I led a party and followed a lead into the hills south of Walwa last evening, from Barber's Dairy where the dairyman had been accosted by Batson. We lost the tracks in the shale near the Mt Alwah tin mine. Sergeant O'Neil and his officers are following through this morning and conducting a pincer movement operation to trap Batson at his hut or flush him out of hiding. I am leading a small party of volunteers to see if the information provided by Batson to the dairyman, Emerson, about hidden supplies on an island, just down river from Walwa, is true, and if so, we will retrieve the supplies. I am just about to leave," said Constable Jolly.

"Good! I understand that Constable O'Connor is on his way to the island, as we speak – keep a look out in case it is a trap! Search, search, search! Report back this evening," said Cook and hung up without waiting for a response.

As the line went dead, Jolly felt a chill slide down his spine... he hadn't considered the possibility of a trap.

By the time Jolly had settled himself in the saddle and the gelding was striding out to the main road, he could hear excited chatter, specifically Paddy Hunt's strident voice, from the front of the police station.

"'Morning fellows!" called Jolly as he came out of the drive and onto the road. The company, comprised of Paddy and his companions, Mr Venner, Mr Taylor, Mr Lowdon and Mr Stewart, chorused a greeting and swung their horses into a rough formation, facing Jolly.

"Lighthorse drills have come in useful," thought Jolly to himself as he admired the party's turn out and their settled mounts. He gave the men the run down as to their task and they set out at a mile-eating canter from the township, Jolly in the lead.

They crested the hill and cut north towards the Murray River. Several gates and the necessity for cutting around lagoons and marsh lands, slowed Jolly's squad somewhat and as they swung around the final coppice of red gums, they saw Constable O'Connor and the Spicer lad sitting astride their horses waiting for them. Jolly felt mildly disconcerted that O'Connor had been kept waiting, but was grateful too, that he had waited. Soon, they were splashing through the shallow sweep of river on the southern side of the island. Once on the island, the men dismounted and hobbled their horses before splitting up to search. It was a beautiful setting, an oasis in the drought ravaged landscape. The river chortled and rushed past the island over shoals of rocks. The chorus of cicadas and the sound of the river isolated the men from one another. Paddy Hunt pushed through the bracken, making his way toward the north side of the island. His shrewd logic drove him to find a possible access point for a river crossing from the north bank of the river. He found himself in a clearing with a towering river red gum holding court. The gum tree was hollow, ravaged by an ancient fire. A glint from the gloomy depths of the cavity caught his attention. Paddy investigated and found Batson's jacket hooked on a shard of wood inside the hollowed trunk.

"Oy, I have his jacket!" he called.

"There is something here, too, in a wombat den!" squawked one of the younger lads with excitement.

After forty minutes of searching, the squad had discovered a jacket, two .303 rifles, three caches of ammunition totalling over two hundred rounds comprised of a mix of .133 and .303 cartridges, two bandoliers, a pair of boots, pair of socks, set of braces, trousers, two tins of biscuits, a box of matches wrapped in greased fabric and three shillings and six pence.

The men gathered and stared at the collection of items. Jolly nudged the tins of biscuits with his boot.

"The carrier mentioned he had lost a quantity of biscuit tins last Friday... fell off the back of his truck!" said Venner.

"Batson must have found them!" said young Taylor enthusiastically.

"There were a total of six tins unaccounted for, so he probably has more stashed in the hills," added Jolly gravely.

"It is odd he didn't retrieve the clothes to wear," muttered Paddy Hunt.

"Or these boots," chuckled Venner, "Although, I did find them on the sand bank, like they were lost in the river and washed ashore."

"Well, he is stuffed now that we have his spare gear!" chuckled Taylor.

"Come on, we had best get these items of evidence secured," said Jolly as he handed one of the rifles to Hunt, the other to Stewart. They took them and slipped them in the vacant rifle boots on their saddles. The remaining items were placed in the Constable's saddle bags.

Cantering back into Walwa young Taylor felt quite proud that he was part of the squad. He caught the eye of a couple of young lasses who were sweeping the footpath outside the Walwa Hotel. He sat tall in the saddle, grinning confidently and saluted.

Walter Webb was waiting outside the Police station when Jolly and his party rode up. Jolly dismounted and tethered his horse to the rail.

"I am certain I saw Batson," announced Webb without preamble.

"Oh, where and when, Mr Webb?" asked Jolly.

The horsemen crowded in to hear the conversation.

"Yesterday afternoon. He crossed the road near Barbers' cottage, I didn't think much of it at the time, I just thought it was young Emerson. The timing was off, though, as I heard later that Emerson would have been in the Jingellic Hotel telling all and sundry about his encounter with Batson at around half four. So, it must have been Batson."

"Was the man you saw dressed?" asked Jolly.

The young lad in the squad sniggered at the thought of a naked Batson swanning about the district.

"Yes, but not as was described on the news ... he had on moleskin pants and an olive or khaki shirt."

"Boots?" prompted Jolly.

"Come to think of it, no, I don't believe so!" said Webb.

"Was he armed?" asked Jolly.

"I couldn't see, but he didn't appear to be carrying any kit," Webb said with a frown.

"Where was he heading?" pressed Jolly.

"Towards the range, topside of Barbers," Webb hooked his thumb down river.

"If he were heading round to his hut, O'Neil's squad should have trapped him by now," said Jolly thoughtfully, gazing up towards Lawrence's Hill.

"Thank you, Mr Webb, I will note your observations - we will secure the evidence and notify Detectives Parker and Cleaver what we have discovered. You fellows, water the horses. We may have to go on a recce up Lawrence's Hill," directed Jolly and, taking the saddle bag with its contents, he hurried up to the police station. So focussed on what he was going to say in his report, Jolly had quite forgotten the two rifles carried by Paddy Hunt and Mr Stewart.

"You might need these!" called Paddy gesturing with the rifle he now had in his hand.

Jolly looked over his shoulder and then waved a hand impatiently for the two men to follow him.

Once the evidence was noted in the register and secured in the lock box, Jolly composed himself and dialled Superintendent Cook. Cook listened to Jolly's report in silence. When Jolly concluded, he thought for a moment and then offered: "Well, that should relieve the locals to some extent... we have secured his weapons, and he is barefoot. He is becoming less threatening!"

"We can't ignore the intelligence that he has caches of supplies in the hills." warned Jolly.

"Certainly, but he has to retrieve them whilst avoiding our search parties and trackers," said Cook confidently.

Jolly frowned and thought to himself that the trackers had been ineffectual to date.

"The fact that he has been spotted, rules out the veracity of his "suicide" note," added Cook, "so it is still an active manhunt. Take your squad up into the hills and see what you can find up at Batson's hut. O'Neil might have flushed him out of hiding, so be cautious! I will relay the information to Inspector Parker. Good day Constable Jolly!"

Cook rang off without waiting for a reply.

Walwa from Wilson's Hill - Arnold Playle collection,
Man from Snowy River Museum

CHAPTER 22

Who is tracking who?

Jacob marched doggedly up the hill. There was very little cover - just a few outcrops of rocks and the occasional tortured tree. It didn't serve to consider what damage a marksman in the tree line above them could do to reduce numbers of the approaching party of volunteers.

"Bloody ill-conceived plan!" he thought to himself, "General Hamilton must be in command!"

He scanned his surroundings and considered the strategy which he would have employed had he been directing operations.

"There must be a track on the ridgeline. We could have taken the horses around, up on the ridge and then descended on Batson's presumed position. A covert and expedient approach!"

The man behind Jacob was breathing raggedly. Jacob turned and viewed his companion.

"Lost a bit of fitness over the past five years have you, Mate?" jibed Jacob.

The man stood, his arms akimbo. He drew in a lungful of air and, pushing his lower jaw forward, he exhaled through his mouth noisily, directing the air up on his ruddy, sweat drenched cheeks.

"I reckon I could still kick some dust if a bullet whizzed past my ear!" he said dryly, "But not fast! ... That's why I am shadowing you... I can use your body for cover!"

His speech was staccato as he sucked in air between phrases. In the finish, his face broke into a mischievous grin.

"Come on, Mate, that tree line looks inviting!" encouraged Jacob.

They pressed on listening to the solid crunching of their companions' footfalls across the sparsely vegetated face of the hill.

Once in amongst a coppice of trees, the group of volunteers pulled up. They raised their flasks to their lips and gulped down drafts of lukewarm water. They mopped their faces with handkerchiefs or sleeves and panted quietly. The two Murray brothers scouted up towards the ridge, hoping to get a view down towards Batson's hut. They approached the ridge cautiously, keeping their heads down. They crawled the final couple of yards and slithered forwards to peep over the ridgeline, down the hill. They were disappointed – they found that a buttress of rock jutted from the lower slopes and obscured their view to the hut, but they could see uniformed troopers cutting through the trees below them.

"O'Neil's lads!" said Ellery to his brother, Stanley, who nodded agreement.

"We need to make our way a little further north, around the hill here and then drop down," continued Ellery.

"Looks like we will be late to the party! O'Neil is bound to get there first," muttered Stanley.

"Couldn't be helped… they sent us the long way round with a bunch of soft, older fellows! It was bound to take us longer to reach the position!" replied Ellery as he looked over his shoulder at the volunteers who were pulling themselves together in the shade. Their shirts were dark with sweat.

"Come on!" said Stanley and the brothers returned to their charges to provide directions.

O'Neil's squad was excited, like hounds on the scent of a fox. The tracker pointed out prints… bare footprints.

"Can only be one bugger!" snarled O'Neil and drew his sidearm. He checked the magazine and then signalled for a silent approach.

The squad paused when they reached the edge of a clearing. Before them, squatting in a lopsided slump was Batson's bark hut. The rock chimney provided the unifying prop to the rustic structure. Rabbit traps and wire pelt stretchers by the dozen, hung from hooks on the front wall and there was a mean verandah supported by stringy bark posts. The front door sagged on its hinges and stood ajar. The men squatted in silence, listening for indications that their quarry was in the hut. Only the sounds of the bush intruded on the silence. A magpie chortled in the tree above them, and orange and brown butterflies flitted across the clearing. A thin wisp of smoke strung out from the chimney.

O'Neil signalled for a couple of men to work their way around to the rear of the hut in the cover of the tree line. After a few minutes they appeared in view, stealthily edging around each side of the hut. They crept up to the makeshift windows. There was no glass, just flour bag curtains and a shutter to keep out bad weather. They cautiously peered into the dim interior. The hut was unoccupied.

O'Neil sent the tracker to scout around the hut before the rest of the squad moved forward and obliterated tracks.

"He bin here, boss," the tracker announced, pointing out scuffed footprints, "Me'be at sunrise. Gone now."

O'Neil entered the hut and scanned Batson's meagre possessions. He opened some trunks, and a cupboard made of flattened kerosene tins. He discovered some shells and a rifle under Batson's bed. He gathered the items into a calico bag and handed the rifle and bag to one of the constables to carry. Satisfied there were no food supplies, he stepped outside and gathered the squad. The sound of clumsy footfalls from the hill above, caught his attention, and Stanley and Ellery Murray appeared from the bush, their squad of volunteers trudged into the clearing behind them. The sting had gone out of the volunteers; they looked hot and bothered. The Murrays stopped and saluted their superior.

"Morning fellows! Anything to report?" asked O'Neil.

Stanley took the lead and responded, "No, Sir. We saw no evidence that Batson had been over the southeastern side of this hill... but then, the ground is gravel and shale, so he wouldn't leave much in the way of tracks. We didn't see him anyways." he ended lamely.

"Boss!" called out the tracker, a huge grin across his face, "Here! He go this way!"

The hunt was back on. Electricity swept through the troops, and they were all on the alert.

"Keep your wits about you, lads!" admonished O'Neil, "this fellow is wound up and unpredictable. We will spread out and comb the hill towards the river. Flush him out into clear ground!"

The combined squad of troopers and volunteers, divided into eight smaller squads and fanned out, setting off with their backs to the hut, descending the hill. If all went well, and if Batson was in the area, O'Neil anticipated his troops would flush their quarry onto the road in the area between the western edge of Walwa and the cemetery.

Jacob Miller and his unfit friend were allocated to the squad led by Ellery Murray. The terrain was difficult. They pushed their way through a dense thicket of tea-tree and wattle before picking up a track made by wildlife, which made the access a little easier. The species of wildlife which commonly used the track must have been wombats and wallabies because the shrubbery closed over the trail quite close to the ground. The men were forced to crouch and risked frequent scratches and impacts to heads and shoulders from flicking branches.

"Fek it," growled Ellery as he mis-stepped and his foot skittered down the incline into a wombat burrow. He landed heavily. Jacob stretched out a hand to help the young constable to his feet. Their hands meshed, and Jacob winced as he felt shards of gravel grind between their palms. They both brushed their palms on their pants and Ellery examined his hands; sharp shards of gravel had chewed into the heels of his hands. He picked out the gravel and brushed his hands again on his pants. He grinned ruefully at his companions.

"As sure footed as a mountain goat!" he chuckled.

The squad lacked the energy to respond with much enthusiasm and simply took the opportunity for a breather.

A shot rang out. Instinctively the men ducked and crouched in amongst the vegetation. They froze, listening for follow up shots or voices. The shot had originated from the lower slopes, closer towards the Walwa township. A slow minute elapsed. Jacob measured it by the trickle of sweat that rolled down the side of his jaw and dripped from his chin.

"C'mon fellas, we will make our way towards the shot. We might intercept Batson. Don't get excited, mind! Safety catches on."

Adrenaline pushed exhaustion to the side, and the squad moved quietly between the trees, concentrating on foot placement to avoid slipping and to reduce noise. Their rifles remained slung across their shoulders as they needed both hands to push branches out of the way and catch onto saplings to prevent slipping down the slope. Voices could be heard up ahead – frustrated, angry tones.

They pushed through a screen of tea-tree and stepped into a small clearing. Jolly stood in front of O'Neil. He had flushed cheeks, more from embarrassment than exertion.

"Of all people, it shouldn't have been you! Safety off and one in the breech?" snarled O'Neil.

"Yes, sir… 'mortified, Sir!" Jolly responded sorrowfully.

O'Neil looked around and confirmed that the entire company was making its way towards the gunshot.

"Well, we would have certainly flushed him by now! False alarm fellas! We will regroup in town and review any incoming intelligence. He won't be within coo-ee of here now!" said O'Neil gruffly.

It was a quiet, dejected march back to town.

From his hiding spot in a small crevice between two massive boulders, Batson watched as the troops withdrew. He chuckled to himself and waved. Memories from his childhood flooded his mind: he and his young chums playing Bushrangers and Troopers up in amongst the rocks of Morgan's Lookout. He hadn't thought of Tom Aspley and Harry Montgomery for years but in his mind's eye he could see them scampering around the boulders and pelting rocks down on him, Batson was a much younger and scrawnier child than his "friends".

"*They* always got to be Mad Dog Morgan and his gang," Batson whinged to himself, feeling the sting of jealousy and the missiles again.

"I'll show 'em now! I am the real Bushranger!" he hissed.

After a moment, he extracted himself from his cramped hiding place and stretched. He flicked a large orb weaver spider from his shoulder and a shard of granite fell out of his lank curly hair. He stared at the shard and then looked up above his hiding spot. He could see the scar on the rock surface from which the shard had been dislodged.

"Hmmm, a lucky shot," Batson mused, "a bit lower and he would have got me!"

He then reached back into the crevice and removed a calico bag. He sat down on a slab of rock and unpacked the contents of the bag: a tin of biscuits, a flask of water and an apple. There was also a small tobacco tin of revolver shells which he had retrieved from his hut. He pulled the revolver from his waistband and spun the chamber. He could see the small shapes of the troopers far down the hill and he straightened his arm and aimed the revolver at their retreating frames.

Imitating the sound of revolver shots he "picked off" the four exposed troopers. He chuckled grimly and put his weapon aside. He opened the tin and ate several biscuits, two at a time. He was starved.

O'Neil stood down the volunteers and his squad when they reached the township of Walwa.

"Go and get a feed and we will muster in the hall at 2pm," he announced. He looked to Jolly with a stern expression and snapped, "You and I will go to Jingellic and review developments with the Officer in Charge."

Jolly's cheeks coloured again, and he saluted sharply and spun on his heel. He hurried off to get the vehicle.

From the vantage point of the bridge over the Murray River, Jolly and O'Neil had an excellent view of the activity around the ford, just east of the bridge. They pulled up and joined the group of eager onlookers at the rail.

"What is going on down there?" asked O'Connor of an elderly gentlemen who had the relaxed attitude of someone who had been watching proceedings for some time.

"Been a bit of excitement, there has!" enthused the gent, "Young Marchant and Coysh were part of a small group of volunteers walking the riverbank, looking for clues... They found footprints in the mud just below Barbers' dairy."

The gent looked a bit affronted when an excited younger man at his elbow took up the story:

"The river is right swift at that point, if someone had gone in, they would be hard pressed to swim - more likely drowned!"

The older gent took back his tale and continued:

"Sergeant O'Connor and an Albury newcomer, Sergeant Cooper, took Barber's old punt onto the river to search for a body. 'Didn't go well! They got hooked up on a snag and the boat tipped over... they did well to get to shore without drowning!" laughed the gent grimly.

"Now they are netting the ford to catch a floater!" crowed the younger fellow.

Jolly and O'Neil resumed their journey to the Jingellic Hotel and headquarters of the search and investigation team.

The ford near the bridge at Jingellic - Arnold Playle collection, Man from Snowy River Museum

Barrow Brothers Walwa-Jingellic Butter factory - Arnold Playle collection, Man from Snowy River Museum

CHAPTER 23

A Dinner date

Emma was acutely aware that Jacob was within reach... well, practically so. Albert had returned from Walwa and brought back the exciting news: a company of ex-AIF troops had arrived in town to volunteer in the Batson manhunt.

Emma knew that Jacob would be one of the volunteers. She had not stopped dreaming about him since her arrival in Walwa and had conjured many a scenario of a romantic encounter. Each delicious imagining brought a swoop to her innards and a smile to her face.

"What now?" she thought to herself: how could she engineer a meeting.

"Confront it all head on!" she decided as she put the basket of laundry which she had just unpegged from the line, on the kitchen table and surged into the sitting room in search of Albert and Minnie.

Minnie had her feet up, reclining on the sofa, her hands gently stroking the bulge of her belly, as she listened to Albert read snippets from the newspaper. The children were at school, so aside from Albert's soothing voice, all was quiet. Emma hesitated at the threshold, gazing at the homely scene. Minnie glanced up at Emma and smiled.

"How goes the toil, slave?" she chuckled.

Emma grinned in response and sat down heavily in one of the remaining armchairs.

"Fair to middling! It is getting warm out there again! The washing is practically dry by the time I finish pegging it out!" said Emma, smiling.

"I have a favour to ask," Emma said after a pause.

"I am sure we would be happy to oblige," said Minnie warmly.

Albert cocked his head enquiringly.

"Do you think we might, well at least, do you think I, could invite Jacob Miller to dinner tomorrow night?" Emma asked hesitantly with colour blooming on her cheeks.

Minnie smiled encouragingly at Emma and Albert.

"I don't think there is anything pressing on our social calendar! What a splendid idea!" Minnie declared with a mischievous smile.

Albert nodded and assured Emma that if it suited Minnie, it suited him.

"Would you like me to track him down in Walwa and issue the invitation... just to do the right thing...." asked Albert.

"To preserve my honour and avoid me appearing too keen?" laughed Emma.

"Well, you know what small towns are like... they will have you married off in the blink of an eye!" chuckled Albert, "or worse!" he added.

"Marriage is not such a bad idea," thought Emma, but she merely smiled gratefully at the Drummonds.

"There is a corned silverside in the crock and the garden is loaded with beans, tomatoes and cucumbers. Maybe turn that big bottle of cherries into a pie, with cream?" suggested Minnie.

Emma was thrilled that her aunt and uncle were so obliging.

"I must go into Walwa again this afternoon to pick up that seal for the windmill, so I'll find Jacob at the same time. I am sure they'll have the volunteers back at the hall by late afternoon," mused Albert.

"Well, with that sorted, I shall just pop into the kitchen and make us all a nice cup of tea!" said Emma before skipping back to the kitchen.

Minnie and Albert shared a conspiratorial smile.

It was after 4pm by the time Albert arrived in Walwa. He parked the truck outside the Walwa Store and popped in to see if the carrier had delivered his windmill seal. Mrs Brindley looked up when Albert pushed through the door, and she wearily pushed strands of greying hair from her eyes. She smiled when she recognised Albert.

"Good afternoon, Mr Drummond!" she hailed him, "How is Minnie? What can I help you with today?"

"We are all good, thank you, Mrs Brindley! Minnie is still a lady in waiting! Has the carrier been in yet? I am waiting on a small parcel," said Albert.

Mrs Brindley sorted through a basket of paperwork and items put aside for customers.

"No, nothing here. The carrier hasn't come by today. Would it have come up on the mail car? Perhaps check with Mrs Hughes," said Mrs Brindley.

Albert purchased a paper bag of mixed lollies for the children before striding down the street to the post office, on the corner opposite the Walwa Hotel. The alluring scent of hops and the chatter of men in the front bar made Albert thirsty as he walked past the windows of the Hotel. He hurried to the post office.

Mrs Hughes was sorting the mail. She stood, sliding letters into the slots of an alphabetical series of pigeonholes on the wall.

She smiled at Albert and greeted him. He enquired after his seal, and she nodded enthusiastically and scooped out the contents of the "D" pigeonhole.

"Just arrived!" she said, "along with this letter for a Miss Payne."

There was a slight interrogative in her tone and Albert felt obliged to explain Emma's presence in their home.

"Minnie's niece, just up visiting..." he assured the postmistress.

Without preamble, Mrs Hughes launched into an update of the search for Claude Batson.

"This morning there was word of footprints in the mud of the river-bank behind Barbers' dairy.... They thought he had swum the river... or drowned! There was a commotion when two police officers capsized a punt looking for a body. They almost became drowning victims themselves! There was a shot which rang out on the hill late morning, but I understand that it may have just been an accidental discharge. Really, Batson could be anywhere! He is so at home in the bush! Makes us all a bit nervous, don't you think? I have had doors locked at night and start at the slightest noise! I don't know what has rattled Batson's chain and now we don't know who his next target might be!"

Mrs Hughes loved to talk, and her position as switchboard operator and postmistress put her in the box seat for collecting information and gossip. The telling was delicious! Sometimes she was accused of telling tales that were scant on facts but in the current situation, she was well supplied with information.

Albert absorbed Mrs Hughes' information and considered the ramifications of a deranged, well-equipped and accurate marksman roaming the district. He considered his interactions with Batson. He had last seen the lad on the previous Friday morning, walking along the road with a sack over his shoulder. The sack was a bit bulky but not heavy from the look of it, and there were intriguing metallic clunks which issued from it. He remembered that Batson was looking well pleased with himself and had greeted Albert cheerily.

"Well, I don't think Batson has an axe to grind with me or my family. He must have just lost his mind.... he was always a sandwich short of a picnic, though, so I hope they capture him soon, before he hurts anyone else.... or himself," said Albert thoughtfully.

Albert slid the envelope and small package into his pocket and crossed to the Walwa Hotel. He pushed through the doors into the bar room. It was crowded for a Wednesday afternoon, particularly so, when it wasn't even a designated livestock sale day. Albert was greeted by locals and examined by the strangers in town. Albert assumed the "foreigners" were part of the volunteer Batson search party company. He scanned the faces in case Jacob was amongst the men.

Albert bellied up to the bar and ordered a pint. The publican was under the pump and scarcely had time to acknowledge him. With a cool frothy beer in hand, Albert turned to see who he might like to share a drink with. He was soon enmeshed in an animated conversation with a group of locals all keen to impart the "latest" on the search for *the Last Bushranger of the Riverina*.

Charles Coysh was keen to be heard, "I may have been the last to see Batson before the shooting!" he announced.

"Where did you see him?" asked a punter dutifully.

"The wife and I were crossing the bridge; a Sunday stroll you know! After lunch it was. We were heading to Redbank and Batson was striding toward us. He didn't look up and didn't see us 'till I hailed him. He was muttering and bristled with guns. He was a confronting sight; my wife was quite disturbed!" said Coysh.

"Where did he get all the guns from?" asked Albert quietly.

Coysh flushed at that point.

"He came and saw me quite late on Saturday night. About nine... He asked to borrow the new Rifle Club .303 service rifle," said Coysh.

"What reason did he give? Why so late?" asked Albert.

"I had been talking to him in the afternoon, whilst watching tennis at the courts in Walwa. I told him about the new rifle which had been supplied to the rifle club, and he said he would like to get some practice with it before the competition in March. I forgot about it and just as I was about to retire for the night, when there he was, banging on the door. He said he was leaving early to go hunting... he knew I would be at church on Sunday morning. I thought nothing of it." said Coysh.

"Was he agitated?" asked Albert.

"Nothing out of the ordinary," replied Coysh carefully, "But funny thing; somebody said they saw him that night, striding up and down in the street, rifle slung over his shoulder...like he was on parade!"

"Well, that sounds like odd behaviour!" suggested Albert.

Albert finished his beer and since Jacob had not materialised in the bar, he felt he should go and seek him out. Albert walked along the footpath and glanced in the Walwa Café window to see if Jacob was there. He crossed to the Coffee Palace for the same purpose before stepping through the doors of the Walwa Hall. The interior of the hall had been converted to a makeshift dormitory. Swags were laid out, chairs next to the swags were hung with jackets and clothes. A few men were resting on their swags, some were reading, others were seated together smoking and chatting quietly. The hall had an all-pervading odour of sweat, tobacco smoke and leather.

Not wanting to intrude, Albert stepped up to the group of men to enquire after Jacob's whereabouts. A tall, sandy blonde young man rose from the group and approached Albert eagerly. Albert smiled with mild relief when he recognised Jacob Miller. They clasped hands with one another and clapped each other on the shoulder.

"Good to see you, again, Jacob!"

"And you, Mr Drummond!"

"Albert, please, Jacob!" smiled Albert.

"How is Emma…. Miss Payne, settling in, Albert?" stuttered Jacob with a slight blush.

"Emma is fine. Such a help to Minnie, well, to our entire family!" said Albert heartily.

"Is Mrs Drummond well in her last weeks of confinement?" asked Jacob carefully.

"She won't be confined!" laughed Albert, "but she is well, thank you!"

Albert looked around and saw that Jacob's companions were watching their conversation with interest.

"Perhaps we could take a stroll?" he suggested to Jacob so that they could have a little privacy.

The two men stepped back into the strong afternoon sunlight. By reflex, Albert batted away a couple of flies with his hat.

"The girls have put me on a task, Jacob," Albert announced with a smile.

Jacob immediately looked pleased and interested.

"I am to invite you to dinner at our home on Thursday evening... tomorrow. I can fetch you in the truck if you do not have transport. Would you be available?" said Albert with a knowing grin.

Jacob laughed and cocked his head at Albert, "I'm sure you know that you don't have to ask twice, Albert! Of course, I would be delighted!"

"Perfect, shall I fetch you at 5:30pm, from here?"

"Thank you, yes!" smiled Jacob, I'll look forward to it!"

Jacob walked Albert to his truck and waved him off. He couldn't stop smiling.

Johns' Walwa Hotel c1926 - State Library Victoria

CHAPTER 24

Stake out

The police officers crowded into the dining room of the Jingellic Hotel for the scheduled 5pm briefing. Again, the bar room was at capacity with curious local men who were keen to listen in on the developments, too. Detective Cleaver was in no mood for dealing with gawkers and cleared the bar room. The publican objected as he could see his profits leaving too, but Cleaver hissed, "If you do not comply with direct orders of an authorised police officer, I shall have your licence!"

Finlay Smith begrudgingly called time and his patrons, with even more animated objections, eventually complied. Parker ordered that the windows were shut, and curtains drawn to further deter the gawkers. In the close, still environment of the dining room the briefing was, indeed going to be brief.

The discussion focussed on a sighting of Batson in the hills above Walwa by a credible witness.

"At 10 o'clock this morning, a message was received here at headquarters that a Mr Walters had been to the Kelly brothers hut near Lawrences' Hill. He discovered that one of the beds had been slept in and a target had been set up in the clearing alongside the hut. It was riddled with bullets and there were shell casings spread about. Mr Walters is convinced it was Batson camping up there and finetuning his aim," said Parker.

An excited stir went through the dining room.

"If Batson was having a spot of target practice in the last few days, the shots would have echoed through the valley! We would have heard him!" suggested Sergeant Tom Morris.

"Granted," said Parker grudgingly, "I believe it demonstrates premeditation!"

"A lot of chaps have target practice without going on to shoot at people... look at the target butts at the rifle club," Morris was determined that evidence provided was accurate.

"We are now confident that Batson is still south of the Murray River. Mrs Oswald Hanna has reported a sighting through her binoculars of a man fitting Batson's description on the face of the hill southwest of Walwa. Local knowledge indicates that the fugitive may well be heading towards The Bluff," said Parker.

There was muttering amongst the police officers who were familiar with the district. Inspector Parker noticed the unrest, and he addressed Constable Ellery Murray.

"Constable Murray, you were brought up in Walwa, I believe you had some association with Batson in your youth, what are your insights into the prospect of Batson making it to The Bluff?"

Ellery stood and puffed out his chest proudly, pleased to have been elevated to ranks of a consultant.

"The Bluff is a fortress. It has steep foothills, sheets of scree and folds and creases so numerous that should Batson make it to the range, it would be impossible to surround him, impossible to track him, impossible to capture him, Sir! Batson is very familiar with the terrain; he could stay well above our trackers and troops and pick us off with a rifle, one by one," said Ellery ominously.

Inspector Parker was annoyed by the absolute nature of Ellery's description and predictions.

"It is never impossible, Constable. However, I acknowledge that it would be tactically disastrous to allow Batson to escape the cordon," said Parker.

"Sir, I would like to add to Constable Ellery's description," said Senior Constable Bunworth.

"The Bluff is like a gloomy mountain fortress. Mountainous country, full of gorges and caves - impassable in spots. I have ridden into areas in this district where the sun never shines – the rays are shut out from the valleys by towering mountains on either side. It would be possible for a man like Batson, to keep an army at bay for weeks from a suitable hiding place. Just like the bushrangers of earlier days. He might escape capture for weeks... months," said Bunworth earnestly.

"Very poetic, Senior Constable Bunworth," said Parker sardonically, whilst glowering at the man.

"We are aware that Batson may well have doubled back to look for supplies. We have collected rifles and ammunition from his caches on the Island just east of Barbers' dairy. Officers have secured another rifle from Batson's hut. The lad, Emerson, reported Batson was only armed with a handgun when he was approached on Tuesday afternoon. Mrs Hanna could not see a rifle with the man she spotted on the hill. So, we can consider that Batson needs weapons, ammunition, clothing and food before taking his chances in The Bluff. Would you concur, Constable Murray?" said Parker.

Murray nodded vigorously, "Yes, Sir!"

"Now this is a little sensitive, but could we expect that Batson may have some sympathisers amongst the local residents? There may be others that might have had a gripe with the victim, Mr Sheppard, or they simply want to buy their own safety. Perhaps he is being harboured and supported in his quest to evade capture," suggested Parker, "To reduce Batson's chances, we must restrict public access to intelligence."

One of the younger constables from Albury sniggered to his mate and said quietly, "I think a lot of these country folk have had restricted access to intelligence for some time!"

"Police movements and activities are not to be telegraphed to the locals... beware of ears!" continued Inspector Parker in a dictatorial and sharp tone.

"I have heard a comment from a local woman that Batson is in a bad way," said Constable Jolly, "I am certainly not accusing her of supporting Batson, but I find it odd that she claimed any direct knowledge of the man's wellbeing without having witnessed it."

"Oh, who was that Constable Jolly? We need to interview her," said Sergeant O'Neil eagerly.

Jolly looked a little anxious.

"She is Mrs Walker. Let me have a word to her. She might clam up and get nervous with an officer with whom she is not familiar."

"Very well but report back immediately!" advised O'Neil firmly.

"Based on Mrs Hanna's information and word from Mr Alf Lawrence that he had spotted Batson on Tuesday night; we could be relatively confident that the man is more likely to be mobile at night and may well be in the vicinity of Lawrences' Hill and his hut somewhere. I propose we set up a couple of discrete outposts of small groups of reliable men, familiar with the bush. They will be stationed at strategic positions across this area," Inspector Parker's finger jabbed at the map displayed on the wall, "the men will camp out overnight. We need to intercept Batson as soon as we can!"

Sergeant O'Neil volunteered: "There are the two Murray brothers, Constables Ellery and Stanley Murray who would be suitable for this task, along with a couple of local volunteers with excellent knowledge of the hills."

"I would suggest four squads of three officers or two and a black tracker, spread over this area, moving silently at night to flush Batson out or to capture him," declared Inspector Parker.

Sergeant O'Neil remembered the activity he had seen from the bridge earlier and asked:

"Is there an update on the footprints and search of the river from earlier today?"

Parker looked grimly at Sergeant O'Connor and Constable Cooper.

"A young lad by the name of Spicer came forward and admitted the footprints were his – he was down there fishing at dawn. His feet matched the prints," said Sergeant O'Connor with a touch of embarrassment as the debacle of capsizing the punt flooded back into his mind.

"Can we be sure that this isn't a ruse to tie up our resources and cover for Batson," asked Inspector Parker suspiciously.

"There is no love lost between Spicer and Batson. The youngster is mortified that Batson effectively held him up and threatened him in his home before the picnic shooting. Batson stole ammunition belonging to the Rifle Club and Mr Spicer," advised Constable Jolly.

"Righto," said Inspector Parker, "O'Neil can select and dispatch the squads to the hills this evening. We will maintain the watch on roads, fords and bridges and if there is no capture overnight, we will muster at dawn in the Walwa Hall to direct parties to scour the hills. Good hunting, chaps!"

Chair legs screeched on the scrubbed floorboards and the police officers dispersed.

Main Street Walwa, looking East -
Arnold Playle collection, Man from
Snowy River Museum

CHAPTER 25

Valentines' Day – 14 February 1924

Batson's eyes opened and he lay still. The birds had ceased their chatter. He listened. He couldn't detect anything, but something had put the birds into a state of silent alarm. He rolled over, slid off the flat rock and shrank his frame under the leafy shroud of a weeping shrub. Carefully, quietly, he arranged his kit around him so that he could lift and run with efficiency, if needs be.

Batson's lack of boots had knocked his confidence. He berated himself for losing his boots in the river. The hills were littered with sun baked, sharp shale which had shredded his feet. Even on grassy patches, the bindii, thistles and other thorny vegetation had further traumatised his damaged soles and split toes. Moving was torturous. Under the cloak of darkness a few hours earlier, Batson had risked a trip to the Murray River. He had sat on a log at the edge of the broad sweep of moon spangled river and soaked his feet in the chill water. He had tried binding his feet with mud, mashed willow leaves and strips of fabric torn from his shirt. Some comfort was provided but it soon wore off, both the comfort and the bindings. He had crossed back through the Drummonds' paddock and found his way to the dairy. In the moonlight, he had managed to find a milk can containing some soured milk – he drank it down greedily, despite the rank flavour. As he stepped forward to replace the can in the cool depths of the shed, he stepped on an unseen object which sent jolts of pain through his battered frame. He dropped the can; it rolled across the concrete landing and fell off the edge and then rolled into the sparse grass below. He froze, listening to see if the clatter had alerted dogs or people at the nearby homestead.

Nothing.

The night sky was fading to the sallow colour of dawn. Batson knew he had to get to cover. He limped up the paddock, over the Upper Murray Road and headed once more, for the safety of the hills. He had worked his way up a grassy shoulder and around to an outcrop of rock which jutted clear of the surrounding hill. He checked the approaches and was confident that he would have an excellent view of the scenery below him, a commanding view of the approaches and a bulky over-hang of rock shielded him from the view of potential observers from elevations above his position. He had not meant to, but as soon as he sprawled on top of the altar-like rock he had drifted off to sleep.

Subconsciously, he had become aware of the absence of bird calls and his reflexes had pushed his body to respond and hide. By the time he had sorted his muddled head and had assessed the situation, he was aware that it was quite late, maybe 9am from the angle of the sun. He realised that the birds were quiet and watchful because a dog was nosing up amongst the rocks on the approach to his hiding spot. It had picked up the scent of Batson's bloodied feet.

Batson immediately thought that it was a police or hunter's tracking dog or possibly, a farmer's work dog. Either way, the dog could reveal his location to searchers. He considered whether he could call it up and keep it quiet, to stop it leading a handler to him. Then he thought glum-ly that he would probably have to kill it because it would doubtless bark. He liked dogs...

He didn't have to ponder the dilemma for long, as the dog looked up and locked eyes with Batson. It startled when it recognised the quarry as human and snarled.

"Fek it, a dingo," muttered Batson.

He had seen the damage that dingoes had wrought on Alf Lawrence's sheep – their throats and guts ripped out, left dead and worse, dying.

Wary of being destined for the same fate and ignoring any concern for searchers, he grabbed his kit and a sturdy stick from under the shrub. He leapt to his feet and challenged the animal. He spread his arms wide, and, with the advantage of elevation, he made himself appear huge and threatening. The lone dingo considered its options briefly before deciding to flee. Batson sank back down on top of the rock. He was sweating and tremors wracked his body. Shock and infection had set in.

Hardwick read the wire transcript which had just been handed to him by Mrs Hughes at the Walwa post office. The journalist thanked the woman absently and scanned the contents:

Need obituary article and update – David Thomas Sheppard, 42, late of Jingellic, fatally wounded 10/2/1924 – Jingellic Picnic Shooting. Leaves wife and two children. Funeral 14/2/24. Moe. 10am. – Mourners to include Employer - Barrow Bros (Butter factory, Jingellic) represented by Mr J Barrow Esq.

Mrs Hughes tapped her fingers on the counter insistently causing Hardwick to look up.

"That'll be threepence, please!" she said brusquely.

"Oh, of course!" said Hardwick apologetically.

He delved into the depths of his trouser pocket and pushed the coins across the counter before continuing to read.

Condition other victims: Major William McGrath – satisfactory - 4 bullet wounds. elbow - permanent disability. Richard King critical – abdominal infection. Police have conducted deathbed deposition. Charles Gainer – shattered knee - permanent disability.

"You know the locals well, Mrs Hughes, what can you tell me about the late Mr Sheppard?"

"I am not inclined to gossip, Mr Hardwick!" said Mrs Hughes waspishly.

"Certainly," said Hardwick in a placating tone, "This is a serious interview for his obituary in the morning paper. Clearly, I will need more than this," he swished the wire transcript in front of Mrs Hughes, "to do the man justice in a tribute piece."

Mrs Hughes was pleased that her opinion had been sought, and considered her words carefully, scouring her memory for details.

"I didn't know Mr Sheppard well. Mr McGrath was probably his closest friend in the district – they were both newcomers, thrown together, I s'pose. Mr Sheppard took the position of manager at the Butter Factory in June last year. He was keen and enthusiastic and seemed determined to boost the business. He put the wind up the workers... sacked a few. He demanded absolute efficiency." said Mrs Hughes.

"Oh, would that have made him some enemies, Mrs Hughes?" asked Hardwick eagerly.

"I can't really say... I suppose so... well, Claude Batson was let go during that time, so... yes!"

Mrs Hughes looked anxious before continuing thoughtfully, "Mr Barber was also forced to let Batson go as a farm worker, last year, I think ... he was unreliable, you know. Although, Mrs Barber, well, both really, remained on sufficiently good terms to continue to give the lad meals and allow him to sleep over on occasion and do odd jobs for a bit of cash..."

Hardwick guided Mrs Hughes back to the topic of Sheppard, "Do you have anything more to say about Mr Sheppard?"

"He was a good, kind man. Very popular. Came to church and sports days, a community stalwart. Very strong...I have seen him lift a 56lb butter pack, one in each hand from shoulder height to above his head. He has lovely little children... Oh, the poor mites to lose their father in such an awful fashion... and Mrs Sheppard, what will she do now?" Mrs Hughes groaned, her eyes glittered and a tear spilled down her cheek.

She unfurled a handkerchief from her pocket and blew her nose, mopped her eyes.

"Sorry to upset you Mrs Hughes, I might leave it at that. Who might be a good person to talk to at the Butter Factory? Was there a foreman..." said Hardwick.

"Mr Davis, I would imagine..." sniffed Mrs Hughes.

"Thank you, kindly, Mrs Hughes! Good day!" Hardwick smiled gently and quickly departed.

Walwa Post Office - Arnold Playle collection, Man from Snowy River Museum

Hardwick walked back down the Main Street. He thought he would just call out to the Butter Factory and see if Mr Davis or the other workers might have something to contribute to his obituary piece. He would collect his vehicle from outside the Coffee Palace and go for a drive, he decided. As he approached the Police Station, which was just opposite his parked car, a dark official-looking vehicle pulled up. A man, Hardwick assumed to be a plain clothes officer and a police constable stepped out of the vehicle and surveyed their surrounds. Hardwick took the opportunity to introduce himself. The senior officer acknowledged Hardwick stiffly and introduced himself and his colleague.

"I am Sub Inspector Connelly and this is Constable Batt. I have come up from Wangaratta to take charge of the investigation into the murder of David Sheppard."

He shook hands with Hardwick in an aloof manner before saying, "A journalist would have his nose on the trail... would you know the whereabouts of Constable Jolly or Detective Cleaver?" asked Connelly.

Hardwick smiled and tapped his nose in a friendly manner, not taking offence from the police officer's words.

"I believe Constable Jolly and several other officers are strategically camped out on the hill... or were last night. Detective Cleaver might well be over at Jingellic, which is acting as Headquarters for the search for Claude Batson ... unless he is out in the field, investigating. 'Can't be more specific than that, I am afraid."

"Where abouts in Jingellic?" asked Connelly.

"The pub!" grinned Hardwick.

The officer was unimpressed and indicated to the Constable, his driver, that they were to leave. He saluted Hardwick and left without another word.

Hardwick was intrigued that there was yet another change of command of the Victorian Police contingent. He had understood that there was a squad arriving from Gippsland after lunch, under the command of Senior Constable Comrie who was to be the Officer in charge. Constable Jolly seemed to be rebounding between members of the NSW investigative team, now led by Inspector Parker, Sergeant O'Neil from St Kilda Road Victorian Police Headquarters, and reporting to Superintendent Cook in Albury. In addition, Jolly was reporting to Detective Cleaver who was making enquiries on behalf of the coroner.

"Who is actually in charge of the investigation?" wondered Hardwick, "No wonder Constable Jolly is on edge," he thought as he stepped into his car.

Hardwick shelved the idea of interviewing Barrow Brothers Butter Factory employees and decided to follow Connelly's car to see what he could glean from the expected briefing between Officers in Charge of the investigation from Victoria and New South Wales.

It was just after 10am when Detective Cleaver and Constable Cooper met with Albert Drummond in the paddock near his dairy. The two lads who were employed to milk, Bill Hore and Percy Emerson, were sitting on the edge of the concrete landing of the dairy shed. Both looked delighted to be "part of the investigation". The police officers alighted from their vehicle and approached Albert. They greeted one another and shook hands.

"What have you got to tell us, Albert?" asked Detective Cleaver.

"The lads here, came down to milk this morning and discovered they were a milk can short. They didn't think much about it until they were cleaning up after milking and it was then they noticed it lying here in the grass," Albert indicated the can.

"It had no way of being accidentally moved from the churn room and pushed off the landing ... we are suspicious Batson has been by for a feed," finished Albert.

Cleaver was thrilled that there was a prospect that Batson was still in the area, despite the nebulous nature of the evidence.

"We will have to take the milk can as evidence and dust for prints to confirm, but I think we can be assured that Batson is getting hungry! I think he will be back!" said Cleaver before turning to the dairymen and advising:

"Go about your tasks as usual over the next day or so. Keep a look out, but don't act suspiciously! If you have an opportunity, detain Batson and send for help. Oh, and keep all this under your hat! Not a word to a soul!"

Albert looked worried.

"Our house isn't far," he said, gesticulating towards the homestead, "I have a heavily pregnant wife, four children and my niece staying with us. I can assure you that the prospect of Batson lurking around in the shadows is highly alarming!"

"I can understand your concern, Albert. I would encourage you to evacuate for a few days and take rooms at the hotel in Walwa, or with friends... just till we have the man in custody," replied Cleaver.

Albert furrowed his brow considering his options. He brightened as a plan came to mind.

"I am sure Minnie will be reluctant to be away from home comforts with the baby about ready to make an appearance. I think our house can be defended from an intruder with a bit of help. I tell you what: I would like to borrow a couple of armed volunteers from amongst the AIF fellows you have camping in the hall, and I will send our children to relatives. Then I think we shall be safe," said Albert.

"I think that might be a plan," agreed Cleaver, "I will contact Constable Jolly and Hugh Hanna and ensure two suitable fellows, and their rifles are dispatched."

"We know one of the fellows, Jacob Miller. Please ensure that he is on the list. We were hosting him to dinner tonight, anyway, so it wouldn't be too inconvenient for him," said Albert and grinned, pleased that he had found such a neat solution.

The investigation and arrangements concluded, the Constable wrapped the milk can in a tarpaulin and placed it carefully in the back seat of their vehicle, before driving away in a swirl of dust.

Hore and Emerson swung down from the landing and cheerily called farewells to their employer, Albert. They collected their ponies from the shade of the acacia tree and cantered off home.

Albert went to tell his family of the morning's events.

Detective Cleaver spoke to Inspector Parker on his return to Jingellic and the senior officer called for an earlier than usual afternoon briefing at Jingellic Hotel, the headquarters of the investigation. Senior Constable Comrie and his party of five officers from Gippsland had arrived and needed an update so an early briefing would be appropriate. In addition, Sergeant O'Neill and Constable Jolly were reporting back in relation to the stake out on the hill near Batson's hut. Wangaratta officer, Sub-Inspector Connelly had arrived and was also awaiting a briefing. Connelly had occupied his time by strutting about and examining the maps affixed to the wall.

Parker called the room to order and smiled beatifically down on the police officers.

"Welcome to those officers and men who have, today, joined us in the effort to apprehend Claude Batson and bring him to justice," said Parker and nodded to Senior Constable Comrie and Sub-inspector Connelly before continuing, "I am pleased to announce that we have evidence that Batson is still in our immediate area."

He went on to describe the finding at Albert Drummond's dairy and remained oblivious to the mutterings from some sceptical officers that the correlation between the upended milk can and Batson's whereabouts was a bit of a stretch.

"In addition, Sergeant O'Neill reports that fresh footprints were detected in the vicinity of Batson's hut on Lawrences' Hill."

Detective Cleaver looked at Parker sharply, "Does this mean the man evaded the squads that were camped out on the hill?"

Sergeant O'Neill looked uncomfortable since the stake out was under his command,

"We were vigilant but saw nothing," he confessed, "Tracks were discovered this morning, some items were missing from the hut."

"Maybe he has some help from the Blacks," whispered one of the constables to the man sitting next to him.

"Not many left here abouts, they were hunted out decades ago!" muttered his neighbour, "Really, it could have been anyone… 'just took their shoes off!"

Parker advised that since the numbers of police and volunteers on the hunt were fortunately of sufficient numbers, they would close the net around Batson's presumed position.

"We have thirty-seven police members and over seventy armed volunteers scouring the hills. I propose we send a group of five men down river on the Victoria side to block the road at the pinch, just east of Mt Alfred. A party should be dispatched to Redbank track on the crest. Block the road west of the Jingellic Reserve near Walkers. We will need several parties to watch the river from the NSW side to ensure Batson doesn't cross back. The sentries at established road-blocks, bridge crossings and fords will be maintained," said Parker.

Parker had been prodding at the map describing the perimeters of his net enfolding Batson as he spoke.

"The fact that Batson has resorted to stealing soured milk, is barefoot and is now presumed to be only lightly armed, since at best, he has a handgun, means that he is getting more desperate and possibly weaker. I am confident his capture is imminent," crowed Parker.

"We need to be mindful of the risk of further innocent victims to a desperate fugitive, and to this end we have requested that residents within the cordon evacuate to relatives or friends for this, hopefully, the final event of the apprehension of Claude Batson. Albert Drummond, owner of the dairy where the milk can was found has requested some additional help from armed ex-AIF volunteers. Constable Jolly, if you can see to it that, umm, was it Jacob Miller he asked for, Detective Cleaver?" Cleaver nodded, "and one other suitable volunteer are dispatched to the Drummonds this afternoon. These men can assist to protect Mr Drummond and his wife until Batson is apprehended."

Sub Inspector Connelly thought he had better introduce himself and assert his jurisdictional authority at this point. He stood, smoothed his jacket and announced his position.

"As senior Victorian Police Officer, I need to point out that this operation, as described by Inspector Parker, is on Victorian soil. I acknowledge that the work that has been undertaken to date, to investigate the case, and search for the fugitive perpetrator, has been, perforce, a combined effort, but now, in terms of legal considerations including prosecution, this operation must be led by the Victorian Police OIC," said Connelly.

Parker was furious.

"Are you intending to steal our thunder, Sub-Inspector Connelly?" he asked tightly.

"Let's not allow ego to hijack a prosecution, Inspector Parker! I am merely directing that we need to follow procedure and ensure that the man does not escape prosecution on a technicality," soothed Connelly.

"With so much blood on his hands, Batson will never be released," growled Parker.

Detective Cleaver could see that the interaction between the two senior officers was unhelpful to the operation and morale of the troops. He stepped in to save the situation.

"Very well then, I think everyone has a grasp on the concept, perhaps Sub-Inspector Connelly can take the reins to organise Victorian officers and volunteers to enact the plan and where necessary, deputise NSW officers to fill the gaps. There is a jurisdictional tangle to unravel, since the fugitive is alleged to have committed murder, grievous bodily harm, robbery under arms, held three women captive for twelve hours and fired at police officers in NSW, and in Victoria to date, he is only wanted on the lesser crimes of burglary, robbery under arms and evading police. This tangle is not ours to unravel and in the first instance, we just need to capture Batson. Sub-Inspector Connelly are you content to provide your orders now or are we to reconvene in Walwa?" said Cleaver diplomatically.

Parker and Connelly glared at the detective, but both could see the merit of his suggestions.

Connelly grudgingly said, "I am happy that Inspector Parker allocate officers to task, since I have only recently arrived on scene, but I insist that reporting come through the Victorian Police system as a priority, for this operation."

Parker rolled his eyes but agreed.

Hardwick had slid into the bar room during the muster of officers for the briefing and had secured a seat at the bar near the door to the dining room. Parker's enthusiasm had caused him to raise his voice, so Hardwick had no trouble transcribing the gist of the briefing. He was ecstatic that cross border rivalry had flared and that there was a frisson of angst in the police camp... it added to the colour and pace of a newspaper article, even if it hindered the police operation.

Emma was just finishing up peeling potatoes when she heard the dogs charge across the yard barking, heralding the approach of visitors. The screen door slammed, and she could hear Albert cross the verandah.

Earlier, when Albert had returned from the dairy, he had told Minnie and Emma about the arrangements for Jacob and another volunteer to come and enhance their defence against an intruder overnight. Subsequently, Emma had been jittery with anticipation to see Jacob, and anxious about the prospect of the fugitive lurking about.

"This will be Jacob and the other volunteer, me dears!" called Albert from the verandah in order to allay the fears of the women.

Emma's heart flipped and she hurriedly wiped her hands, smoothed her hair and took off her apron. She went to her aunt in the sitting room, flustered and excited.

"Do you think I should go out and meet them or hang back discretely?" Emma asked sheepishly.

Minnie laughed, "Come on, haul me up and we will both go out and welcome our guests and defenders!"

Emma complied with a giggle.

The two horsemen clattered into the yard and dismounted. They saluted and called greetings to the ladies who were waving from the verandah. Their voices were lost in the excited yipping of the dogs that were swirling around the legs of the strangers. Albert roared, scattering the dogs and hastened to meet their guests and help them sort their mounts.

When the horses had been attended to, the men came to the house for more formal introductions. Jacob was accompanied by his unfit friend, Mark Barton. Both had rifles slung over their shoulders. Jacob and Emma locked eyes. Emma blushed prettily. Noticing the exchange, but aware of priorities, Albert took charge:

"Excuse us, Ladies, but I will just provide the fellows with a run down on the defence of the homestead ..." said Albert.

This reminder that the gathering was not entirely a social activity, sobered the group. Emma returned to the kitchen to finalise dinner; Minnie set the table in the dining room.

Not surprisingly, Jacob elected to eat dinner with the family, whilst Mark Barton was happy to eat on the verandah, maintaining watch. He sat on a chair at the corner of the verandah which afforded sweeping views across the paddocks and towards the hills that described the southern margins of the Murray River valley. The light was softening towards dusk, and a light breeze provided some relief from the oppressive heat of the day. His rifle rested against the verandah rails. Barton hoped he wouldn't be required to use it.

Emma served dinner, plates of corned beef and white onion sauce, on a bed of fluffy mashed potatoes. Beans, sliced tomatoes and cucumbers provided appetising colour to the plate. A homemade, still warm loaf of bread and a dish of golden butter rounded out the homely meal. Conversation rattled around the activities of volunteers and police trying to capture the fugitive, Batson. Jacob tried to lighten the topic by sharing anecdotes of officers falling in wombat holes, the discovery of aboriginal rock paintings whilst investigating caves, and the comic failings of policemen navigating the Murray River in Barber's punt.

"Apparently the hull split, and the punt rapidly filled with water and sunk. Constable Cooper was terrified. I don't think he has ever had a bath before, let alone been for a swim!" laughed Jacob, "He was thrashing about in the water crying that he was about to meet his maker when Sergeant O'Connor grabbed him by the collar and told him to put his feet under himself! They were on a shoal of rocks and the water was only three foot deep! They waded to shore quite unharmed."

Albert took the conversation away from Batson and he told some tales of watery misadventures on the Murray and huge fish hauled from its depths. Jacob, an enthusiastic fisherman, marvelled at the size of the Murray cod which Albert described and soon, Albert escorted him to the sitting room to admire the preserved head of a monstrous cod mounted on a polished red gum plaque and suspended above the fireplace. Emma shuddered. She found the trophy grotesque; the maw of the fish had a width of nearly twelve inches. She could imagine such a fish engulfing her foot and dragging her into the depths of the river. She shuddered again and began to clear the table.

Albert and Jacob joined Mark on the verandah, taking him a pint of ginger beer. They studied the hills and Albert said, "I wonder if he is up there somewhere, watching us!"

The men were quiet, contemplating the disturbing thought of being watched.

Emma and Minnie stepped through the screen door. Emma was bearing a tray with plates, cutlery and a cherry pie. The men gathered some chairs and set them down so that the group could watch the sunset over the hills whilst enjoying dessert. Emma sat on a chair next to

Jacob and revelled in the delicious proximity to the man with whom she was so infatuated. After they had finished eating and the conversation lulled somewhat, Albert suggested to Emma that she and Jacob might like to go and tie up the dogs for the night.

"Take your rifle, mind… just in case," he suggested mildly with a wink.

As Emma and Jacob stepped off the verandah, whistling up the dogs, Jacob said, "Well, the rifle stifles the romance of an evening stroll on Valentine's Day!"

Emma giggled. Jacob paused as he opened the house yard gate for Emma and picked one of Minnie's roses.

"A red rose, perfect for you, Emma!" he said sincerely as he carefully flicked off the thorns with his thumb nail and handed the perfect bloom to Emma. Their fingertips met on the stem of the rose. The sensation was electric. As they wandered down the drive towards the sheds where the dogs were already waiting next to their tie-ups, Jacob gently took Emma's hand and squeezed it.

From his position up on the hill, Batson could indeed look down on the Drummond homestead. He watched the glow in the windows as the lamps were lit. He wondered what the family was doing, what they were eating for dinner… his stomach grumbled at the thought of food. He took a swig from his flask; the warm water was tainted with the eucalypt tannin and flavour of moss from the stream in which he had last filled the flask. He didn't mind. It was wet and it quelled his cramping stomach. Batson was miserable: his swollen feet hurt, he was sunburnt, hungry and had endured a night of bizarre dreams followed by a hot and uncomfortable day. He had rested up, trying to regain his strength.

Batson stretched out a leg and he adjusted the cushion of his swag in the small of his back as he leaned against the rock face.

"Just four more biscuits... two now, two for breakfast."

He opened the tin, selected two biscuits and nibbled at the crispy edge, trying to make the meal last.

CHAPTER 26

Day 4: Capture in a Cowshed

Bill Hore and Percy Emerson were whistling as they worked. The rhythm of the milk jetting into the pails and the steady munch of the cows eating grain in the bails provided soothing sound effects. Bill finished with his cow first and stepped up to release her from the head bails. The milk in the pail was heavy, the rich frothy goodness slopped as he moved towards the cool churn room to add his contribution to the milk cans. A shadow loomed at the window, startling Bill. He looked up to see the gaunt and sunburnt features of Claude Batson.

"For God's sake, give us a drink of milk!" said Batson hoarsely.

"Ohh, Good Day, Claude!" said Bill carefully.

"Good day, Bill," mumbled Batson

Percy Emerson stood up and shifted his pail of milk from under the cow. He released her and joined Bill Hore.

"Come around to the coolroom, there is a cup you can use," Bill suggested to Batson.

The dairymen eyed each other, and Percy whispered, "Watch out, he might have that pistol, still!"

Batson stumbled around to the churn room. When he shuffled through the door, Bill was tipping his pail of milk into a milk can. Percy had placed his pail on the floor and was reaching up to a shelf for a tin mug. He rinsed it under the tap before handing it to Batson. He motioned that he should fill the cup from the pail. Batson squatted and filled the cup. He guzzled a cupful of still warm milk. Milk was spilling over his chin in his haste. Percy and Bill looked at one another - they saw their opportunity and jumped the fugitive. There was a clatter as milk pails tipped and clanged, and the tin mug went skittering across the concrete floor. Batson grunted as the weight of the lads pounded him into the concrete. He squirmed and resisted but in his weakened state he was no match for the combined enthusiasm of Percy and Bill. They had him.

"Aww, let me go!" Batson whined, "I have done you no harm!"

"That may be, Claude, but you have done harm to others! You would have been caught in the long run!" grunted Hore as he twisted Batson's arm behind his back.

Batson sagged; all the fight had left him.

"Yeah, I know, ... just a matter of time..." he whispered forlornly.

The dairymen allowed Batson to slip down until he was sitting in a dejected heap on the floor.

"I am just about settled now, Bill.... Yes, settled!" muttered Batson.

Batson was a woeful sight. He was filthy and his clothes were tattered. Percy's khaki riding breeches had rents at the knees, his shirt had been sacrificed to make temporary bandages for his feet, and a shabby dark coat hung from his lean frame. A grey cap adhered to his sweat matted hair and his feet were bare, battered, and bloodied. The dairymen felt sorry for their captive and gave him some more milk.

"We will have to get you to the Drummonds' house and call the police, you know, Claude," said Percy carefully.

Batson nodded miserably.

Bill Hore looked around the churn room and found an old towel.

"Will it help to bind up your feet, Claude? Make it easier to walk?" asked Bill.

Batson nodded and Bill made a fair attempt at binding the fugitive's feet whilst Percy let the cows out of the dairy yard to return to their paddock.

WILLIAM HORE AND PERCY EMERSON, the lads who lured Batson in with a bowl of milk, and then captured him.

Bill Hore and Percy Emerson - The Sun (Sydney, NSW (1910 - 1954), Saturday 16 February 1924

Leslie Osborne was moving a mob of Drummonds' sheep, pushing them up to the yards for crutching later in the day. His dogs were circling the mob and easing them up through the gates. Leslie stood in his stirrups to get a better view of the odd sight of three figures making their way up the slope to the house yard. His curiosity was piqued and, leaving his dogs to finish the task, he cantered up to the trio.

"What are you up to?" he called as he reined in alongside.

It was only then that he recognised Batson.

"You've nabbed him, boys!" cried Leslie with excitement.

"Claude came back for some more milk... he is starved. We are going to see if the missus can give him a feed whilst he waits for the police," said Emerson.

"I can ride to get the coppers," volunteered Leslie, not wanting to miss out on the excitement.

"Righto," agreed Bill, "You better just shut the gate behind those ewes, though!"

Leslie looked over his shoulder and saw the dogs had just pushed the last straggler through the gates, so he cantered back, shut the gate, whistled up his dogs and set off across the river flats to Jingellic.

Jacob and Barton saw the group in the paddock from the elevation of the verandah.

Jacob stepped to the door and called through the screen door to Albert, "The lads might have caught Batson!"

He then shouldered his rifle and followed Barton as he hurried down to meet the trio. Albert stepped back inside to telephone the police.

Batson was struggling to walk. He was pale, gaunt and trembling. Jacob pitied the man and he and Barton each took one of Batson's arms over their shoulders, hitched him up and chair-lifted Batson the rest of the way to the homestead. They settled him down on the grass in the shade of a large mulberry tree. Albert assessed the pitiful fugitive and called out to Emma to fetch Batson a drink and some food.

Emma hurried to make sandwiches from thick hunks of bread, with some cheese and homemade relish. She then loaded a tray with a peach, a jug of ginger beer, a glass and the sandwiches and set off to take the refreshments to the prisoner. Once she had pushed through the screen door though, she hesitated. She was curious to see the notorious bushranger, but she baulked, knowing the trauma he had inflicted on innocent people, an imitation of the devastation wrought by Norman List in the Botanic Gardens. Jacob noticed Emma's reticence to come out and strode up the steps to meet her. He took the tray from Emma with a grateful nod and comforting smile.

Batson ate and drank hungrily. Minnie noticed the fugitive was not wearing a shirt under his aged military tunic and, with motherly concern she called out to her husband, "Albert, I am just getting Claude one of your old shirts!"

"Sorry, Missus, my decency has been shredded...I shouldn't be in view of ladies without a shirt... I tried to make bandages..." said Batson shyly as he hitched his jacket closed over his bare chest.

It wasn't long before the police arrived in a Ford Motor car. A plume of dust pursued them down the drive. Sub-Inspector Connelly, Senior Constable Bunworth and their driver, Constable Harry Roxburgh scrambled from the vehicle and pushed through the house yard gate. Connelly was ecstatic that he would get the kudos of being the arresting officer of *the Last Bushranger of the Riverina*. He imagined the newspaper headlines as he joined the group standing around Batson. His vision was a bit deflated by the lack of opportunity for a show of heroism and bravery, as he looked down on the pitiful fugitive sitting on the grass determinedly eating a sandwich, Connelly saw that there was no fight in the man.

Connelly introduced himself and his officers before asking the dejected Batson to identify himself.

"Claude Batson," he muttered, his mouth full.

"Claude Valentine Batson?" asked Connelly sternly.

Batson nodded.

"I am arresting you on suspicion of murder of one, David Thomas Sheppard and the felonious wounding of three other men, last Sunday, tenth of February 1924. There are several other charges pending relating to the case, but the primary matter is sufficient to warrant your arrest. Do you have anything to say?" said Connelly.

"I didn't know Sheppard was dead," muttered Batson.

Batson looked up at the officers and, recognising Senior Constable Bunworth, Batson said, "I knew I would be caught... soon. I didn't want to give myself up. Didn't expect to be caught this morning. I thought I could trust these two!" Batson swung his head and glared at Emerson and Hore.

"Where is your revolver, Batson? The one with which you threatened Percy Emerson," asked Bunworth.

"I wasn't going to hurt anyone else. I am sick of my gun! I don't want to see it again!" said Batson wretchedly.

"Did you stash it somewhere, Claude?" insisted Bunworth.

"I jammed it under a log... near the well at Barbers'," muttered Batson reluctantly.

The Constables lifted Batson to his feet. Bunworth patted down the prisoner to ensure he was unarmed, before the two constables helped him to shuffle towards the police vehicle. Batson looked up at the verandah to where Emma and Minnie were standing together. Minnie had her arm through Emma's providing her with some moral support, as her young niece was unnerved by her proximity to a murderer.

"Thank you for the food and the shirt Missus," Batson said with wretched gratitude.

Claude Batson - sitting in the sun - Source: National Library of Australia

CHAPTER 27

The Bushranger in custody

Once confined to the police vehicle, the odour emanating from Batson was unbearable. Connelly was in the front seat alongside the driver, Roxburgh, and had his window wide open, but still gagged.

"Good God man, we will have to remedy this or the journey to Wodonga will be unpleasant for all of us!" declared Connelly.

"We might call in to the Walkers' - he could have a tub, they have a telephone so we can report to headquarters," suggested Senior Constable Bunworth from the backseat. Connelly agreed and, not far up the road from Drummonds, Roxburgh turned into the Walker driveway.

As the group of men stepped away from the vehicle in the drive outside the Walker homestead, Mrs Walker appeared at the door.

"Good morning, Missus!" called out Batson, before Bunworth jerked his arm to silence him.

Connelly explained their intentions, but Mrs Walker was less than pleased that her home had been selected to provide ablution facilities for a prisoner and expressed her displeasure in no uncertain terms.

"Well, he can't come in," she finished her tirade determinedly, "the laundry is just there, the copper is not long boiled and there is soap and a towel."

As the prisoner was led towards the laundry, his shuffling, painful gait pricked Mrs Walker's Christian conscience. She went and fetched a bowl of salted water so that he could soak his feet, and she provided some clean clothes and bandages. Batson smiled gratefully as she passed him the bundle. Roxburgh was designated as Batson's guard whilst the man cleaned himself up as best he could.

Mrs Walker turned to Sub Inspector Connelly and declared, "Privation has reduced him to a wreck of his former self! He must have been quite harmless in the finish."

Connelly considered that Mrs Walker was taking some of the shine off his triumph and snorted, before changing the subject:

"I will need to requisition the use of your telephone, Mrs Walker, can you direct me to it, please?" said Connelly.

The phone call to Inspector Parker at the Jingellic Hotel headquarters was terse. The tug of war over custody of Batson had begun in earnest.

"He will have to be processed in NSW since his most serious crime was committed in this state," emphasized Parker.

"Yes, but we have arrested him in Victoria, so he will need to be processed in Walwa, then Wodonga," asserted Connelly.

Parker could see a stalemate looming.

"Bring him here and we will take a statement which can be used in both jurisdictions and whilst we do that, we can seek directions from above!" said Parker.

The suggestion seemed logical and appeased Connelly. He also considered it as an opportunity to strut in front of the large contingent of police officers and community members.

"Maybe an interview with a journalist or two will be advantageous to promotion," he thought to himself.

Once Batson was cleaned up, Mrs Walker bandaged Batson's feet herself whilst Roxburgh secured Batson's clothes in an evidence bag. Roxburgh and Bunworth bundled the prisoner back into the vehicle as Connelly settled himself in the passenger seat, and then they drove off to Jingellic Hotel.

Word had spread via the bush telegraph about the capture of Batson and there was great excitement across the district. Businesses closed their doors, and it seemed like the entire community rushed to the Jingellic Hotel to catch a glimpse of the *Sniper of Jingellic*. When Roxburgh drew up in front of the hotel, there were crowds of people assembled in the street outside the establishment. Journalists armed with cameras jostled to be front of the throng.

"Pose for a picture, Sirs!" called out Bruce Courtney.

Courtney had an enviable reputation as a newshound and his photographs had been splashed across many a front page. His editor was anxiously waiting for a batch of images of scenes from the hunt for the Jingellic Sniper. The first picture of the monster with his captors would be gold for Courtney. He was so excited that he had to force his hands to stop quivering as he directed the officers to stand near the motor vehicle with Batson sandwiched between Senior Constable Bunworth and Sub-Inspector Connelly.

Batson and an unidentified police officer outside Jingellic Hotel - source Trove National Library of Australia

To muted applause, Bunworth and Connelly then escorted Batson through to the dining room and sat him down at a table in the middle of the room. Gawkers pushed and shoved to get a position from which they could watch proceedings. The doorways and windows were crowded. Inspector Parker and Sub-Inspector Connelly took seats opposite Batson, Detective Cleaver and Senior Constable Bunworth sat on the edge of tables flanking the prisoner and the remaining officers jostled for a position nearby so they could hear the interview. Batson looked around furtively. He had the appearance of a cornered wild animal. He quivered, both from nerves and a fever of infection.

"Very well, Mr Batson, you are facing some very serious charges. Consequences could be very dire, very dire indeed. Your cooperation in the investigation process could mean the difference between the noose and a prison cell," said Inspector Parker with malice in his tone.

"Indeed," said Sub Inspector Connelly, not to be outdone on grandstanding, "We need to understand your motivation, whether there are possible mitigating circumstances..."

There were several audible snorts from the assembly and one of the junior officers whispered to his mate: "Is there any excuse for murder in cold blood?"

"Maybe they are just softening him up for a full confession," replied his mate.

"So, Mr Batson, your full name, address and date of birth for the record, please," said Parker nodding at Constable Batt who was officiating as clerk.

"Claude Valentine Batson, 29th of August 1900," replied Batson in a lacklustre voice.

"Address," prompted Connelly.

Batson hesitated, genuinely unsure what his address might be.

"My mail comes care of the post office, to Mrs Hughes in Walwa... when I have mail," said Batson.

"Where is your home, Mr Batson," insisted Connelly sternly.

"I don't have none ... not a real home. I have a hut up on Lawrences Hill, a bed at Barbers' sometimes..." Batson frowned when he thought of the Barbers.

Parker looked to Constable Jolly who had been gingerly sorting Batson's possessions which had been removed from his pockets during an initial search of his clothing retrieved from the evidence bag. The items were now laid out on the table in front of him.

"For the record, please itemise the prisoner's possessions, Constable Jolly," directed Parker.

"Five cigarettes, a boot lace, a small bundle of receipts in the name of C Barber, a three-penny piece and a small tin containing what looks to be cyanide," said Jolly.

Jolly looked to Batson who nodded miserably in confirmation.

"So, you did *take* some cyanide," grinned Detective Cleaver, "but you didn't swallow it!"

There were some sniggers from the police officers.

"Did you intend to suicide, rather than be captured?" asked Connelly, with a sneer.

Batson looked towards the man and hesitated as if choosing his words.

"Would have been cowardly..." he said quietly.

"Tell me about Sunday last, 10 February," said Parker.

Batson sighed wearily.

"I was going to hunt some rabbits. I picked up a rifle and some ammunition from Barbers ... I was going hunting." Batson muttered.

"Did you know of the plans for a picnic on Jingellic Creek?" asked Parker.

"No. .... Well, not when I planned to go hunting... Mrs Barber told me later of the picnic, when I saw her... when I was in their home collecting my other rifle and ammo," stuttered Batson.

"Did you decide then and there to go and ambush the participants of the picnic, Mr Batson?" asked Connelly.

"No!" said Batson with anguish in his voice.

"What was your relationship to the Barbers?" Parker asked.

Batson struggled with constructing a reply.

"Were you on friendly terms?" prompted Parker.

"Yes," said Batson quietly, "most of the time."

"Most of the time?" queried Connelly.

"Well, we were real good, but then that Richard King moved in," growled Batson, "He was quarrelsome... he was always looking for trouble, looking to get me kicked out and to take my place..."

Batson spat the words and, under the sunburn, his cheeks flamed and eyes glittered, "I was driven to do it!" Batson snarled.

"By whom?" pressed Parker.

"Those that riled me, nobody knows what I have suffered..." wailed Batson.

He was clasping his hands together. His knuckles were white.

"Are you aware of Norman List?" asked Connelly.

Batson stared at his hands and thought. His mind picked over the name and a face emerged in his memory.

"List?" he said finally.

Batson looked up at Connelly and cocked his head.

"He has been in the newspapers of late, involved in a serious matter," said Connelly.

"Don't read newspapers, heard no radio or gossip, don't know no List," answered Batson sullenly.

Constable Jolly, as the Walwa police officer, considered that he knew Batson and felt that he had a relationship with the man. He had a burning question. He interrupted the proceedings and weathered a glare from Parker for his trouble, "I have a query, Inspector Parker, may I?"

Parker was concerned that his interview might be going off track but reluctantly agreed to the request.

"Claude, you have been the champion marksman at the Walwa-Jingellic Rifle Club for over two years now. I have seen you shoot in competitions. You and your rifle are like one. What did you intend, when you had the victims in your sights at Jingellic Creek?"

"I knew I would be caught ...I didn't want to shoot," said Batson quietly.

"Are you saying you didn't intend to kill anyone?" asked Parker with surprise.

"I am sick of my gun; don't want to see it ag'in. I had no intention of harming anyone," said Batson vehemently.

"Bit late, now," whispered the junior officer to his mate.

Batson's eyes were becoming wide and wild. He glanced around at the officers sitting in the room. His skin prickled as he felt the pressure of being the centre of attention, the confinement in a room amongst a crowd of strangers. His eyes settled on Constable Jolly.

"You! You shot at me the other day! I did not think you would fire at me... I had nothing ag'in you!" snarled Batson.

Batson glared at Jolly who looked entirely confused and said nothing.

"It was wide... took off a shard of rock above where I was hiding, I was watching you lot," he gestured at the police officers and glowered, "as you searched my hut. I could have shot the lot of you! Then again, yesterday evening, twenty men walked past me, with ne'er a look sideways to see me!" Batson's voice was high and strained.

It dawned on Jolly and O'Neill that Batson was referring to the accidental discharge of the constable's firearm on Tuesday. Jolly coloured with renewed mortification but held his tongue.

"I bet *The Prince* put you up to it. He would like to see me dead!" snarled Batson with spittle foaming at the corner of his mouth.

Batson was suddenly on his feet, raging. Bunworth and Cleaver sprang at him, grasping him by the arms and pulling back down into his chair.

"Steady, Batson, this isn't going to do you any good!" growled Bunworth.

Batson flinched, pulling out of the officers' grasp and he reached for his foot. He rocked backwards and forwards, clasping his foot which Cleaver had apparently kicked during the scuffle to restrain him. He was moaning quietly.

Cleaver was remorseful that he had inflicted unintentional pain on the prisoner.

"Are your feet that sore?" he enquired knowing what the answer would be.

"Yes," sobbed Batson, "so would anyone's walking through that country..."

Batson was now muttering incomprehensibly between quiet sobs.

"I think his foot has festered," said Cleaver noting the bloody, foetid discharge oozing through the bandages that Mrs Walker had applied.

"We should have him examined by the nurse or doctor, before we continue," suggested Connelly his nose wrinkling at the stench of the ruptured abscess.

Constable Jolly suggested that Batson be taken to the lock-up at Walwa police station and have a medical review there. Parker agreed since Batson was now clearly beyond making a statement. Connelly couldn't face being confined to a vehicle with Batson's reek, so he quickly suggested that Constable Jolly and Detective Cleaver take Batson to the Walwa lock-up and arrange for the nurse to attend, whilst he and Parker finalised their reports together.

"Detective Cleaver and Sergeant Morris will remain in the Upper Murray to finalise their investigation and report to the coroner in relation to the death of Mr David Sheppard. The inquest is scheduled for next Tuesday, the 19th. All other officers and men are discharged from this case and are to return to their stations post haste," stated Parker.

Over the racket of the men scraping chairs and jostling to disperse, Parker quietly said to Cleaver and Morris, "By all accounts the country is deteriorating into a bloodlust-fuelled epidemic: First List, then Batson, now there is a gunman running amok in Goulburn district, setting fire to property and shooting at victims in cold-blood. All this on top of the push gangs and gangsters of the cities. We are at war, gentlemen. A war on crime!"

Constable Jolly and Detective Constable Cleaver escorted the limping, miserable Batson through the tap room to the police vehicle. The crowds jostled to see the now pathetic figure of Batson. Some scowled, some sympathetic, some were just curious, but nobody said a word.

Sergeant O'Connor of Tumbarumba with Batson's rifle Trove/National Library of Australia

CHAPTER 28

Jacob

As soon as he was discharged from his capacity as a volunteer to the police search team, Jacob hurried back to the Walwa Hall. Inside, there was a jostle of men collecting and packing their kit, accompanied by raucous discussions as to the intriguing topic of Batson. There was wild speculation as to his motivation and what the next few days would bring for the erstwhile fugitive. Jacob focussed on collecting his gear before he slipped out of the hall and hurried to the post office.

"I would like to place a call to Albert Drummond's residence, please Mrs Hughes," Jacob declared to the postmistress.

"This isn't a public telephone, I will have you know, Sir," said Mrs Hughes stiffly.

"Well, could you direct me to the closest public telephone in Walwa, please?" Jacob asked.

"There isn't one..." muttered Mrs Hughes, before sighing and adding, "I suppose it is a local call. Just this once, and mind you are no more than two minutes, I have a business to run, you know!"

Mrs Hughes opened the flap of the counter and showed Jacob through to the parlour and the telephone.

She left the room but didn't shut the door.

Jacob was conscious of Mrs Hughes eavesdropping but was unconcerned. Mrs Hughes made the connection through the switchboard and announced, "Mr Drummond, I have a young man here who wishes to speak to you... go ahead, Mr Miller," she called and put down her earpiece. She hovered at the rear of her office, near the door, ostensibly sorting some mail, but listening curiously.

"Jacob, how are you? Are you and Mr Barton discharged from duty?" asked Albert.

Albert was relieved that the district was released from the siege of uncertainty and fear, which was created by the unknown whereabouts of a demonstrably dangerous fugitive. His voice reflected upbeat positivity.

"I am well, thank you," said Jacob matching Albert's levity, "Yes, Barton and I rode to the Jingellic Hotel and were there when the officers brought the wretch in to make a statement. He was interviewed but he became distressed and started raving. They carted him off to the lock up in Walwa and called for medical assistance. The volunteers and out-of-district police officers were all discharged."

"Didn't Batson look dreadful? Not the monster we had conjured in our heads... just a dejected derelict man!" said Albert soberly.

Jacob agreed and then dropped his voice and added hesitantly, "I have a favour to ask, well permission, I suppose, Albert. May I call on your niece, please. May I drop by in, shall we say, an hour?"

Jacob had rapidly calculated how long it would take to walk out to the Drummond homestead; just in case he was unable to secure alternative transport.

Albert chuckled.

"Stand by, sir, I will just go and find Emma to ascertain if she is available!" he said with mock formality.

Without muffling the receiver, Albert put the telephone receiver on the table and called, "Emma, it is for you! Jacob is on the telephone!"

Emma burst through the screen doors. Eavesdropping had given her the advance notice that she was wanted on the telephone. Giddy as a schoolgirl, she clutched the phone and caught her breath before speaking into the mouthpiece carefully.

"Hello, Jacob, so nice that you called!" she said.

"I am dying to see you again, Emma, ... before I am sent back to Albury. Would it be suitable if I dropped by to see you?" said Jacob earnestly.

"Oh, that would be lovely," cooed Emma, "do you have a ride out?"

"No, it is all a bit of bedlam in Walwa, everyone is celebrating, packing, or swirling around gossiping. I was just going to walk out. About an hour I think..." said Jacob.

Albert wandered through from the verandah casually, as if he hadn't been following the conversation, "I will put the pony between the shafts and you can go and fetch the lad, Emma!" he announced.

Emma smiled at him gratefully.

"Perfect, thank you!" she called to Albert's retreating frame, and to Jacob, "It is awfully warm, Jacob! You wander down to the willows on the bank of Walwa Creek, at the second bridge and I will meet you there shortly with the pony trap!"

Jacob grinned to himself.

"Sounds like a plan! Now, don't you gallop that poor pony, Emma," he laughed.

Emma was excited as she trotted the pony down the road in the direction of Walwa. She smiled and hummed to herself. The earth had rotated to a very favourable position: The sun shone, the fugitive sniper was in custody, her concerns had evaporated, and Jacob was ... well, Jacob was interested in her and was coming to visit, again, but it would be a *proper* visit this time... and she would have him all to herself on the drive home. The feeling of butterfly wings swooped through her core. She gazed across the flood plain towards the Jingellic Bridge, despite the summer heat, the land here was green with summer grasses and she could see the sparkle of the broad sweep of the Murray River. The whitewashed wood of the bridge span and the small Customs House building was set off against a backdrop of luxuriant willows. It was a beautiful vista. Beyond the approaches to the bridge were the sprawling buildings of the original Redbank Hotel and not far away the

Jingellic Police station. It never failed to amuse Emma that the Jingellic Police station was located in the wrong state, since the Murray River formed the border between NSW and Victoria. Her attention snapped back to the road as the whine of engine noise alerted her to the rapid approach of a dark motorcar. The pony skittered a little and snorted. Emma was not a confident horsewoman, and her grip tightened on the reins.

"Easy Neddy, easy!" she crooned to the pony.

Fortunately, the driver of the vehicle was considerate and slowed to walking pace to pass the pony and trap. Emma had an opportunity to gaze at the occupants of the vehicle. A pale face returned her gaze from the back seat. The man's eyes were wide and anxious. It was only when she noted that the other occupants wore police tunics that it dawned on Emma that she was looking directly into the eyes of the killer, Claude Batson. She blanched and shuddered and hurried the pony along.

From the back seat of the police vehicle, Claude Batson's eyes were drinking in the view of the Upper Murray countryside. Instinctively he knew he would never see his country again. He shivered as fever wracked his body, and he shifted in his seat to settle his feet into a more comfortable position. As he moved, the chains attached to manacles on his wrists which in turn linked to a belt around his waist, jingled. Bunworth, who shared the back seat with the prisoner, shot Batson a warning look and he tapped his truncheon on the seat in a threatening manner.

Batson ignored his captors. His injured feet had been attended to by the Walwa Bush nurse. She had bathed and flushed the wounds before packing them with sulphur powder. She gently inserted cotton wool padding between his toes, made a sole of cotton wool and then bandaged his feet with Vaseline impregnated gauze and cotton bandages. The attention had reduced the pain, and a dose of laudanum had made him comfortable and relaxed. He was a very compliant prisoner for Sub Inspector Connelly, Senior Constable Bunworth and Constable Bell, who was driving the party to Wodonga Police Station.

A couple off to town - Jim Harvey collection

CHAPTER 29

Emma

Emma and Jacob would have limited time together, since he was reliant on a lift back to Albury with Mark Barton and his fellow ex-AIF volunteers. Despite the time constraints, the afternoon would still be idyllic in Emma's view.

When Jacob and Emma arrived back at Albert and Minnie's farm, Emma was blissfully happy. As the two young people had jig jogged along the dusty road in the pony trap, their conversation had been comfortable and, at times, animated. They found themselves in tune with one another and the knowledge that the dark threat of the fugitive sniper was eliminated, enhanced the joy. They drew up at the hitching rail near the shed and Jacob took on the task of unhitching the pony from the trap, rubbing the animal down before turning him out into the paddock. All the while, Emma leant against the rail, gazing at the young man, drinking in his image, capturing it to sustain her through the next few weeks of separation. Every now and then, Emma would smile or laugh in response to their conversation and the sight would make Jacob's heart skip.

"I am done for!" he thought to himself, "I will marry this treasure!"

They wandered up to the homestead to have a cup of tea with Minnie and Albert. Minnie was putting a tray of teacups, teapot, and glasses down on the table and Albert was swinging through the screen door bearing a plate of fruit cake and jug of ginger beer as Jacob and Emma climbed the steps to the verandah.

"Well done, Jacob!" cried Albert. "You captured the last Bushranger of the Upper Murray!"

Jacob laughed, "I am sure they will mention my name in dispatches and the future history books on the incident!" he chuckled, "I was definitely the hero!"

He nodded to Minnie and asked with concern, "How are you, Minnie? The excitement of the last week and this warm weather must be adding to your burden!"

Minnie smiled warmly, "Thank you for asking, but since Emma arrived, I have been treated like the Lady of the Manor and am quite comfortable!"

Emma poured tea for them all before handing around cups and slices of cake. It was a pleasant afternoon, viewed from the cool shadows of the verandah and they enjoyed a few minutes of casual conversation before the clatter of hooves and the squeal of children shattered the peaceful afternoon.

"Oh no!" said Albert affably, "here come the hoards!"

"They are home from school early!" said Minnie with concern.

The children pulled up at the garden gate, singing out "Hello" to the adults and giggling. The smaller children slipped off from behind their older sibling who was dinking them, two to a pony. The children ran to the verandah, satchels banging against their small backs. The older children took the ponies to the paddock and hauled off saddles and bridles before leaving the ponies to roll and wade out into the dam for a cool down and a drink.

Once the full complement of children had joined the adults on the verandah, the fruit cake and ginger beer didn't last long.

Edna announced that their teacher had heard that Batson had been captured and was keen to go to Walwa, so he had given the students an early mark from their lessons.

"Can we go swimming?" pleaded the little girl, Kate, "It is so hot!"

Emma took it as an opportunity to spend time with Jacob beyond the watchful eyes of her uncle and aunt and volunteered to take the children to the river. The children squealed with delight and shot off into the house to change and gather towels and sunhats and flasks of ginger beer.

"Are you sure you will be right with the rabble?" asked Minnie with grateful concern.

"We will be fine; Jacob can wrangle the boys, and I will manage Kate and Edna! You put your feet up and have a rest, Minnie!" said Emma reassuringly.

"We shall be back by four o'clock," said Jacob checking his pocket watch, "Barton should be here by then, to pick me up."

Emma slipped Jacob a small look of regret that their time together would be so truncated, but then smiled and called out, "Come on, you lot, we need to get going if you are to get wet!"

Time slid past in a sublime, magical combination of laughter, deep connection, sunshine and happiness. Emma felt a warm glow, "...what is this? ...could it really be love, so soon?" she thought to herself.

At 4:30pm, Emma waved vigorously but regretfully as the car driven by Mark Barton and containing Jacob and two other fellows drew away from the homestead. She could see Jacob hanging out of the window waving furiously in return. Grasping the opportunity with delight, Emma had boldly planned another date with Jacob. They had agreed that Emma would take the mail bus to Albury on Friday week and spend the weekend in town.

"A whole weekend with Jacob!" thought Emma gleefully.

For the sake of propriety, Jacob had said that he would book Emma a room at Sodens Hotel, but they would be unchaperoned, and that thought was exciting.

Emma strained to see the car through the dust cloud, to glimpse Jacob one more time and hugged herself with delight. She knew in her heart that she was destined to be with Jacob, and her imagination took flight, dreaming of their future together.

Customs House on Victorian side of the Jingellic Bridge - State Library Victoria

CHAPTER 30

To and Fro'...

It was late afternoon by the time the Ford Motor vehicle arrived at Wodonga Police Station. The police officers unfolded themselves from the vehicle, stood stiffly, and stretched. Constable Bell opened the door for Batson and helped him out of the vehicle before providing him with a shoulder to lean on and to assist him to walk. Senior Constable Bunworth led the group into the police station.

Batson was now shuffling awkwardly on his bandaged feet. He was forced to stand at the charge desk and answer questions and complete some forms. He was then charged with "Wounding with Intent". Batson was then bundled back into the police vehicle and transported to Albury Police station for processing in the NSW jurisdiction.

An hour later, Batson crossed the Murray River again into Victoria, and at 7:20pm, he appeared before the magistrate in Wodonga Court. He was flanked by Sergeant Kersley and Constable Bell and a group of newspaper reporters. CT Kearn and WR McLeish were the duty magistrates who heard the charges. Prosecutor Senior Constable Glowski charged Claude Valentine Batson on a provisional warrant with, "Feloniously wounding David Thomas Sheppard with intent to murder and feloniously wounding three others, Richard King, Charles Gainer and William McGrath."

Senior Constable Bunworth and Constable Bell gave evidence. The magistrate set the court hearing for the Supreme Court in Albury for a date in April, six weeks hence.

A newspaper colleague of Phillip Hardwick had pursued the entourage of police vehicles and witnessed the warrant hearing. He noted for the *Albury Banner* readers:

"The accused was dressed in a blue striped twill coat, gaberdine breeches and a rough tweed cap. He was not wearing boots. Batson's face was pallid, and he looked dejected and worn out."

The reporter went on to speculate that the prisoner was drugged as his responses in court were sluggish and sometimes incoherent.

Constable Bell reported back to his superiors that, when asked to complete some documents at the Albury Police station, Batson had written slowly, but in a legible hand, which was a significant observation in relation to the note left on the Barber's kitchen table earlier in the week.

Richard King was still on the critical list in Albury hospital and the NSW police were determined for King to identify his assailant. So, after his Wodonga Court appearance, and despite the late hour, at 10:45pm, the weary Batson was again driven interstate and escorted to the Albury District Hospital to meet Richard King.

Mr JB Scobie, Justice of the Peace, presided over the bedside court hearing. In the crowded hospital room were Superintendent Cook, Sergeant E. P. Kersley, Dr C MacKnight, (the doctor who had attended the victims of the shooting), and the matron, Sister Drury, who was crammed behind the door. At the back of the room a constable sat with a notepad at the ready, prepared to be the official scribe.

Batson felt that his feet were blocks of molten lead. The pain was intense, and he was bone weary. His head throbbed and the fever was causing his thoughts to muddle, and the bright lights in the hospital startled him. Constable Bell and Senior Constable Bunworth practically dragged Batson through the door into the hospital ward and presented him to the bulky figure shrouded in white bed sheets and the attentive audience that clustered around the bed.

Richard King was weak and pale. His breathe rattled and wheezed through parted, thin, grey lips. Spittle accumulated at the corner of his mouth. Yellow, rheumy eyes swivelled to view the visitors. His eyes narrowed and his hands, which had been resting at his side on top of the bedlinen, clenched into fists when he laid eyes on Batson.

"Batson... you, you madman!" he choked.

Nurse Searle, who had escorted the men to the room, hurried to King's bedside and placated King.

"Mr King, settle, you cannot afford to fuss!" she remonstrated with her patient and glared at the police officers, "I think you have your identification, gentlemen," she said sternly.

Bunworth ignored the nurse. He glanced at the scribe to ensure he was attentive and said, "To be clear Mr King, and for the record, do you identify this man as Claude Valentine Batson and are you absolutely convinced, that he is the man who raised a rifle and shot on your picnic party and yourself and Mr Sheppard in particular, last Sunday, 10 February 1924, in Jingellic, NSW?"

King's eyes were locked on Batson. His face had a disturbing mottled colouration, and beads of sweat had formed on his lip. Batson stared doggedly at the floor.

"Yes.... That is Claude Batson... the Sniper!" croaked King.

"That's enough gentlemen!" said Nurse Searle sharply.

The matron, Sister Drury stepped forward in solidarity with her colleague, "You will have to leave, gentlemen. You have your answer!"

Justice Scobie ignored the women.

"We are here this evening to present the charges made against the accused, Claude Valentine Batson and to hear the evidence from the witness and victim of the shooting, Richard King. We are meeting here, under the unusual circumstances of a bedside hearing, since Mr King is so unwell," Justice Scobie said solemnly before he produced a sheaf of documents.

He selected a particular document and pulled himself up to his full height of five foot four and announced, "I will, for the record, read Mr King's dying deposition recorded on Monday, 11th February 1924,"

The doctor flicked a worried glance at his patient. He feared the term "Dying deposition" would have a negative impact on his patient's wellbeing. King continued to glower at the pitiful figure of Batson who was propped up by the flanking officers.

The Magistrate read the brief statement in a clear sombre voice.

Shortly after the midday meal, the men in the party set out for the river to fish. Just before we reached the river, I felt a pain in the stomach but did not know that I was shot. Gainer immediately came to me but fell, shot in the knee. Sheppard was also shot. I heard Gainer call to the women to get into the creek. I believe that I was the first man shot.

The magistrate turned to Doctor MacKnight, "Doctor, please can you describe Mr King's injuries for the record and so that Mr Batson is aware of the extent of harm he is alleged to have inflicted."

MacKnight glanced at King. He was still a very unwell patient, and the doctor was concerned that a full description of his wounds would certainly depress the man. He elected for an abbreviated account:

"Suffice to say, gentlemen, Mr King has suffered a through and through wound, most likely a gunshot wound, with an entry wound in the anterior left thorax and exit wound on the right side of his back below his ribs. The projectile penetrated his stomach, liver and left lung. He is still gravely ill," said MacKnight.

Richard King did indeed look worse after the reiteration of his injuries.

Sergeant Kersley persisted, "Did you actually see Batson shoot at you, Mr King?"

King's eyes slid to appraise Kersley. He huffed in frustration before saying:

"I heard the first shot and then the second hit me. I went down and from my position and due to my distress, I didn't have a clear view of the shooter. I heard Mr Barber call out to Batson and that is how I knew it was he who shot at us," King wheezed.

"Do you have any thoughts on why Mr Batson may have felt compelled to attack your party, or yourself in particular, Mr King?" Bunworth pressed King.

"I had no quarrel with Batson," croaked King, "I cannot give any reason why Batson should shoot at me."

King hesitated and looked pained and thoughtful before adding cryptically, "What I think, I cannot say, because it is outside the question."

He grunted and moved his body as if to relieve a pinch point before continuing.

"I never attempted to do him any harm. I do not think that there was really anything between us. There is no ill-feeling on my part towards Batson."

Justice Scobie looked at Batson sternly and declared:

"Claude Valentine Batson, you are charged with feloniously wounding Richard King with an intent to murder. Do you have anything to say for yourself?"

Batson rallied and spat at King, "You knew the way I have been stirred up in the last three months!"

Sergeant Kersley stepped towards Batson and said quietly, "Settle yourself man! Do you have any questions for Mr King? Have you anything you wish to say?"

"No! I have no words for him!" snarled Batson.

Bunworth pulled the official copy of King's dying deposition document from an inner pocket of his tunic and approached the bed, "A signature, please Mr King..."

"Enough! Go!" screeched the nurse as she shooed at the police officers.

They finally followed her orders.

Batson was taken from the hospital to the Albury Courthouse, where Justice Scobie insisted on completing the hearing in the early hours of Saturday morning. He demanded a summary of evidence from the police, represented by Sergeant Kersley.

Kersley outlined the case but asked to defer the presentation of evidence in its entirety as it would take some time to assemble all witnesses, and the investigation was still on going.

"Of course, Sergeant Kersley," said Scobie before sliding his eyes towards the dock.

"Mr Claude Valentine Batson, what is your plea in relation to the charges of felonious wounding of Richard King, Charles Gainer and William McGrath and felonious wounding causing death of David Sheppard?"

Batson stood shaking his head numbly.

"In addition, there is a lesser charge for which you are to be tried: that of shooting at police officers with malicious intent and as an attempt to evade arrest. How do you plead on all counts?"

Batson was bone weary and wracked with feverish chills.

He mumbled, "I am not guilty, I was driven to it..."

"The prisoner must speak up! How do you plead Claude Valentine Batson?" roared Justice Scobie

"Not guilty," said Batson.

He then looked to Colonel Wilkinson, who appeared in a legal capacity on Batson's behalf, and enquired, "Will you be applying for bail on behalf of your client?"

"No, I presume that it would not be granted even if I were to apply," said Wilkinson.

Scobie raised his brows before frowning and continuing,

"I concur with the prosecution and recommend that Claude Valentine Batson be remanded in custody at Albury Gaol and will reappear in Albury Police Court on Tuesday, 19 February 1924. Evidence will be provided for the Coroners' Court sitting at 10am. Thereafter, we will reconvene to formalise the charges in light of the outcome of the findings of the coroners' inquiry."

The Magistrate gathered his paperwork and rose as the Clerk directed, "All rise!"

Chapter 31

Behind bars and analysed by an alienist

The steel door clanged as the prison guard and police officers left Batson to himself for the first time in over twelve hours. Batson, now dressed in the drab grey tunic of a prison inmate, stretched out on top of the hard, narrow bed. His body was soaked in sweat, both from the stuffy environment of the Albury Gaol cells in late summer, and the fever which raged through his system. The throb of his wounded feet was incessant, a sharp pain in his head had settled behind his eyes and felt like a steel band across his skull. He shut his eyes, sullenly banished thought from his mind and waited for sleep to descend.

A grey light was filtering though the bars of the small window high above Batson's head when he opened his eyes. He was groggy after a fitful period of dozing. His eyes roamed around the cell. It was a small gloomy rectangle. A pail in one corner and a simple bed with an itchy lumpy mattress were the only furnishings. The drone of men's voices began to break into the uneasy silence. He could hear an occasional shout, muttering, banging on steel doors and distant sobbing. The air was stale and rank: Batson realised that he was responsible for most of the odour. Suddenly the clang of metal announced the arrival of a visitor as the hatch in his door opened.

"Oy, Batson, stand clear of the door! Be at the back of the cell! I am opening the door."

He could see a small portion of a face peering through the hatch. Batson swung his legs over the side of the bed and groaned and shuddered as circulation rushed through his bruised and swollen feet. When the guard opened the door with the Governor of Albury Gaol looming behind him, Batson was a miserable form hunched on the edge of his bed.

"Attention, man!" snarled the guard as the Governor stood, backlit by the corridor lamp light, surveying the prisoner.

Batson looked up and realised that the prison officers were truly insistent that he be upstanding as the guard stepped forward and jabbed a baton in his ribs. He struggled to get up and finally ended in a near upright stance, with one hand providing some support by gripping an uneven stone that protruded from the wall.

Batson didn't look at the officers.

"I am Mr Wicks, Governor of Albury Gaol. I have come to remind you that you are a guest of His Majesty the King and that you are in remand until your trial date. I will not tolerate any ill manners or bad behaviour. You will receive three meals per day, the privilege of forty minutes of exercise in the yard once per day and time to empty your night soil pail and have a shower once per day. Under no circumstances are you to touch or interfere with another prisoner. Any divergence from rules or inappropriate conduct will result in solitary confinement and withdrawal of privileges. Do you understand Mr Batson?"

"Yes..." muttered Batson.

"Yes, Sir, Mr Wicks!" said the guard with another savage jab of his baton in Batson's rib cage. The guard was standing immediately opposite him, glaring in a vindictive manner. Batson gasped and repeated the prescribed answer.

"Very good, Mr Batson. Later today you are to expect a visitor, Mr John MacPherson. He will be here to assess you," said Wicks.

Batson really wasn't interested. He just wanted to sit and take the weight off his feet.

"Yes, Sir, Mr Wicks," Batson muttered as the guard twitched his baton in his direction.

"Very good!" said Wicks and spun on his heel to leave.

"No trouble, mind, Batson!" hissed the guard before following his superior and slamming the door shut.

Batson collapsed on his bed in a foetal position, hugging his now smarting ribs. His tongue was thick with thirst and his guts ached with hunger. He drifted off into a miserable doze.

A clang startled Batson to wakefulness again.

"Oy, your breakfast!" announced a rough voice.

A tin mug, and bowl was shoved through the hatch and left to teeter on the narrow platform.

Batson stood and shuffled up to retrieve his rations. There was a tin mug of moderately hot black tea and a bowl of a dubious grey gruel with a hunk of bread slowly drowning in the paste. He was so hungry that the unappealing aesthetics of the meal didn't faze him. He scraped up the gruel with the bread and ate ravenously. The tea was sweet with sugar, and he felt much better after downing the brew. The tea made him think of the Barbers.

"The Missus..." he whispered to himself thinking of the cups of tea she had made and which they had shared across that well-scrubbed kitchen table. His mind's eye scrolled through a rosy illusion of peace and happiness, before it clouded into blackness when Richard King stepped through the imagined door.

"You arse!" Batson hissed "and you, you disloyal cow, Ruth Barber!" he muttered.

A jumbled, jerky vision of the events leading up to the picnic skittered through his head before imploding in a red fog.

"You made me do it.... I was driven to it!" he lamented as he rocked on his bed.

Sir John MacPherson was shown into an interview room at Albury Gaol by the Governor, Mr Wicks, himself.

"It isn't often that this establishment has a visit from such a luminary of the criminal investigation and justice system," he gushed to the fine featured but sallow looking fellow who was now seated before him.

Wicks admired the cut of the man's suit, his crisp shirt and his fashionable tie.

"I have followed your work, Sir! Well, the reports we are privy to, anyways. You are always headlined as Sydney's Best Alienist!" declared Wicks.

MacPherson inclined his head in acknowledgement of the praise, but coughed discretely and said, "Yes, quite so. I am very busy, Mr Wicks, will the prisoner be along shortly?"

"Of course, Sir! Officer Wall is just escorting him from his cell now. Batson has injuries to his feet, you understand, so he can't move at pace. Please excuse the delay," said Wicks.

The alienist frowned.

"Has he been afforded medical attention since coming into your care, Mr Wicks?" MacPherson asked.

"Ummm, I believe his wounds were dressed by the nurse in Walwa, yesterday," said Wicks, who was taken aback that MacPherson seemed to be questioning his management of a prisoner.

"Yesterday? He needs a doctor! The man cannot be considered in sound mind and fully culpable if he is harbouring an injury or infection," scolded MacPherson.

MacPherson eyes were narrowed and cold as he regarded the Governor. Just then, there was a knock at the door. It opened to reveal Batson and his accompanying prison guard, Frank Wall.

MacPherson took in Batson's appearance, his sweaty sheen, marked limp, tattered soiled bandages on his feet and overall miserable demeanour. He glared at Wicks but before he could add to his tirade, Wicks offered: "I shall summon the doctor immediately, Sir John!"

Wicks then scuttled from the room. In the corridor, Wicks regained a modicum of his composure and turned to advise MacPherson:

"The prisoner is manacled as you can see, Sir John. Do you want the guard to remain in the room with him or just outside?"

"I will speak to the prisoner alone, thank you," said MacPherson stiffly.

"Very well. Officer Wall will monitor the interview via the observation window. If there is any sign of the prisoner becoming difficult, the officer will step in," said Wicks sharply.

Frank Wall tapped his baton in the palm of his hand and glared at Batson with an undisguised threat, before withdrawing, shutting the door and standing to attention watching the occupants of the room through the observation window.

MacPherson invited Batson to take a seat. With relief, Batson sank into the chair, his feet were again, throbbing. MacPherson asked after Batson's injuries and treatment in the Gaol before introducing himself and providing Batson with an outline of his profession and what he was seeking to clarify during the interview.

"I am Sir John MacPherson, Chair of the Department of Psychology, Sydney University. I consult as an Alienist on cases to provide insight to the courts and Police. Today, I have been asked to assess your condition and to make recommendations for your treatment whilst in custody. I will need to ask you some questions, Mr Batson. May I call you Claude?" said MacPherson. Batson nodded his understanding and agreement.

MacPherson drew from Batson a description of his upbringing and descriptions of the challenges he had faced as an abandoned child and a marginalised adolescent in a remote, rural community.

"So, at school in Holbrook did you learn to read and write?" MacPherson asked directly.

"Enough...," said Batson.

MacPherson rifled through his satchel and withdrew a copy of The Daily Telegraph newspaper. He flicked through the pages, carefully avoiding the page with the article about Batson's exploits in the Upper Murray, and finally selected page three. The page had articles about the building boom in Sydney and graphic advertisements in type-settings of different styles and font sizes. He folded the paper to reveal the single page and smoothed it flat as he set it in front of Batson.

"Can you read a paragraph aloud for me please, Claude? How about the first paragraph of this advertisement?" he tapped his finger on an advertisement for KFB Foundry which had an ecclesiastical quote as its heading.

"Why?" Batson muttered sullenly.

"As you know, I am investigating your capacity to stand trial, and I would like to ascertain your capability in relation to literacy and comprehension." MacPherson spoke quietly but persuasively.

Batson studied the paragraph silently before opening his mouth and speaking each word deliberately. The longer words were sounded out with his forefinger doggedly following the lines of script.

"The only Mon-u-ment worth-while for any man is the Mon-u-ment-al Work he can do to his own Ch-a-rac-ter – cer-tain-ly that is all he can take with him into the next world," Batson recited.

Batson continued to stare at the words, frowning.

"Do you understand the meaning?" asked MacPherson.

Batson was silent for a moment. He shuffled anxiously in his seat before offering uncertainly,

"A man will be the same person in heaven... or wherever...when he is dead ... as he was on earth," said the prisoner.

Batson's gaze crawled across the table before coming to rest briefly on MacPherson's face. Their eyes met momentarily before Batson retreated to looking at the paper in front of him.

"What about this paragraph?" MacPherson's finger described a circle around an advertisement for emery grinders.

"Em-ery grinders sim-pli-fy many problems of sharp-'ning your knives, sciss-ors, Chisels, Garden tools... A grinder is a house-hold neck-issity these days and the one we illus-trate will meet all re-quire-ments."

Batson's reading was much more fluent for this exercise and his eyes flicked to examine the picture of the grinder with interest.

"Do you read newspapers often, Claude?" asked MacPherson.

"Not really, I don't buy papers. Sometimes I look at the paper at the Barbers' ... 'read the headlines and look at pictures," said Batson.

"Do they get a paper every day?" asked MacPherson.

Batson was confused about this line of questioning; he was thinking more about MacPherson's motivation than the question.

After a minute, he said, "Mebbe a cuppla times a week. There's always something to read and use in the dunny!"

Batson's face cracked into a grin at the thought.

"So, you saw the headlines over the last fortnight? There were detailed descriptions of the Norman List affair in the Botanic Gardens," said MacPherson.

Batson looked at his interrogator with a blank expression.

"Dunno... List?" Batson said and looked puzzled.

MacPherson had seen the headlines in the Sydney newspapers, and he had followed the story of the Melbourne Botanic Garden tragedy of 24 January 1924, with a keen professional interest. Norman List, the perpetrator, would have been on death row by now had he not committed suicide a few days after shooting five random innocent victims in the Gardens. MacPherson assumed that the Albury Banner and Wodonga Express had granted the crime as much column width as its city-based counterparts. There were blow-by-blow accounts in The Sydney Herald.

"Very well, on another matter, Claude, can you please write down your full name, date of birth and your parents' full names?" asked MacPherson, determined to demonstrate a link between Batson's handwriting and the script on the note found in the Barbers' kitchen, allegedly written by Batson.

MacPherson withdrew a pencil and notepad from his satchel and slid them across the table to Batson. Batson opened the notepad to a fresh page, dabbed the tip of the pencil on his tongue and carefully wrote down the details as he had been asked.

MacPherson watched as Batson held the pencil awkwardly in his fist and pressed firmly into each stroke. The letters were misshapen but legible. He put an "s" into Florence, his mother's name, and missed an "n" in his father's name. MacPherson was reading Batson's notes from across the table.

"Dennis Kennedy is your father? Dennis Vincent Kennedy?" asked MacPherson.

Batson cocked his head curiously and nodded.

"I never met him, mind!" Batson assured the psychologist.

"Did that concern you, did you feel rejected by your father?" asked MacPherson.

"By all accounts he was a bad egg.... Anyways, me mam didn't want me neither," said Batson sullenly.

MacPherson looked at Batson with a sympathetic frown and considered that there surely couldn't be two men of that exact name. He had been called to assess one Dennis Kennedy just over a week previously. The man was in remand in Goulburn Gaol. As a result of his assessment, Kennedy had been recommended for incarceration in the Goulburn Lunatic Asylum for seventeen years. MacPherson didn't share these thoughts with Batson.

MacPherson replaced the notepad, pencil and newspaper into his satchel. Batson watched quietly before asking, "Are you finished with the newspaper, Sir?"

MacPherson cocked his head and studied the man.

"Would you like to read it?" he asked with a renewed suspicion that Batson was more skilled in literacy than he was letting on.

"Nah!" laughed Batson gleefully, "There is nothin' to wipe my arse on in the cell!"

He grinned again, his stained and broken teeth on display.

MacPherson was about to hand Batson the paper but then considered that it was inappropriate for him to read the article about his case. He shook his head.

"It is not permitted," he said apologetically.

MacPherson was genuinely regretful that he was unable to help Batson with his ablutions.

"Now then, Claude, we come to last weekend. How were you feeling on Sunday morning?" asked MacPherson quietly.

"Awright," mumbled Batson, his face had clouded again, and he dropped his head so that his unruly locks obscured his expression.

"It was a pretty day last Sunday, late summer sunshine, a day of rest," suggested MacPherson.

"Always things to do..." said Batson.

"What do you do on Sundays," asked MacPherson, "Church service? Visit friends? Fishing?"

Batson shuddered at the mention of Church. MacPherson made a note.

"Went to see the Kelly brothers," said Batson without enthusiasm.

"Are they good friends of yours?" asked MacPherson.

"Nah, not really. Not mates. Just know 'em, you know," replied Batson.

"What did you get up to? Did you have a cuppa, chat about plans for the week?" pressed MacPherson.

"The Kellys were smirking, they knew something was up," said Batson.

Batson was fidgeting, making the chain on the manacles squeak and jingle.

"What do you mean, something was up?" queried MacPherson his head was cocked, and he held an encouraging expression on his face.

"They were part of it... talking behind my back. I was a joke to them. I showed 'em though .... I shot the mistletoe out of the gum, and it dropped into the tray of the pony trap. It frightened the crap out of the dog that was asleep underneath it!" the words tumbled from Batson's lips, and he grinned at the mental image of the incident.

"I had heard that you were a champion marksman, Claude," said MacPherson soothingly.

"Can shoot the buttons off of a tunic at a hundred and fifty paces," boasted Batson.

MacPherson's astute mind worried at this comment. He had no doubt about the young man's degree of marksmanship, it had been confirmed by numerous sources, yet, when presented with easy human targets at the picnic, he had only wounded his victims. Granted he had inflicted grievous injuries, but no true sniper would have left a target with a still beating heart.

"So, when you arrived at the Barbers' home on Sunday morning, what were you intending to do?" asked MacPherson quietly.

"Dunno, I just ended up there. Wandered down from the hill after leaving the Kellys and just went to the Barbers. By habit, I s' pose," said Batson.

Batson was concentrating on picking the dirt out from under his fingernails, one tattered thumbnail scraping under the fingernails of the other hand.

"Were you angry with the Barbers," probed MacPherson.

"Fed up… fed up with Mrs Barber, not angry. She had let that bloody Richard King in… King was just a clown, a know-nothing know-all. He pushed me out of the way," said Batson darkly.

Batson's voice was edgy now, and he was breathing hard.

"Did you plan to go to the picnic, Claude?" asked MacPherson.

"Didn't know about it…well, not 'till the missus said summat. I was just going to get some pelts. The Rabbitoh comes Mondays," said Batson quietly.

MacPherson nodded.

"You were certainly armed to the hilt, Claude. Charles Barber's statement indicates a couple of rifles; you took ammunition from the Barbers and the Spicers...a handgun, too, I believe," said MacPherson.

Batson stared at MacPherson, who met his gaze steadily before asking quietly, "When did your plans change, Claude? When did you decide to go to the picnic?"

"When I wasn't invited but King was..." spat Batson, "I just went to look, to see what King was up to... and that's when I saw... saw they were all there, Sheppard, King, the missus. I thought *The Prince* would be along soon, too."

"*The Prince*?" queried MacPherson, quietly thinking Batson was now slipping towards delusional.

"He behaves like he is so far above us, so high and mighty! He is an arse! Percy Bloody Barber," said Batson malevolently, his voice rising with spite.

Batson's brain was screening a chaotic series of images. A kaleidoscope of persons against whom he harboured a grudge, real or perceived.

MacPherson noticed the wild eyes and spittle accumulating in the whiskers at the corner of Batson's lips.

"Did you mean to kill them, Claude?" MacPherson asked quietly.

"No! No... not at first. I wanted to frighten them. Maybe hurt them. Give them some of the pain... some of the pain they caused me!" Batson's voice had become staccato.

"I fired a shot near them. King ducked, then, as I pulled the trigger a second time, he moved into the bullet. I... I panicked; I had done it now! I had hit one of them! I aimed at Sheppard, then. I just wanted to wing him, but he moved too, and it went clean through him. I went to finish off King, but the fat oaf was behind the other fellow, I didn't want to shoot that fellow, 'had nothing ag'in him. Didn't know him. I hesitated and then I decided to puncture King's fat gut since he was sprawled on the ground. I loosed a bullet. The other fellow moved, and I shot him in the leg ... by accident, it was. When McGrath ran, I knew it was going to be him or me... I tried to bring him down, but he wouldn't stop, then he came back with a gun ... he was in the 8th Lighthorse, you know... at Gallipoli. I respect him. I got out of there."

Batson's voice was again, staccato. He was sweating profusely and rocking in his seat. Suddenly, he crashed his forehead into the table. The violent movement brought Officer Wall running.

"I was driven to it, they all had it in for me..." Batson started to rant incoherently before grunting as Wall laid his baton into his ribs and jerked on his elbow forcing him back into the seat.

"Settle down, laddie!" growled Officer Wall menacingly.

Batson subsided.

MacPherson stood, gathering his satchel and hat.

"I think that will do for present, Claude," he said gently to Batson and to Officer Wall, MacPherson said sternly, "I have advised the warden that Mr Batson needs medical attention immediately. I am sure he is delirious with a fever. I will expect a medical report this afternoon!"

With that, MacPherson stalked out of the room, finding his own way through the dim corridors and back to the reception area.

MacPherson reported back to Detective Cleaver, the lead officer investigating the death of David Sheppard, the erstwhile Jingellic Butter Factory Manager, on behalf of the deputy coroner. His initial report was by telephone. Mrs Griffiths at the Jingellic exchange connected his call to the Detective Cleaver at the Jingellic Hotel. Cleaver was initially terse, as he was busy dismantling the temporary police headquarters in the Hotel's dining room. Finlay Smith, the publican, was anxious to reclaim control of his business and relieve the dining room of its role as a police incident room.

"Detective Cleaver here, what can I do for you?" said Cleaver with a sharp tone.

MacPherson reminded Cleaver of his role and the fact that he was reporting as requested. His voice was stiff. Cleaver apologised.

"What is your impression of Batson, then? Culpable? Mentally fit to stand trial?" said Cleaver.

"I am concerned for Batson's wellbeing. His capacity seems to be impaired by a raging infection and delirium. I have ordered that he be examined by a doctor and treated appropriately. However, I am confident that the man has culpability and he has exercised a degree of premeditation. I was able to demonstrate that he is literate and would have been capable of writing a short letter and reading newspapers, so there is a potential that he may have been following the events in Melbourne and may have had some aspirations to mimic Norman List's activities. Batson could well have desired similar notoriety and the public attention as has been lavished on Norman List, the Botanic Gardens shooter. Batson also referred to his admiration for Bushrangers of the past, particularly Mad Dog Morgan. There is a syndrome which encapsulates such motives, Detective Cleaver."

MacPherson hesitated for grand effect, causing Cleaver to ask, "Oh yes, Sir John, and what might that be?"

"*Trago-suggestion*," said MacPherson emphatically, "The affected individual, a weak-minded or mentally damaged patient, exhibits tendencies to abandon their moral compass and will strive to emulate the activities of a hero-figure. Usually that *hero* is steeped in infamy. In this case, Batson's potential heroes have been murderers, criminals of the most evil persuasion. Norman List may prove to be responsible for inducing a copycat cluster of criminal activity," MacPherson finished dramatically.

Cleaver was confused, "If he has lost his moral compass and is victim of a "syndrome" is he then culpable, will he be fit to stand trial?"

"That is for the court to decide, Detective Cleaver!" said MacPherson primly.

Phillip Hardwick, the journalist who had been doggedly following the Batson case, had struck up lucrative arrangements with the telephone exchange operators of the district, and it was paying off. From these sources, he was able to discover the most fascinating news scoops. A transcript of Cleaver and MacPherson's conversation was forthcoming with extreme efficiency. Hardwick was lurking on the verandah of the Jingellic Hotel during the two men's telephone conversation and Mrs Griffiths, the post mistress and exchange operator next door to the Hotel, spotted the journalist from her front window. She dutifully transcribed the conversation between Cleaver and MacPherson and hand delivered the transcript to Hardwick within minutes of the conclusion of the conversation.

Later, Hardwick gleefully quoted Sir John MacPherson, Sydney's best alienist:

"Norman List's massacre in the Melbourne Royal Botanic Gardens has influenced the Jingellic Sniper, Claude Batson via *trago-suggestion.* This incident may well be part of a copycat cluster."

Hardwick extrapolated on the consultant's comment and drew in the activities of Robert Fenwicke to be part of the copycat cluster. Fenwicke had been terrifying the residents of the Goulburn environs during the preceding few days. Fenwick set about robbing properties, before razing them to the ground and randomly shooting people. He was referred to by the press as the *Goulburn Incendiarist.* Just that morning, Fenwicke had calmly surrendered himself to the police in Goulburn and his tyranny of terror was concluded peaceably.

Hardwick had a powerful memory, and he recalled an incident on which he had reported in late 1923. It detailed an altercation between passengers on the Corryong to Tallangatta mail bus. He had already concluded that the central character to that report matched Norman List's description, and the police evidence had corroborated that Norman List was working at a sawmill in Koetong during that time. He clicked back through his mental filing cabinet drawing out the salient points: A man fitting List's description, and a friend had joined the mail car at the Koetong Hotel pick-up point in September. The driver reported that the passenger was surly and behaved erratically. He began to quarrel with his mate, forcing the driver to pull over in Tallangatta to evict the two quarrelsome men. The situation deteriorated and a physical fight broke out next to the car and the windscreen was smashed. A shard of glass gashed the driver's cheek. An attempt was made to restrain the belligerent passenger, and police were called but the man escaped before police arrived on scene. Later he was believed to have chased some young lads, before disappearing from the district. Hardwick drew a very long bow and thought it would be neat if Batson had been List's battered mate on that fateful mail bus trip. He made a note to try and make a solid connection between the two shooters. Had Batson been employed at the sawmill in Koetong? Had the two felons cooked up the picnic shootings as a blood thirsty scenario as they laboured and drank together? Hardwick found the concept of a copycat crime exciting, and he was confident that he would be able to concoct an article exploring the theme that would be a reader magnet for newspapers and please his editor.

Hardwick's editor was indeed congratulatory on such a scoop, and the copy was published immediately. Fortunately, however, MacPherson's *trago-suggestion* effect didn't gain traction amongst the criminally inclined within the audience of Hardwick's newspaper copy: in the short term, there were no similar incidents after the surrender of Fenwicke. MacPherson's terminology of *trago-suggestion* was similarly unpopular amongst other psychologists and was not adopted as a clinical term.

CHAPTER 32

A medical opinion

Dr (William) Cleaver Woods, an eminent local doctor and contracted Government Medical Officer, was called to consult with Batson. Escorted by a prison guard, he entered Batson's cell and found the man standing awkwardly, leaning on the back wall of the cell. He looked most unwell.

"Sit down, Batson, before you fall down," Woods said kindly.

The doctor laid a hand on Batson's forehead.

"He has a marked fever!" he announced, "we will have to have him transferred to the infirmary immediately. Clearly, his wounds are infected and will need redressing."

Woods glanced at the rank, dirty bandages on the prisoner's feet and his nose wrinkled at the stench. The prison guard stepped forward to force Batson to his feet.

"No," said the doctor authoritatively. "Fetch a bathchair or stretcher, don't make him walk!"

The guard looked uncertain.

"Go! Batson poses no threat to me, look at him!" snapped the usually calm doctor.

The guard glared at Batson who was now slumped on the edge of the bed, his head in his hands, before he reluctantly left the cell to fetch another officer and a stretcher.

"Now then, Mr Batson... Claude, may I call you Claude?" said the doctor.

Batson looked up sluggishly and nodded in a dispirited fashion.

"We shall take you to the infirmary and get you some treatment for your injuries. You seem to have a fever, too."

"Make me well enough to face the noose?" asked Batson grimly.

"You will have a fair trial," said the doctor encouragingly, "mitigating circumstances, a moment of madness, delirium… Have you been unwell for some time?"

Batson shrugged and said heatedly, "Self-defence it was, they drove me mad!"

"Who antagonised you?" asked Woods calmly, "The victims at whom you shot? I can't see self-defence being a viable argument when the picnic party was unarmed… but a diagnosis of reduced culpability due to a psychotic episode may get you dispatched to an asylum rather than death row at Pentridge."

Woods felt mildly guilty about the direction their conversation had taken, but his personal beliefs tended to interfere with his attention to legal protocols. He abhorred the death penalty. In his opinion, only God could determine who was to die, not mortals. He could hear footsteps on the approach; the guards were returning. He looked at Batson. He could see that the man was deep in thought.

"Lie down, Batson, the guards have a stretcher, they will roll you onto the stretcher and take you to the infirmary," said Woods.

The guards were sour and rough with Batson. Neither felt compassion for the man's plight and both felt aggrieved that they were being asked to carry him.

Once in the well-lit and airy infirmary and laid out on the examination couch, Batson felt cooler and vastly more comfortable. He detached himself from his physical body and concentrated on the strange smells of disinfectant before his imagination took him to a different plane. The doctor, assisted by an orderly, gently unwrapped his feet. The bandages had to be sponged away as the discharge from the wounds was clotted into the fibres of the dressings. The smell was rank, and the two guards hastily stepped out of the room, muttering that they would be "Just outside" as they left.

Woods debrided the wounds, then flushed with an iodine solution. Once done, he announced cheerfully, "I think your feet are on the mend! We shall just need to change your dressings daily and soon they should be more comfortable under load."

He dusted the wounds with sulphanilamide powder, applied a petroleum jelly drenched gauze across the sole of each foot before applying padding and then he carefully bandaged Batson's feet.

"Sit up, please, Claude," said the doctor.

The voice eventually penetrated his reverie and Batson responded sluggishly. He carefully slid his legs over the side of the couch and sat up. His feet did feel better. The doctor placed his palm over Batson's eyes, one at a time, checking his pupillary reflexes. Then he popped a thermometer under his patient's tongue and stood back wondering to himself if Batson could be a victim of syphilis. He read the thermometer, noticed that Batson was still mildly febrile and drew a blood sample.

"I will send your blood off for a Wasserman test," said Woods, carefully watching the patient for signs of recognition of the name of the test and the implications, but Batson sat immobile, deep in thought.

"Do you have any symptoms of ... the Pox?" asked Woods outright.

"Pox? No... no, I don't think so," answered Batson uncertainly.

"A rash, sores on your privates, lumps in your armpit or groin..." suggested Woods.

Batson coloured, realising that the doctor was referring to a form of venereal disease and muttered, "I thought you had to be with a woman to get it... I, I haven't ... well not really..."

Batson looked flustered and then scowled as he remembered his thwarted romance.

The doctor went to the cabinet and shook two small tablets from a vial. He filled a cup with water and handed tablets and water to Batson and advised, "There you go, a couple of these and you will feel much better!"

Woods asked the orderly to fetch the guards.

"Can he walk now, doctor?" asked the sour, older guard as he entered the room.

"I may be a good doctor, but not that good!" laughed Woods, "stretcher him back to his cell and he should be a lot better tomorrow."

Both guards looked furious but complied. Batson had a very rough ride back to his cell and was unceremoniously dumped on the floor of cell.

"Git up Batson!" growled the guard, "don't expect any favours!"

The cell door clanged shut.

Dr William Cleaver Woods, a leading medical practitioner and Mayor of Albury 1911 and 1917-18 from the Albury City collection.

CHAPTER 33

Court matters - 26 February 1924

Batson was feeling better. The provision of three meals a day had renewed his strength and refreshed his mindset. His feet were much improved, his sunburn had faded, although his nose was tatty with peeling skin and his lips were crusted. The Humane Society had provided Batson with some clothes for his court appearance, and he dressed carefully in the near-new clothes - a grey tweed suit, a crisp white shirt with a soft collar and simple black tie. He combed his unruly, lank hair with the thick wooden comb that had been included in the care-pack from the Society. It proved impossible to smooth, so he opted to slick his hair down with some water. The guards had refused to allow Batson access to a razor, so his jaw was rough with a dark stubble. He was still unable to wear shoes, so apart from the bandages, Batson's feet were bare.

The guards arrived promptly at 9:30am and applied manacles to the prisoner's wrists which were in turn, connected to a chain around his waist.

"Move out, Batson!" said the senior guard gruffly and shoved Batson in the small of his back.

With one guard ahead and one behind, Batson was led through the corridors to the waiting transport vehicle which was parked under the portico near the front gate of the gaol. Batson hesitated as he stood near the vehicle, uncertain how to negotiate the steps with his hands restrained. One of the guards hooked a hand under his armpit and boosted Batson, helping him to mount the steps and climb into the compartment behind the cab of the truck. Batson landed awkwardly on one of the bench seats which lined the sides. The guard then reached in and swiftly padlocked the prisoner's manacles to the ring on the bench and slammed the door shut. The compartment was a dim, confined space. Batson started to sweat, his breathe came in gasps. Butterflies swooped around in his guts and his thoughts swirled. Snatches of the conversation from earlier with his defence lawyer jumbled with Dr Woods' words of advice. Batson felt confused and anxious, and the walls of the small compartment were pressing in on him.

The vehicle took off with a jolt. The manacles pinched Batson's flesh, and his shoulders strained as he struggled to maintain his seat. The rough ride took his mind off claustrophobia.

Soon the vehicle lurched to a halt, and the door was wrenched open. The guard glared in at Batson and warned, "I will not tolerate any funny business, from you Mr Batson!"

Batson nodded sullenly and muttered, "Yes, Sir."

"Now you sit still while I unclasp the padlock," growled the guard.

Batson nodded again and the guard reached in and keyed the lock and unhitched Batson's chain.

"Righto Laddie, step lively!" said the guard, as he stood to one side and his colleague stepped up to flank him. Batson scrambled awkwardly from the vehicle and stumbled on the bottom step. He lurched towards the senior guard, who grabbed him by the arm and landed a swift blow with his baton into Batson's hip. As he flinched and struggled to regain his footing, Batson became aware of the crowds milling around the entrance to the courthouse. The case had become a spectacle, and many people had skipped work and responsibilities for the day to come and watch the court proceedings, the trial of the *Last Bushranger.*

Batson dropped his head and steadied himself. The guards led him through the heckling crowds and into the main foyer of the courthouse. They approached a green door marked Interview 1 and the guard knocked, opened the door and announced Batson's name to the occupant. The guards ushered Batson through the door, pushed him down into a seat and, as the door slammed shut, they stood to attention on either side of the door. Batson recognised the man on the opposite side of the desk as his newly appointed solicitor, Colonel J Wilkinson.

"Just a few items to discuss before you are required in the dock, Mr Batson," murmured Wilkinson, inserting some documents into a manilla folder.

"As mentioned earlier, today you are required to face two hearings. The first will be the conclusion of the Coronial Inquest into the death of David Sheppard. The second will be your preliminary appearance in the Albury Police Court on criminal charges of felonious wounding of four persons and firing on police with the intent of evading lawful arrest."

Wilkinson gazed at Batson trying to assess if the man was following. Batson returned his gaze with a resigned expression. Wilkinson continued:

"The point of the inquest is to determine the cause of death of David Sheppard and to identify if there is culprit against whom charges can be brought. Seems to me that it is undeniable that you will be identified as the causative agent, and it is my job to defend you in the subsequent trial."

Batson continued to look unmoved. Wilkinson battled on,

"The coroner will call for evidence from the witnesses and then you ... or at least I, on your behalf, will have the opportunity to present your evidence and call for additional witnesses. Since we haven't had an opportunity to discuss the case in detail, we have obviously not yet built a defence. So, we shall opt to say *nothing* at this point, do you understand?"

Batson studied his solicitor and then merely nodded.

"It is in your best interest to listen to the proceedings but say *nothing*. No outbursts, no demonstrations of emotion!" reiterated Wilkinson sternly.

"I have already stood before a magistrate, Sir," said Batson stiffly.

"Yes, that was for the Victorian Judicial system," said Wilkinson mildly.

"And here on Friday before..." said Batson.

"That was your warrant hearing" answered Wilkinson.

"How many times...." muttered Batson and smacked his palms on the table.

The guards made a move towards Batson, but Wilkinson shook his head and raised a hand in a placating fashion.

"It is procedure, and it is a complicated by both states wanting a piece of you! There may well be adjournments, and the case may only be concluded after multiple hearings, so get used to it!" said Wilkinson harshly.

The two men glared at each other before Wilkinson relaxed and said quietly, "Look, Batson, I can probably save you from the gallows, but our only gambit is to do all possible to assure you of fair treatment before the courts - to encourage lenient sentencing due to any possible mitigating circumstances that there may be. If you get riled, you *will* be convicted and if you escape the noose, you will doubtless end up in an asylum and frankly, that may be the worst outcome!"

Wilkinson shuddered. He had visited several asylums to interview clients and witnesses in the past, and the experience was the stuff of nightmares.

"There is some public sympathy for your cause, Claude. The Walwa and Jingellic communities have initiated a *Batson Defence Fund*. I can also reveal that my services have been procured on your behalf by Mr James McBrien, a landholder from Bowna. Do you know him?" asked Wilkinson.

Batson looked puzzled and then offered hesitantly, "I think my mother may have worked for him. I trapped rabbits down that way for a while..."

Wilkinson also looked puzzled and slipping a sheet of paper from the folder on the table in front of him, he said, "In this letter, addressed to me, Mr McBrien wrote,

"I am extremely sorry for Batson. I have known him since he was a boy. I feel strongly about the treatment he has received from some men in the district and most of his prospects for happiness have been cruelly wrested from him. I am prepared to stand by him in his present trouble and intend to brief the best counsel I can procure to defend his case."

Wilkinson looked up at Batson and examined his expression carefully before saying, "Mr McBrien is clearly a staunch supporter, Claude."

"At least some people can see through the lies and gossip, then," said Batson looking relieved.

Wilkinson gazed at his client wondering how best he could defend such a monstrous act of violence against a defenceless picnic party. He also found it curious that the community would rally and seek to defend him after rallying, just a fortnight ago, to hunt him down.

"Very well, you will be called to the coroner's court in a few minutes. The guards will accompany you to the dock. Please remain standing until the Deputy Coroner advises you to be seated. Do not anger him!" advised Wilkinson sternly.

"Yes, Sir," muttered Batson.

"This will be a mere formality, shouldn't be gone long!" murmured Mr Decimus H Mott, JP, as he kissed his wife goodbye and strode off down Kiewa Street toward the Albury Courthouse.

Justice Mott had followed the details of the Batson case in the newspapers, particularly the Border Morning Mail of which he was a co-owner. Like most of the Albury populace, he had already concluded that the death of David T Sheppard, late of Jingellic South near Walwa, was unnatural and unlawful and that his alleged assailant, Claude Valentine Batson would be required to stand trial for murder.

Mott entered the court, settled himself into the elaborately carved chair behind the bench and waited for the clerk to call the assembly to order. He then looked with interest at the accused and found himself disappointed. Batson was not the monster he had first imagined. He was a short, swarthy fellow with barely controlled lank, curly dark hair. He was dressed in a grey suit which hung on his lean frame and in which he looked very uncomfortable. Mott drew his gaze back to the gallery, cleared his throat, asked the assembly to be seated and intoned the objective of the sitting.

"At the request of the Coroner Mr I.W. Williams, I, Deputy Coroner, Decimus H Mott, do hereby proceed with initiating an inquisition for our Sovereign King George V, taken at Albury, in the State of New South Wales on this, the 26th day of February 1924, upon the circumstances of the death of one David Thomas Sheppard, late of Jingellic South, via Walwa, who died on the 11th of February in Albury District Hospital subsequent to wounds received at Jingellic on Sunday 10 February 1924."

He glanced across the court room and re-examined the accused. Batson did not meet his gaze, he merely sat in the dock, eyes downcast. He looked tired and pained.

"For the record, Sergeant Kersley, can you say who identified the victim?" asked the deputy coroner.

Kersley responded, "Mr Sheppard's wife and next of kin had accompanied him on admission to hospital, so medical records confirmed his identity, but as a formality, Albert Ashcroft, the driver of the motor-lorry from Jingellic to Albury, identified his body in the morgue of the Albury District Hospital on Monday 11 February."

Mott nodded gravely.

"Sergeant Kersley on behalf of the Police department, who do you wish to call first, to give evidence?"

Sergeant Kersley stood and looked towards Charles Barber.

"Mr Charles Barber, farmer in Walwa and participant of the picnic in Jingellic on that fateful day. A principal witness to the shooting, your honour," said Kersley.

Charles Barber took the stand. His limp was more marked today. He had been sleeping badly and his knee, a chronic issue, had flared up. He was sworn in by the clerk.

Sergeant Kersley asked Barber to describe the events leading up to the shooting. Barber wondered to himself how many times he would have to recount this tragic tale but dutifully reiterated the statement he had provided to police and the evidence he had provided to the previous hearings.

"I was standing next to David Sheppard. I heard, what I later realised, were rifle shots. I saw Richard King fall and he was groaning in agony. I looked up to where the shots were coming from - which was on top of the opposite creek bank, and that is when I had a clear view of Claude Batson. I saw him pull the trigger of his rifle and heard Sheppard say, *Oh, God I am shot! I am dying! Do not leave me!* I knelt next to Sheppard and tried to comfort him. I shouted: *It is Claude, Claude Batson!* I looked towards King and saw him collapsed and bleeding. Just then, another shot found its mark in Charles Gainer's leg. He had been standing over King... he pitched forward landing on top of King and rolled off down the bank," said Barber and then cleared his throat.

Barber looked devastated as the memory of the incident flared across his mind. He glanced at Batson to assess his reaction. The gallery gasped as their collective imaginations conjured gory images.

"I told Sheppard that I would have to go and get help and save the women and children. I crossed the creek, and, under cover of the embankment, I made my way to where my horse was tethered. I rode to Jingellic for help and a rifle," finished Barber breathlessly.

Sergeant Kersley called Ruth Barber next, she corroborated her husband's evidence and added: "Mrs Gainer was so heroic! She shouted at Batson that he was cowardly - shooting on unarmed men, and then she ran across the creek to assist her husband who was slumped in the shallows under the embankment."

Ruth paused before continuing:

"I scooped up George Poyntz, my nephew, and together with the other ladies, the terrified children and I scrambled into the creek and hid amongst the willows," Ruth said in a meek, quiet voice.

The trauma was still raw and was etched across her features.

"Did you see Claude Batson shooting his rifle? Did you see him shoot Mr Sheppard?" persisted Kersley.

"I heard the first shot and ignored it ... I thought the men had shot at a snake, there are so many about this year... but then there was another shot, and another... I looked up to the embankment opposite the picnic site and I could see a figure lying in the grass shooting. When Mr McGrath took off and the man stood up, I had a clear view of Claude Batson. It was definately Claude Batson shooting!" Ruth stated firmly.

The women in the gallery gasped dramatically. Ruth looked at Batson across the court room and then her face crumpled, and she sobbed quietly. After a moment, she sniffed and added:

"No, from my position I did not see Mr Sheppard fall. I did not see him shot... but later, when Mr McGrath called to us and encouraged us to move upstream to gather where the men were... he said Batson was gone and we were safe... It was then that I saw Mr Sheppard lying wounded on the grass. I rushed to help him, comfort him. He said to me, *I am done for, I am shot through the spine,* ... it was awful!"

She was now sniffing and sobbing intermittently.

"Thank you, Mrs Barber, that will do," said Sergeant Kersley gently.

William McGrath was next to give evidence. He took the stand wearing his injuries like a badge of honour. He leant heavily on a crutch and his arm was swathed in bandages. Despite his pitiful appearance, his bearing and succinct replies to the questions asked by Sergeant Kersley, evidenced his fortitude and military background. He expanded on the statement that he had provided to the police and added definitively that he had a good view of Batson shooting at the party. He refuted the suggestion from Kersley of the possibility of a second gunman.

"No, Batson acted alone, I had clear vision of the man on the embankment," stated McGrath forcefully.

Other witnesses were called and depositions read. As they went through the same evidence that had been delivered before at the hearings in the Wodonga magistrates court, and at the bedside hearing of the Albury Police Court at the Albury District Hospital, Batson's face became more fixed and expressionless. For extended periods of time, he sat with his head in his hands, shielding his face from the multitude of eyes that watched him. When Dr Conway MacKnight took the stand, Batson's interest was piqued by the evidence provided by the attending doctor. Batson sat up straight and watched the doctor closely as he spoke.

"I examined Mr David Sheppard at Albury District Hospital at 4am, soon after he had arrived at Albury District Hospital, on 11 February 1924. I found him to be in a great deal of pain with a penetrating wound at the left side of the border of his seventh rib and another penetrating wound in the lumbar region of his back. I concluded that the wound was a through-and-through gunshot wound. Symptoms indicated a serious injury to the spine and spinal cord. He had paralysis of his legs and obvious abdominal organ damage. His condition deteriorated over the next nineteen hours, and he died at 11:20pm that night," said MacKnight

The audience sighed and some women paled and sobbed as they considered the drawn-out suffering experienced by Sheppard.

MacKnight continued, "Postmortem examination the next day, 12th February, revealed that the bullet had passed through the thoracic cavity, abdominal cavity and exited via the back, severing the spinal cord, fracturing the spine and penetrating numerous organs. Cause of death is directly attributable to the gunshot wound: shock, sepsis, peritonitis and division of spinal cord."

Batson hid a smile by dropping his head into his hands again.

Police who had been involved in the arrest of Batson at the Drummond property and those who had interviewed him, provided their version of the events to the coroner. When Percy Emerson and William Hore were on the stand, Batson glared malevolently at each lad. Finally, the honourable John R Scobie, JP who, together with Sergeant Kersley had taken David Sheppard's dying deposition at his bedside on the 11th of February, provided his evidence and read Sheppard's deposition to the court.

Batson was then asked to provide his version of events, but he refused, shaking his head sullenly and looking towards his solicitor.

Colonel Wilkinson leapt to his feet and reiterated his client's position, "My client wishes to reserve his defence and plea ...."

Mr Decimus Mott swept a look across the room imperiously and then glared at Batson.

"Very well, I have heard the evidence and statements, and I conclude that David Thomas Sheppard did indeed die from the effects of a gunshot wound feloniously and maliciously inflicted by you, Claude Valentine Batson. I find that the said, Claude Batson, did feloniously and maliciously murder the deceased. You, Claude Batson, will be committed for trial at the next sitting of the Supreme Court in Albury. The date will be 23 April 1924, at 10am," Mott announced before he looked for confirmation of the date and time from his clerk, who nodded.

Justice Mott then stood, nodded to the court and strode from the bench. The clerk raised his voice and announced:

"That concludes the Coronial inquest, into the death of David T Sheppard. The Police Court will convene at 1pm this afternoon to hear the case of Crown versus Claude Valentine Batson on charges of felonious wounding with intent on Richard King, Charles Gainer, William

McGrath and David Sheppard in addition to firearms offences and attempts to evade lawful arrest. All witnesses and parties are to be present in the court no later than 12:45pm."

There was a general clatter and hubbub as the gallery exited the court room. Batson was escorted by two guards back to the holding cells in the bowels of the building. Journalists hurried off to write up their notes and deliver copy to editors.

It was like intermission at the theatre for the members of the public gallery, and nearby cafes did a roaring trade of refreshing the palates of customers intent on dissecting aspects of the evidence that they had heard during coronial court session.

In the holding cell, Batson leaned back against the cold plaster wall. He considered all that he had heard in the court room and the information that Wilkinson had tried to impress upon him.

The coroner had said "Murder", he thought.

"I am done for!" he muttered to himself, "they'll hang me, like Ned!"

He knocked the back of his skull rhythmically against the wall.

"I was driven to it ..." he repeated in time to the thuds of his head against plaster.

After several thuds, Batson froze and pondered the defence that Wilkinson would devise.

"What did he say the options would be," he thought, "The noose, life in prison or a lunatic asylum."

He shuddered.

The Kelly boys had been laughing at him last Sunday morning - he could still hear John's strident voice, jibing at him:

"Your old man is a well-dressed fella!! He is back in a straitjacket!"

A goading laugh, then one of the others piped up with,

"Dennis Kennedy is a guest of His Majesty at the loony bin in Goulburn!"

"Are you a bit batty too, Batson?" asked John Kelly.

Agitation was raging through Batson; he clenched his fists and pummelled them into the flesh of his thighs.

"Oy, Batson! You have a visitor!"

The guard's voice broke into Batson's maelstrom of thoughts.

Colonel Wilkinson stood at the door of the cell watching Batson solemnly. He carried a brown paper bag. After a moment he turned and smiled at the guard.

"That's all right officer, give us some privacy, I need to talk to my client."

The guard looked dubious, "I can wait just here in the corridor. You can call if you need."

Wilkinson entered the cell and sat on the chair which was bolted to the floor. He gazed across at the clearly agitated Batson. His client was sitting on the bunk, rigid and pale.

"I brought you something to eat..." Wilkinson said softly.

Wilkinson reached out and handed the brown bag to Batson, who nodded appreciatively and opened the bag. Inside was a round of sandwiches wrapped in greaseproof paper, a fruit bun and a bottle of lemonade.

"Eat, whilst we talk, Claude," said Wilkinson with a smile.

He waited whilst Batson unpacked the bag and laid the items out on the surface of the bed. He unwrapped the sandwich and bit into it hungrily.

"As you heard, the coroner has committed you for trial on a charge of murder, that will be heard in April. This afternoon, you will be brought before the magistrate to face three charges of felonious wounding and evading the police," said Wilkinson calmly.

"We will stick to the plan - we will defer your plea and defence until we have had an opportunity to work out a strategy. We need to tease out some mitigating circumstances, to engender some sympathy for your cause and get your head out of a noose. So, in the first instance, keep your head! Keep calm and polite. We are not going to cross examine or make a plea. Do you understand Claude?" said Wilkinson with emphasis.

Batson had his mouth full, so, merely nodded.

"Alright, then. Rest up and I will see you in court shortly," said Wilkinson.

He stood up and left the cell wondering to himself which would be better, asylum or gaol. Batson shared that thought.

By 12:30pm, the courthouse gallery was again, packed. The case had drawn the interest of the newspapers whose sensationalised copy had in turn, captured the attention and imagination of the public. In attendance were the idle and the unemployed who were simply there for entertainment value but in addition, there were many attendees who had a vested interest: those who had participated in the manhunt for Batson, those who were related to the victims, and many who felt traumatised by the five days of living in fear of a *marauding killer*. All were keen to see the case to its conclusion and hoped for some sense of vengeance to mitigate the impact that Batson's crimes had inflicted upon his victims and the community. There was an increase in the volume of chatter as Batson was secured in the dock and faces turned to peer at him. For many it was their first view of *The Last Bushranger*.

Phil Hardwick, reporter for The Albury Banner, noted for his newspaper copy that Batson had combed his hair and was looking very tidy and well presented in the dock. He sat tall and calm and was interested in the proceedings, although a little shy as he scanned the crowds.

"He is a different man from the quivering wreck I saw being questioned by arresting officers in Jingellic," Hardwick thought to himself.

The magistrate entered and there was scraping of feet and chairs as the assembly stood in response to the clerk's direction of, "All rise!"

The magistrate, the honourable Mr JB Gibson PM, nodded and everyone regained their seats.

"Very well then, we are here today for a preliminary mention of the case against Claude Valentine Batson, 23 years of Walwa, in the State of

Victoria. Please stand Mr Batson," said the magistrate, his eyes drilling into Batson.

"You are charged with feloniously wounding with intent to murder, four men, David T Sheppard, Richard King, Charles Gainer and William Lachlan McGrath on Sunday, 10 February 1924 at or near Jingellic in the State of New South Wales. In addition, and subsequent to, the initial charge, you are further charged with the Murder of David T Sheppard."

Seargeant Kersley stood, "Permission to speak your honour," he said.

The magistrate nodded.

"The Deputy Coroner, Mr Decimus Mott, has this morning, committed the accused, Claude Batson, to trial by the Supreme Court on 23 April 1924 on the charge of murder of Mr DT Sheppard. Hence, the prosecution wishes to apply to withdraw the charges against Claude Batson in relation to offences against the said, Mr DT Sheppard at this hearing."

The judge agreed and restated the charges, "Claude Batson, you are charged with feloniously wounding with intent to murder, three men, Richard King, Charles Gainer and William Lachlan McGrath on Sunday, 10th February 1924 at or near Jingellic in the State of New South Wales. All three charges shall be considered concurrently. How do you plead, Mr Batson?"

Batson's eyes slid to his solicitor questioningly.

Wilkinson hopped up and said, "Permission to speak, your Honour?"

The judge's head slid on his bulky shoulders and his gaze fixed on the solicitor.

"Yes, ...Colonel Wilkinson, is it?" said the magistrate gravely.

"My client has not had sufficient time to brief me, and we would like to reserve the defendant's plea and defence until his next appearance."

"Will this apply to the other charge of Firing on Police Officers with the intent of causing unlawful wounding and avoiding lawful apprehension."

"Yes, Your Honour," agreed Wilkinson, nodding.

"In the absence of a plea, we will still hear evidence from the prosecution," said Justice Gibson, "Sergeant Kersley, who do you wish to call as your first witness?"

In turn, the prosecution called as witnesses, Charles Barber, Ruth Barber, Dr W Cleaver Woods, William McGrath, Lizzie McGrath, and Gwendoline Gainer. Inspector Parker was also called to present the police evidence that had been accumulated to date, including some photographs which had been obtained by police of the scene of the shooting. The series of images included posed scenes of a re-enactment of the incident. Parker presented the statements from the victims who were still confined to hospital.

Sir John MacPherson was called and asked to present his opinion, as consultant alienist, of the culpability of the accused. MacPherson described Batson as being reasonable and cooperative. He waxed lyrical in relation to his theory of *trago-suggestion*. His enthusiasm and verbosity was sufficient to annoy the magistrate.

The magistrate interrupted MacPherson's dissertation.

"So, what is the short answer, Dr MacPherson? Is the accused fit to stand trial?" barked the magistrate.

MacPherson said with chagrin, "Batson is not mad. He understands what he is being accused of...."

"So, the answer is yes... Batson is fit to stand trial?" said Justice Gibson emphatically.

"Badgering the witness!" muttered Colonel Wilkinson under his breath to his clerk.

MacPherson's cheeks flushed with suppressed rage. Unable to speak, he nodded.

"You are excused, Dr MacPherson, said the magistrate severely before looking to Sergeant Kersley, "Prosecution?"

Sergeant Kersley cited some complications to the full presentation of the facts as two of the three wounded victims were still inpatients of

Albury District Hospital, and time and road conditions had interfered with the availability of some other witnesses.

"In point of fact, one of the police vehicles in which Sergeant Cooper was a passenger, was involved in an accident subsequent to the wheel studs shearing due to the wash aways created by the severe rain event of Friday last, ..." said Kersley before being interrupted by Justice Gibson.

"I do hope your officers were not injured and I do understand the difficulties," sighed the magistrate, "We will adjourn the matter until March 30."

As the court cleared, Hardwick remained in his seat for a moment longer considering the evidence that had just been presented. He was particularly interested in the medical opinion on Batson's mental state and culpability. He noted that the Government Medical Officer, Dr Cleaver Woods, had declared that since medical treatment of the accused's wounds had commenced, and his febrile state had been controlled, the accused was, in the doctor's opinion, of sound mind and was conscious of his actions. When pressed as to the accused state of mind during the shooting, the doctor declined to make comment since Batson had not been his patient at that point in time and he had no knowledge of Batson's state of mind prior to his consultation with the man on the Saturday immediately after Batson's arrest.

The prosecution was anxious to prove Batson culpable and had relied on Sir John MacPherson's evidence. An alienist's view of the mental status of the accused. Hardwick reviewed MacPherson's words which he had scribbled on his notepad. He had written CAUTIOUS in capitals across the page and then a quote:

"I understand that Mr Batson was under extreme mental stress for an extremely prolonged duration. This was induced by the perceived slights upon his reputation by others. He was certainly the victim of early childhood trauma and poor circumstances, and these factors may have provoked a reduced resilience to stress and had weakened his mind, however, my assessment of

the accused during an interview on Saturday, 16 February 1924, revealed him to be conscious of the extent and ramifications of his actions but was none-the-less intent on blame-shifting to his victims. I would need further investigations to ascertain if the accused was culpable at the time of the shootings."

"That statement is full of smoke and mirrors," said Hardwick grimly.

He hadn't realised he had spoken aloud and was startled by a chuckle from the seat behind him. Hardwick turned and smiled apologetically to the man, who still had a sardonic smile on his lips. He stood, offered his hand and introduced himself. The fellow clasped his hand firmly, and responded affably, "Jacob Miller, pleased to meet you. I agree with you, a very reserved assessment of Batson's culpability!"

"What is your specific interest in the case, Mr Miller?"

"I was part of the ex-AIF volunteers who went up to Walwa to help with the search for Batson. I suppose, since I was invested in the case, I wanted to see the conclusion."

"That won't be today, Mr Miller!" said Hardwick glumly.

"No, clearly," agreed Jacob.

"Would you be interested in providing some insight into the search, and your activities whilst engaged in the manhunt, Mr Miller? I like to provide my readers with a well-rounded report, a true reflection of the intricacies of a story!"

Jacob regarded the journalist steadily, considering the offer, before admitting, "I have an additional interest in the case and can see a parallel with that of Norman List in Melbourne last month, are you familiar with that case?"

"Indeed, Mr Miller! I have already made the connection in a piece in the newspaper last week – I referred to a statement made just last week by Sir John MacPherson, the alienist, on the topic of trago-suggestion and the fact he considers Batson to be a copycat!"

"I have the afternoon off from work, so perhaps we could go and get a spot of lunch and take the discussion further," suggested Jacob.

The journalist leapt at the suggestion, "My shout!" he said happily, and the two men left the court room together.

Hardwick suggested the Albury Club, since he was a member, and he could guarantee that their conversation would be uninterrupted and private. He hoped that his companion would be impressed by the exclusive venue and be encouraged to talk freely. He was thankful that it was to be a business expense as exclusivity was reflected in the menu prices.

The two men approached the grand doors of the Albury Club on Kiewa Street and were met by the liveried doorman. He greeted the familiar Hardwick and his guest and swung the doors wide, ushering the pair through to the dining room. The Maître de, who recognised Hardwick, guessed that an interview was intended and whisked them through to a quiet alcove. He seated the men and murmured a description of the specials of the day before offering to fetch a drink for the pair.

"I might have pint of lager, please, Herman," said Hardwick and looked questioningly at Jacob.

"Make that two, thank you," said Jacob with a grin.

The Maître De nodded and carefully placed menus in front of the men.

When they were alone, Hardwick eagerly enquired, "So, what is your connection to the Norman List affair?"

"I was in the Gardens during the shooting. Circumstances put me in the company of a young lady from Walwa..." said Jacob gravely.

"And they say lightening doesn't strike twice!" said Hardwick, "don't tell me this poor lady was at the Jingellic picnic?"

"Fortunately not, but Batson was captured on the property where she is currently residing with relatives," said Jacob.

"Good heavens, that must have been terrifying for the young lady.... Can you give me her name?" said Hardwick with pencil poised over his notebook.

"I would have to ask her permission, particularly if you were intending to include her name in an article," said Jacob cautiously.

He went on to detail his account of the tragedy which had unfolded in front of him during Norman List's rampage through the Botanic Gardens.

"I understand that List saw action in France and was afflicted with syphilis – both of these aspects may have addled his brain," suggested Jacob.

"Yes, my contact in the Melbourne office, thought that shell shock, and diseases and injuries such as syphilis and head injuries could certainly have triggered a psychotic episode. Apparently, List's previous employer reported that List complained that he was hearing voices. One of the investigating officers drew a long bow when he discovered that List was quite academic and read texts on mathematics and astronomy; he suggested that this had contributed to a brain strain injury!" enthused Hardwick.

"Hmmm, I think the fellow just snapped! Some of the stories from returned AIF servicemen, even my own experience, to a lesser extent, leads me to conclude that the war left more than just physical scars on participants," said Jacob sadly.

Both men sat quietly reflecting on the tragedy of war.

"What about Batson?" asked Hardwick, "He can't blame his behaviour on the war."

"No, but I wonder about the poison he was experimenting with.... I understand from talking to some locals whilst up in Walwa, that Batson was inventing a rabbit poison, perhaps a form of gas. He and another fellow tried to patent a formula and method of delivering it to rabbit warrens. Rumour has it that the poison was like the gas the Huns were so keen to distribute across the trenches of the Somme. Perhaps he poisoned himself in his eagerness to prove the efficacy of his invention... in the same way that mustard gas may contribute to war terrors and shell shock, maybe his form of rabbit poison has corrupted Batson's mind," said Jacob.

"An interesting observation, Mr Miller, I will follow up that theory!" said Hardwick enthusiastically.

"Do you think Batson was in contact with List? Did he know of the Botanic Gardens tragedy?" asked Jacob.

"My understanding is that during police interviews, he denied any knowledge of List, and I don't believe he would have read newspaper reports or listened to the radio. However, there is a potential that the two encountered one another in the last six months. Batson roamed the district quite widely and List was employed by a sawmill at Koetong and frequented Tallangatta..." suggested Hardwick.

Hardwick noticed Jacob frowning at the unfamiliar locality names.

"Koetong is about twenty-five miles south of Walwa and Tallangatta is west of Koetong on the Murray Valley Road, on the way to Wodonga. It isn't too much of a stretch of imagination to consider the two may well have come face-to-face," said Hardwick emphatically.

The Maître De returned with two frosted glasses of beer and took their lunch orders. Alone again, the two men explored the coincidence of two very similar murder scenarios and the motivation for such monstrous acts. Hardwick scribbled copious notes and asked questions of Jacob to flesh out his descriptions of the man hunt in the Upper Murray hills. Finally, whilst tucking in to their meals which had been served during a lull in conversation, Hardwick asked Jacob's opinion on the topic of gun registration and restrictions.

"Oh, I agree, the situation needs to be brought under control. Firearms need to be secured and registered, particularly now there is the deadly combination of a rise in unemployment and a high population of men suffering from the after-effects of war. I notice that most of the crime element in Melbourne, particularly the push-gangs are war damaged men," said Jacob.

Hardwick nodded and remembered the Crutchie-Push gang members he had seen operating on the streets of Melbourne. The gang members were amputees yet seemed uncompromised by their anatomical deficiencies: their crutches were wielded as weapons and the speed at which they were able to flee from police or chase down their victims was astonishing.

"The criminals will always find a way around the legalities of gun ownership,' suggested Hardwick.

"Yes," said Jacob, "But restrictions and registration might shrink the pool of firearms available to the criminals and increase the difficulty of acquisition. If it was illegal to carry a firearm unless for legitimate reasons of hunting or gun club activities, then criminals in possession of firearms could be arrested on the lesser charge of a firearms offence before they escalated to armed robbery, or worse,"

Hardwick smiled, happy that Jacob was in his camp.

"There will be an outcry of indignation in relation to impinging on an individual's rights...but these two picnic massacres, the recent Goulburn Incendiarist and the fact that crime has never been more rampant and blood thirsty in Victoria and NSW than at present, will certainly push the argument towards increased regulation," said Hardwick grimly.

"*Goulburn Incendiarist,* is that what you newshounds are calling that mad man who was on a spree of arson, robbery and ... did he shoot someone as well?" asked Jacob.

"Yes, he was confirmed to be mad! Robert Fenwick was an escapee from Gladesville Asylum. He gave himself up peaceably on Saturday... just walked into the Marulan Police station, I believe," said Hardwick.

"Will he be included in MacPherson's list of copycat criminals?" asked Jacob.

"Hmm, MacPherson's term is *trago-suggestion,* by which I understand him to mean that susceptible brains can be influenced to mimic the criminal activities of another person... If Fenwick was such a copycat, he certainly added his own signature and an escalation to the trago-suggestion activities, with arson included!" said Hardwick.

"Tell me, Hardwick, with all due respect, what role do you think newspaper reports have on such susceptible criminals?" asked Jacob solemnly.

Hardwick frowned.

"I take your point Mr Miller. I noticed that MacPherson was concerned about this aspect of influence, too! In one of his press-releases," Hardwick flicked back through his notebook as he spoke until he found the relevant page, "he said, the glorification of mad and brutal offences by sensationalised reporting or even gossip, may have an inspiring impact on melancholy brooders and those with a pathological grudge against society. He even pointed the finger at popular crime fiction and the American film industry! Emulating *Deadwood Dick*, you know!" chuckled Hardwick.

"Deadwood Dick... now there is one I am not familiar with!" laughed Jacob.

"It is probably better that you steer away from that character and form of trashy fiction!" suggested Hardwick.

The rest of the lunch was spent in a wide-ranging discussion of criminal psychology and the triggers that push ordinary people to become unlawful. Jacob was interested in criminology and had read widely on the subject.

Jacob chuckled grimly as he said, "In the words of the popular author, Agatha Christie, nobody is ever as they seem! In the current era, with the economy in tatters and so many disturbed returned servicemen, all of whom have been well and truly blooded on the battlefields of Europe, no wonder there is rampant crime."

His companion agreed.

"Well, thank you for an interesting discussion and agreeing to lunch with me, Mr Miller. I would be happy to hear of any further insights you may have on the Batson case … and that of Norman List," said Hardwick.

Hardwick handed Jacob his calling card. Jacob took the card and smiled.

"Hopefully, the next time I speak to a newspaper man, it might be on happier subject matter," he suggested, whilst thinking to himself that the occasion might involve an announcement of an engagement to one, Emma Payne.

The thought made him smile broadly as he shook Hardwick's hand, and they parted company.

CHAPTER 34

Snake!

Alexander Drummond cantered down the drive to Albert's property and waved to the figures he could see on the verandah. He was intrigued to hear Albert's firsthand account of the capture of the *Last Bushranger of the Upper Murray*. He hoped it would make up for the disappointment he felt that he had missed out on the excitement since he had been away for the duration of the search as a patient of a Melbourne Hospital. Alexander was keen to discover if the reality matched the hype of the newspaper reports and gossip.

Albert was glad to see that his brother was back to health and they greeted one another enthusiastically. After introductions, Emma slipped off to the kitchen to make the obligatory pot of tea for the family.

On her return to the verandah, bearing a tray with tea things and a generous plate of biscuits, she overheard the brothers' conversation.

"It was all a bit pathetic in the end... Batson was far from the menacing bushranger as depicted in the newspapers. He was just a dejected, hungry young man. I think the police were sorely disappointed. They were hoping for a battle... a shootout which would cover them in glory," said Albert.

"The police could do with some glory, the wrong 'uns are running rings around them at present... seems to me that the papers are full to overflowing with pages of murderous gunmen running amok and then there was all that bother in November, with the Melbourne Police strike! The criminal element crawled out of their holes and had a ball in the absence of law and order!" said Alexander.

Minnie glanced towards Emma, reassuring herself that the conversation wasn't upsetting her niece. Emma smiled back wanly.

"How are you, after your troubles, Alexander?" Minnie said, pointedly steering the conversation away from Batson, "You had a few days in hospital?"

"They were just being cautious... I was perfectly fine, really! Dulcie was just being a worrier," said Alexander gruffly, "I think she was just keeping me away from the hunt for Batson!"

Minnie smiled gently, "Someone with heart trouble doesn't need to march up and down the hills in summer heat! You should take a holiday!"

"I just had one... in hospital!" laughed Alexander.

The men went on to discuss some farm matters, including plans for crutching another mob of ewes, and the price of butter fat before Emma and Minnie lost interest in agricultural topics and the two women excused themselves and went into the kitchen to prepare lunch.

As soon as Emma was out of earshot, Albert shared what he had overheard when Batson was carted away by the police.

"Batson said to Senior Constable Bunworth that he had hidden a revolver. He said it was out the back of Barbers'! We should go and look for it," suggested Albert.

"Why not leave it to the police?" said Alexander cautiously.

"They have cleared out of the district. Most have gone back to their usual stations, and Constable Rice and Jolly have been busy with court appearances and paperwork. I would worry that it might fall into the wrong hands...," said Albert virtuously.

Inspired by a sense of civic duty and keen for a challenge, the brothers decided to go on an excursion. They called out to Emma and Minnie to say they were just popping out to look at some stock, before riding off to the Barbers' home.

The Barbers were out of the district, staying in Albury with relatives to be on hand as required, to present their evidence for the Coroners' inquiry into David Sheppard's death and to the Albury and Wodonga courts in relation to Batson's case. So, with Richard King in hospital, the Barbers' home was unoccupied.

"Batson said he had pushed the revolver under a log near the well," said Albert as they dismounted and tethered their horses to the rail in the Barbers' yard.

"Where is the well?" asked Alexander scanning the yard.

"Up the back there," said Albert as he marched off behind the house.

The dry grass crackled underfoot; the Upper Murray had missed out on the rainstorm that had welcomed Batson to Albury on Friday evening. In the space of just a few days of Ruth Barber's absence, her garden was already beginning to look neglected. Her geraniums and roses were wilted, and the vegetable patch was in a bad way. Some washing, forgotten in all the drama of the past fortnight, flapped lazily on the line. The brothers found the well; rows of red bricks defined the perimeter, and a windmill towered over it and creaking listlessly in the scant breeze.

"There it is," cried Alexander seeing a likely looking log a few feet away from the well.

He stepped up to it and without thinking, he bent down and rolled the log to one side. A coiled black snake was revealed, and it reared up in a threatening manner. Both men froze, sucking in their breath with horror. The startled snake seemed satisfied that no further threat was intended and slipped off silently into the shrubbery.

"Bloody hell, Alex, that was close! Lucky it was a black, a brown would have come at us!" laughed Albert, "How is your heart now?"

"Pounding! It still works!" said his very relieved brother.

A canvas bag lay where the snake had been, moments before. Alexander stooped and picked it up. He undid the drawstring and eased out a Webley pistol.

"We seem to have found it!" said Alexander, "Now what?"

"Best take it to Detective Cleaver, although I think he has gone to Albury for the court case, along with Constables Rice and Jolly," said Albert, "we might need to send it on the mail car. I will phone the Police and advise that we have found it."

"It's a handy piece," said Alexander hefting the pistol, testing its weight and balance, "I wonder where Batson got it from, it looks like military issue."

"No idea. Although it is one of the few things you wouldn't be able to buy in the Walwa Store! He could have pinched it ... Batson is a different sort of fellow, but I wouldn't have thought him a thief. Mind you I wouldn't have thought him capable of murder either... what could have spurred him on to commit this atrocity?" mused Albert as the two brothers wandered back to their mounts.

"Persecution, they say, can scramble a fellow's mind. All that bother about the rabbit poison and the patent. Batson was humiliated when the demonstration cocked up. Some of the fellows just took the jibing too far, and to top it off, Batson was convinced that someone stole his idea and put in a patent application ahead of the one he and Lawrence put together. I hear that there is some sympathy for Batson's dilemma. McBrien down at Bowna has put up the funds for a smart legal counsel."

Albert nodded in agreement.

"And on the opposite side of the argument, Detective Constable Cleaver and Constable Bell are raising funds to help the victims. Even the Gadds and Councillor Jephcott have put their hands in their pockets to start up a charity fund to help the wounded and to have the heroes recognised: William McGrath and even Percy Emerson and Bill Hore," said Albert.

The men swung up into their saddles and trotted off. They elected to head to Jingellic since that route would take them past the Jingellic Police Station at Redbank and if Constable Rice was indeed away, they could go on and check if there were any police officers remaining at Jingellic Hotel. Failing both options, they would arrange with one of the Smith girls at the post office to send the Webley to Detective Cleaver in Albury via Holbrook, with John Kennedy, the carrier.

As they were crossing the bridge, heading for option two, The Jingellic Hotel, Alexander asked, "Why do you think it took so long to track Batson? I heard that the police brought in black trackers."

Albert laughed, "A canny bunch, those trackers! If it were a child or a woman lost, the tracker would have sniffed them out in a couple of hours. The police made the mistake of telling all and sundry that Batson was armed and dangerous. The trackers didn't want to be in the lead when they got to the end of the tracks... they were afraid of being peppered with lead!"

"I can understand their perspective," agreed Alexander.

"I heard one of the police officers griping ... last Wednesday it was, that when those tracks were picked up on the riverbank... Despite perfectly formed footprints, the tracker, Gilbert, was insistent that the person who had made the tracks was heading in the opposite direction. As soon as they tried to question him, he could no longer understand English!" said Albert.

The two men laughed.

Finlay Smith greeted them as they pushed through the doors into the tap room. The aroma of hops and polish enveloped the men.

"Are you still hosting the police contingent, Finlay?" asked Albert noting the hotel was quiet with just Ted Plunkett sitting up at the bar. Ted was grinning lopsidedly at the brothers with a tide of froth festooning his whiskers and a schooner, half full of beer, warming up on the bar in front of him.

"Thank the Almighty, they have all gone! I have my hotel back under my control!" Smith grinned broadly.

He had been entirely fed up with the heavy police presence for the last week. His staff had been under the pump trying to keep the meals up to police and gawkers. The hotel's limited accommodation had been stretched to overflowing with some of the troops resorting to "hot bedding" or sleeping on the floor. The kitchen had been forced to operate at all hours to feed the searchers who came back to the "Operational headquarters" long after usual mealtimes but still expected to be fed. He appreciated that the furore had brought more punters to his bar and more income to his pocket, but overall, it was an excessively busy week, and his supplies and staff were exhausted.

"Well, since we are here, can we trouble you for two pints?" asked Alexander hopefully.

Plunkett looked towards the men equally hopefully and grinned a toothless smile.

"You better give Plunkett a top up whilst you are at it!" said Alexander affably.

Settling themselves on to bar stools, they chatted to the barkeep as he pulled three beers.

They showed Smith the Webley revolver they had just found and discussed where Batson might have come by such a weapon.

"As I said to Albert, it looks like military issue," said Alexander.

Smith peered at it with interest.

"Batson didn't serve, so I am not sure where he might have got it," said the Smith and then thought for a moment.

"Although he was chummy with Richard White down at Burrowye Station, wasn't he, Ted. Could he have got the pistol from White?" suggested Smith.

Plunkett looked a bit apprehensive.

"That White is a bit of a wrong 'un," said Plunkett, "wouldn't surprise me if he had a pistol... funny thing, not long ago, the manager of Burrowye Station, Webb, you know? He had his dogs poisoned ... I think the poison was meant for his family. Then soon after, there were shots fired at his house. Small bore, like a pistol. Maybe White gave his pistol away so he couldn't get pinged for the job," suggested Plunkett.

"Yes, maybe he gave it away to Batson!" concluded Smith.

"Not sure Batson and White were too chummy in recent times," mused Albert, "I am pretty sure that White may have been the man who tapped Batson on the shoulder and scrubbed him off that lass' dance card - the one he had his heart set on!"

"Poison, random shots fired... sounds like Batson could have had himself a practice run for a crime spree," suggested Alexander.

"Y-eeesss," said Albert enthusiastically, "and set White up to take the blame! I think John Houston let White go... he might be working on the roads now. I haven't seen him around for a while!"

Smith laughed at the brothers' conversation, "I think you two might have been reading too many books... is Arthur Conan Doyle or Agatha Christie to your taste?"

The Drummonds grinned.

"Don't you go telling White I said 'owt about him," whined Plunkett looking even more anxious, "Don't want him comin' after me next!"

The two brothers pondered the mystery of Batson and revolvers and downed their beers.

"We better get this parcel off to the post office, then Alex," said Albert, "It could be a vital clue!" he grinned at Smith conspiratorially.

They called their farewells and pushed through the doors back into the sunshine.

"Can the police match the weapon to bullets lodged in the Webbs' walls?" asked Alex of his brother.

"Hmm, not sure. Not sure if we should even mention a possible connection. You heard Plunkett. He is worried that any talk might make him a target, if it was White doing the shooting at Webb's," suggested Albert.

Still musing on the topic, the brothers went next door to the post office, to post the parcel.

CHAPTER 35

Batson on the brink...

Claude Batson had been moved to the remand cells. His new cell was more spacious and, although it could accommodate two bunks, he was the sole occupant. There was a small footlocker for each bed, a more permanent privy arrangement in one corner and a table with an enamel bowl and a jug of water. Batson had adapted to the routine of prison life. He was fed, sheltered, participated in work details to split wood and had plenty of time to think.

Batson had overheard and participated in hurried conversations with fellow inmates whilst on work details, in the exercise yard and in the communal dining room and it was apparent that he was the principal topic of conversation for the bored, under stimulated men. There was a hunger to hear the details of the *Sniper at the Picnic* incident and speculate on the outcome of Batson's hearing when the Supreme Court sat in Albury in April.

"There hasn't been a hanging at Albury Gaol since the 1880's," said one swarthy, old hand in the dining hall one afternoon. He pushed a piece of bread into his mouth and munched noisily whilst regarding Batson with curious eyes.

Batson tried to ignore him and hurriedly shovelled the last of the greasy grey stew into his mouth.

"You could pinch Henry Wilkinson's claim to fame, and *you* could be the last man hanged here!" persisted the man malevolently.

Batson shot the fellow a dark look and stood up, snarling, "Shaddup, Ryan!"

The sudden movement caught the guards' attention, and they moved briskly towards Batson in a pincer movement. Ryan looked at Batson with a challenge on his face, but Batson recognised that he would feel the batons before his persecutor, so he merely gathered his bowl and cutlery and moved off to deposit them in the wash bucket before joining the queue of men waiting to return to their cells.

Hanged - The word echoed in Batson's mind. He thought about Ned Kelly. He searched through the stories he had been told, including Kelly's last words to the hangman when told that the time had come: *Ah well, I suppose*, or sometimes reported as *Such is life*. Batson admired the fact that Kelly was stoically resigned to his fate, but he felt resistant to his fate. In his mind's eye he could see Kelly standing on the trapdoor, a calico bag over his head. He could feel the rough hemp rope snug around his neck, the swoop of his stomach as he fell...

"It would have been quicker to take the cyanide I had in my pocket..." he thought to himself with anguish coursing through his being.

He thought of the rabbits he had seen poisoned by cyanide, the froth and the agonising contortions. Then he remembered James Gordon... It was a decade ago, and Batson had been a young lad at the time, but he recalled the incident vividly. He and his employer at that time, had been loading bags of grain into the dray outside the store at Smiths' Hotel when James Gordon came wobbling up the road on his bicycle. His eyes were wild, his face pale and sweating, foam on his lips. He pulled up and fell from his bike in a mess of limbs and a clash of metal. He managed an explanation in short gasps before he was overcome by the seizures. A container of strychnine which he was using to bait the dingoes, had spilled in his pocket alongside his Woodbines. He had put a fag to his lips and inadvertently, the strychnine too. He died kicking in the dust ...

"I don't want to be kicking on the end of a rope either," Batson thought.

Round and round the thoughts of death swirled as he walked through the corridors back to his cell. He flung himself on his bunk and balled his fists into his eye sockets. He tried to sink into the blackness, escape from the turmoil in his head.

Later that afternoon, when his section was released into the exercise yard, Batson noticed that his swarthy persecutor, Ryan, was amongst the group of men marching around the quadrangle. Their eyes met and the fellow winked lasciviously at Batson and smirked. Batson dragged his eyes away and concentrated on putting one foot in front of the other. The men were expected to walk the perimeter of the quadrangle in single file, ten minutes clockwise, ten minutes anticlockwise and ten minutes of free time. The yard was bare, just a bricked surface, defined by tall stone walls. It was sun drenched and kiln-like in summer, damp and cold in winter. A watch tower looked down on the yard and the exercise group was monitored by three guards, who usually stood by the door gossiping and idly watching the prisoners. Batson noticed that there was a grate in the floor towards the southeastern corner of the yard. It broke up the monotony of the brickwork. Batson deliberately walked on the grate for a couple of laps, testing its fastness. It was initially a distraction from counting his steps and finding patterns in the bricks, but then he stepped on it because he liked the noise from the grate as it clunked in its housing. He heard hurried steps behind him and turned slightly to discover that his persecutor had extended his gait to overtake some fellow prisoners and had fallen into step just behind Batson.

"I met a fellow once in Albury, Batson," muttered Ryan quietly, so that the guards wouldn't hear, "his name was Dennis Kennedy. Know him?"

Batson ignored the fellow.

Ryan persisted, "Heard tell, he was your Da'."

The circle of prisoners continued their monotonous tramp.

"Bonkers he is... Silly as a wheel, ... locked up in an asylum now, I hear!" Ryan cackled in a low menacing manner.

Batson gritted his teeth and tried to ignore the swarthy troublemaker. They completed another circuit.

"Must be in the blood, you and Kennedy - both bonkers!" sniped Ryan.

A red haze was pulsing through Batson's consciousness. It was always the same; always someone interfering with him, goading him... Batson found himself again in the southeastern corner. He stopped suddenly, causing the swarthy man to cannon into his back and to lose his balance. The column of men lost its rhythm and formation, and chaos prickled. Batson stooped and slid his fingers through the bars of the grate at his feet. His muscles bunched and jarred at the sudden exertion necessary to wrench the grate from its housing. He swung around and the grate became a formidable weapon. Using centrifugal force to his advantage, Batson swung the grate and collected Ryan with the full force directed into the side of his body. Ryan vainly tried to protect himself and flung up an arm to shield his head. The sickening crack proclaimed that the bones in his arm had shattered on impact. The force caused Ryan to cartwheel into the stone wall. There was a dull thud, and his body slithered down the wall into an untidy pile on the ground. The noise built to a crescendo: the guard in the tower triggered the siren and trained his rifle on Batson, the prisoners were yelling, "Fight, fight!", and the guards were yelling at Batson to drop the grate. They surrounded him batons in hand and threatening. The fight had gone from Batson; the red haze was withdrawing and he let the grate slide from his fingers. It clanged onto the brick paving. Ryan began to writhe and moan.

"Not dead, yet, then," was Batson's last conscious thought before a baton crashed into his skull.

Batson woke with a dull ache through his brain and a sharp pain at the back of his head. He found he couldn't move to touch his head as his arms were restrained across his body. His entire torso was hugged by an uncomfortably tight sensation. He was shrouded in darkness. He felt the chill of a paved surface against his cheek. He struggled to right himself and with a degree of contortionism, he was able to sit up. Postural change made his head thump harder. He struggled to order his thoughts and figure out his situation and concluded that he must be in solitary confinement, the straitjacket was foreign to him, so he was unable to reconcile that aspect of his situation. He shuffled backwards until his back met with the wall. Surprised that the wall was comfortable to lean against, he swung his head and felt it with his cheek and concluded that he was in a leather padded cell.

"Maybe Ryan was right," Batson thought miserably, "I am mad."

The absolute darkness, absolute silence was eating at Batson. To a man who had never been truly confined, and who usually fell asleep caressed by the silver of moonlight and stars, or in the glow and crackle of a comforting fire, surrounded by the whispers of nocturnal animals, wind in the leaves and the creak of his poorly built hut, the absence of sound, absence of light was terrifying. He screwed up his eyes to conjure the jagged colours that were induced by optic nerve pressure, and he tried humming, then singing. His repertoire was restricted, and he ran out of verses, the situation was compounded by a maddening thirst, so he quit singing after a few minutes. Batson felt the anxiety creeping up on him again. He shook his head and in a deliberate and determined fashion, he forced his memory to recount every step of the pathway from his hut to Walwa. With his mind's eye, he saw the specific rock formations, he identified animal tracks, the wattle blossom, small delicate orchids, birds. He pictured the massive gum trees with eroded fissures in the bark, some with scars where the original inhabitants of the Upper Murray had taken sheets of bark for canoes. That thought took him to the caves and rock surfaces up in the hills and ridgelines around Walwa and Jingellic, where he was quite sure, he would have been the first white man to see the handprints and art of the aboriginal first inhabitants of the district. He was comfortably lost in his imagination when there was a metallic clatter and light streamed through a small port.

"Batson! Are you awake?" growled an ominous voice.

"Yes...yes, Sir," Batson responded hoarsely.

"No sudden movements mind! Sit against the wall, I am opening the door," said the voice.

The door opened, light sliced through the blackness, making Batson squint in defence of the sudden stimulation of his retinas. A guard was silhouetted in the doorway.

"The doctor wants a look at you. We are going to the infirmary. No trouble, Batson!"

"Yes, Sir," mumbled Batson.

"On your feet then, man!" snarled the guard.

Batson pulled his legs under himself and levered his body to an upright position by pushing off the wall. It was awkward and the effort aggravated his throbbing head. He grunted in pain and frustration. The guard moved away from the door, backing into the corridor.

"Off you go, Batson, head to the end and turn right,"

They set off, with Batson's eyes still struggling to accommodate the bright light in the corridor.

Dr Cleaver Woods was on duty when Batson arrived at the infirmary. He looked at Batson and smiled kindly.

"Good morning, Claude. I understand you were involved in an episode in the exercise yard, yesterday."

Batson gazed at the doctor whilst trying to assemble the memories of the "episode."

Finally, he admitted, "Ryan provoked me, Sir."

"You could have killed the man! Threatened the guards..." Woods frowned at Batson in disappointment.

Batson looked at the floor blankly and mumbled, "He stirred me up... like the others, wouldn't shut up. Shouldn't stir me up."

"Sit down," said Woods, indicating a steel chair bolted to the floor, "I need to examine your head."

Woods was brusque now, frustrated that the man was unremorseful. Batson sat down awkwardly, unbalanced by the restriction of the straitjacket.

The doctor examined the wound to the back of Batson's head.

"Apparently your head hit the wall when the guards were trying to disarm and restrain you," commented the doctor as he looked accusingly at the guard.

The guard shrugged.

He cleansed the injury and carefully closed it by knotting strands of hair together across the wound. He applied a gauze compress and wrapped a bandage around Batson's head to maintain pressure on the wound.

"How are your feet now, Claude, you are walking better and wearing shoes, so I assume they are back to square?"

"Yes, sir, all good," said Batson listlessly and then more urgently, "I need a piss, Sir, and so thirsty."

Woods frowned and looked to the guard, "Has he not been allowed to visit the privy? Has he been fed?"

"He only roused this morning. No time to sort," said the guard with some affront.

"Take him to his cell, remove the straitjacket, give him a feed and a jug of water. I will come and assess him in an hour," advised the doctor.

"Out of solitary, then, Doctor?" asked the guard dubiously.

Woods nodded. The guard huffed and hauled Batson roughly to his feet before marching him back to his cell.

Released from the straitjacket and into the comparative freedom of his cell, Batson stretched and went to use the privy as soon as the guard left. He then washed his hands and face and drank a huge draught of water. Refreshed, he started pacing up and down between the bunks and flapping his arms about to stretch out muscles that felt fixed and stiff. His brain was whirring again, and he dissected the events that led to his current predicament. He revisited his issues with Richard King, he grieved the disruption of his relationship with Ruth Barber and seethed as his persecutors flashed in succession through his memories. He heard again the rifle shots and experienced the satisfaction as his targets collapsed, their blood spilling on the grass. He was so focussed that he didn't hear the door open behind him. The guard's voice crashed through his consciousness,

"Batson! Attention! Stand clear!"

Batson swung around, startled. There were two guards framed by the doorway. One was holding the straitjacket.

Batson started swinging his head side to side as he backed up to the back wall of his cell.

"Nooo, no please, not that thing..." he moaned.

The guard, glared at Batson.

"The doctor had no authority to have you released from solitary confinement. No authority to have you out of the straitjacket, neither. Guv orders you back in!"

The two guards approached Batson.

"Now, Batson, we can do this the easy way, or we are happy enough to cop the slog of putting the jacket on an unconscious body..." said the guard with quiet menace.

Batson's eyes were wide with fear, fear of the darkness, not of the guards. He rushed them. The guards were experienced and had predicted the move. In the confined space between the bunks, they braced, one jabbed a baton into Batson's solar plexus and the other slammed his baton against Batson's temple. Batson crumpled to his knees, gasping for breath.

The guards applied the straitjacket with practiced efficiency to the incapacitated prisoner. They were dragging Batson to his feet when Doctor Woods walked in.

"What the devil is going on here?" he demanded.

"Guv'nor wants the prisoner back in solitary and restraint," said the senior guard stubbornly.

"I haven't assessed him yet to determine if such measures are necessary," reasoned Woods.

"Sorry Sir, but we have to take directions from Guv'nor, not you."

Woods could see the set of the guard's attitude. They would not be swayed, so he spun on his heel and announced, "I shall go and speak to Governor Wicks, then!"

The guards bundled Batson off back to the padded cell. Although groggy from the blow to his head, Batson tried to resist, as the fear of the darkness filled his head.

By the time the guards shut the door on Batson, he was blubbering and muttering in an incoherent fashion.

"Batson is bonkers!" laughed the guard callously to his colleague.

Albury Gaol - image courtesy of Albury Wodonga and District Historical Society

CHAPTER 36

A fine romance and friendship

It was a perfect late summer afternoon. The Murray River was lazily swirling, drawing the small boat downstream. Jacob was merely dipping or stroking the water with an oar just occasionally to keep their course true to the centre of river. Emma was mesmerised by the scenery and fascinated by the variety of birds that she could see. She leant back against the side of the craft, watching tall spoonbills as they fed in the shallows, a variety of ducks glided passed as if in an impromptu regatta, whilst a multitude of species flitted over the water feeding on insects or squawking and calling in the trees that overhung the river. She trailed her hand overboard in the cool water and scanned the scenery as they slid passed on the tranquil waters. Every so often, she would exclaim excitedly and point out whatever had caught her interest to Jacob. He acknowledged her enthusiasm, but had eyes for Emma alone, although every so often, he would check the course the boat was taking.

"This is glorious!" enthused Emma, "such a good idea!"

Jacob smiled. He was besotted with Emma, and he would do anything to make her smile.

"We won't have the opportunity to do this for much longer, the weather will turn against us soon, so we have to make the most of it!" declared Jacob.

A large fish breached, flipped and splashed near the shore.

"Goodness, he was huge! It was a *Feed-a-family-of-six* size! Perhaps you should have brought your fishing rod."

"One must be serious about fishing," declared Jacob solemnly in a prim voice, "no talking, definitely no giggling, and full focus."

He laughed and added earnestly, "I wouldn't be able to pay you sufficient attention if I had a rod in my hand!"

"Well, we can't have that!" teased Emma, "We will have to go hungry!"

"On the subject of dinner, I hope you don't mind, but I have arranged for us to dine with Mr Hardwick and his wife, this evening... just a casual meal at their home."

Jacob was anxious as he awaited Emma's response. He regretted that he had forgotten to mention the engagement to Emma before they set off. He need not have worried: Emma found the fact that he was so keen to show her off to his new friends, charming. She had heard all about Phillip Hardwick from Jacob and had read many of his articles in the newspaper. She was also keen to meet the eminent journalist because she wondered if she too, could become a professional writer. Emma loved literature and had always kept a detailed journal. From an altruistic perspective, she imagined that writing articles for newspapers might be the best way she could help some of her erstwhile clients at the Repat Office.

"I could highlight their predicaments, the challenges they face... I could expose the inadequacies of the system. I could fight for a better system!" she enthused to herself.

On another tack, Emma dreamed of writing a novel one day, perhaps an epic, featuring a star-crossed-lovers style romance with an intriguing plot twist.

Emma suddenly realised that Jacob was looking at her with a puzzled frown and realised that she hadn't replied.

"Oh, sorry, Jacob, I was lost in my daydreams! Of course I would love to spend the evening with the Hardwicks. Do we need to dress for dinner?"

Emma started to mentally review her wardrobe, wondering if she had a suitable outfit amongst her meagre collection of clothes.

"No, don't be silly! Providing we don't capsize, what you are wearing is perfect! Like you!" said Jacob.

His voice caught as his eyes raked her form.

"Oh, you are so sweet!" laughed Emma, "...and no, let's not capsize!"

After a moment she added: "I might have to put my shoes back on for dinner, though!"

She picked up her feet and wiggled her bare toes at Jacob playfully. Jacob caught a flash of her long lean legs under her skirt and smiled appreciatively.

They basked in the warmth of the early Autumn sunshine and luxuriated in the ambience of boating on the Murray River.

After a moment Emma asked, "When are we expected for dinner?"

"It's very casual, as I said. Whenever we get there!" said Jacob lightly.

"What time is it now?" asked Emma thoughtfully.

Jacob hooked his pocket watch out from his fob pocket, "Just after three."

Emma was eyeing a cluster of willows and a small beach-like inlet.

"Do you think it might be nice to pull up in the shade of those willows for a while?" she asked innocently but with a coy smile on her face.

Jacob looked sharply at Emma to see if what he had thought he had heard in her voice matched her expectations.

"Why of course, Madame, your wish is my command!" he laughed.

He settled himself into a more active position on the bench seat, grasped both oars and manoeuvred their craft expertly towards the little beach. He ran it aground and shipped the oars. He picked up the tether rope and stepped over the side onto the silty sand. As Jacob hauled the boat more firmly up onto the beach, Emma giggled, as the motion caused her to rock wildly in her seat. Once the boat was secure, he steadied it with one hand and offered the other to assist Emma ashore. She gathered up the picnic blanket and the two towels they had brought along, before rising. She wobbled on the unstable surface of the boat, which made her giggle again, before clasping Jacob's hand and stepping out of the boat and joined him on the beach.

Electricity seemed to surge between their hands. Emma felt she was being drawn into the depths of Jacob's eyes. He drew her hand to his lips and kissed her fingers, so gently, like a butterfly landing.

"Pick a spot in the shade and lay out the blanket Emma," he said, his voice husky, "I will just tie up the boat, so the current doesn't take it, and we are left marooned!"

"I wouldn't mind spending my days on a desert island with you Jacob!" said Emma playfully, before hugging the blanket and towels to her chest and making her way up to the grassy bank under the willows.

She selected a spot where a fringe of foliage created a secluded arbour. She spread out the blanket and arranged the rolled-up towels as pillows, before stretching out on the makeshift alfresco day bed. She looked up to find Jacob standing over her with that look on his face, the one she had come to recognise...

Emma reached up a hand and drew Jacob down on to the blanket alongside her. Leaning on one elbow he reached a hand to her face, his fingers slipped up her cheek and ran through her hair before he tilted her head towards his. He swooped to meet her mouth with his, their lips were hungry for one another. A tide of mutual passion was unleashed.

As it turned out, Emma and Jacob were late for their dinner date with the Hardwicks. Phillip Hardwick smiled knowingly at his wife, Doris, when the pair arrived a little flustered and excessively cheerful. The Hardwicks' maid had shown the guests through the house and out into the garden where their hosts were relaxing in wicker chairs under a wisteria draped gazebo, The scene was lit by rose-gold twilight and long shadows stretched across the perfectly manicured lawn. Phillip Hardwick got to his feet and greeted the pair. He introduced Emma to his wife.

"What have you two been up to for the afternoon?" he asked with a mischievous grin.

Emma glanced at Jacob and blushed slightly as she said, "Boating on the Murray!"

"How was the fishing?" asked Hardwick of Jacob.

Jacob grinned broadly, as he caught the flash in his host's eyes, "Didn't cast a line… sightseeing, you know!"

"Phillip, you are incorrigible, where are your manners?" scolded Doris, "May we offer you both some refreshment? We are on our second Gin Fizz! Would you like to join us… I am sure Phillip would love to show you his skill with the shaker and swizzle stick!" Doris laughed.

The men went to the drinks trolley and organised refreshments whilst Doris swept Emma off into the far reaches of the garden to show off her roses. By the time the ladies returned, they were chatting like old friends. Doris had gleaned the entire tale of Jacob and Emma's unusual path to a relationship and Emma had decided that Doris' beauty was more than skin deep. Jacob and Hardwick were engrossed in a conversation about the latest details about Batson. They looked up as the ladies approached and each stood to pull out a seat for their partner. Emma sat down and found a tall, frost-beaded glass in front of her. A slice of lemon and a small sprig of rosemary floated amongst the shards of ice on the top of the drink.

"We are fortunate to have had an ice delivery today! A very chill Gin Fizz is delicious on a warm day, is it not, Emma?" enthused Doris.

Emma thanked her hosts and took a sip, savouring the aromatics and luxuriating as the cool fluid dcrosse her tongue.

"I overheard your comments as we approached," said Emma seriously, "I don't mean to be crass, but I am curious about the case, what is the latest on Batson?"

Hardwick glanced at his wife, ensuring that she was comfortable with the topic before saying, "I think Batson has completely run off the rails. He was obviously disturbed to even contemplate the atrocity he committed on a party of innocent picnickers, but now, he has launched an attack on fellow inmates and guards with an iron floor grate!"

"Oh, my goodness, did he injure ... or kill anyone?" gasped Emma.

"He broke a fellow's arm... another inmate. The guards subdued him... which you can interpret as knocked him out cold, and he has been in a padded cell for the past three days, in a straitjacket."

Jacob frowned, "Such severe methods of punishment would only create more derangement in an already disturbed mind," he observed.

"I agree. I often worry that prisons are not aiming to rehabilitate criminals, just make them worse," said Hardwick before adding grimly, "I have visited the gaol on occasion to interview an inmate, and it has occurred to me that there is little difference between prisoner and guard. Some of those guards are psychopaths!"

"So, if Batson continues to demonstrate aggressive, irrational behaviour, will they just convict him out of hand and hand him the death penalty... or is he likely to serve a life sentence?" asked Emma with a concerned furrow across her brow.

"What if he was just defending himself, the only way he knows how, against a predatory fellow inmate?" asked Doris, "I have heard from bits in the newspapers and from Phillip, that Batson is a bit of a simpleton who has been subjected to horrendous bullying. Prisons are dangerous places."

"Yes, that is the gist of what I heard whilst up in the Upper Murray, too, that his behaviour and violence is out of character. There is a fair bit of local sympathy for Batson, despite his actions of shooting up the picnic party. One of the big landholders down Bowna way has financed legal representation for him," said Jacob.

"Counsel will have his job cut out for him trying to defend such murderous intent at the picnic site and now, with this attack on a fellow inmate!" mused Hardwick.

"Well, I suppose there is a slight mitigation of his intent, from the perspective that by all accounts he was a crack shot, yet he only wounded his victims, other than poor Mr Sheppard," suggested Emma.

Jacob responded earnestly, "I don't think he meant to harm Mr Sheppard to the extent that he did... I fear Sheppard may have lost his balance as he climbed through the fence and intercepted the bullet meant as a warning shot... Well, that is my impression from Batson's statement."

"That would be hard to prove!" laughed Hardwick.

"I understand Batson was examined by doctors... including the Chair of Psychology at Sydney University," said Emma, "apparently Mr MacPherson consults on behalf of the Police... an Alienist, they call him!"

Emma cocked her head and smiled – she thought the term strange.

"Yes, Sir John MacPherson, has had a chat to Batson and the press! He initially considered Batson quite sane. He did wax lyrical on the topic of his favourite phrase: Trago-suggestion," said Hardwick.

He emphasised the term with a pompous tone in his voice.

Emma laughed at his dramatics and asked, "And what, pray tell, might that mean?"

"MacPherson has hypothesised that a person with a weak or damaged mind might be prone to being unduly influenced by the actions of others, the power of suggestion and copy their activities. He thinks it is particularly so of those with a criminal bent," said Hardwick solemnly.

"At the moment he has plenty of fuel for that fire," suggested Jacob, "Norman List in the Botanic Gardens, the maniac who was shooting people and burning down property in Goulburn and in addition, Mr

Batson. The headlines in The Truth, last Sunday was *State's terrible and tragic toll of Blood Lust Epidemic!"*

"His theory wobbles in relation to Batson, though. Several of his employers and associates vow and declare that the man is illiterate, and he has stated that he has never seen an article about List or heard a wireless report. He rarely socialises and is unlikely to have been influenced, if he had genuinely never heard of List," said Hardwick.

"Someone suggested that he might have been in bad company… Dear, remember your chat to the fellow from Burrowye?" Doris looked to Emma and said in a conspiratorial manner, "he said that Batson fell under the influence of a man called White, who worked for Houston's at Burrowye Station. He is a bad egg. 'Reads penny-awful novels about bushrangers and gunslingers and although not proven, he might have been involved with shooting up the manager's house and poisoning his dogs!"

"Heavens, the Upper Murray is supposed to be *God's Own Country*! Now you are making it sound like a haven for criminals!" said Emma with alarm.

Jacob laughed, "Settle down, Emma, there is a lot worse going on across your hometown of Melbourne: Squizzy Taylor, Push Gangs and the like! I think a few skeletons in the closets of country towns is inevitable…. Human nature, unfortunately. However, the Batson affair was the most excitement that Walwa and Jingellic has seen for years!"

"So, is Batson mad or methodically malevolent?" asked Emma, "Is he likely to have a noose, a long term in prison or a trip to an asylum in his future?"

"Nice turn of phrase!" grinned Hardwick, "*Methodically malevolent*, I might steal it as a headline!" Emma felt chuffed and wondered if she should ask Hardwick to mentor her career in journalism.

"None of the options presented to him are pretty!" sighed Doris, "I travelled to Mayday Hills with the Red Cross a few months ago. I was there to fetch a little baby born to a poor, deranged young woman who was an inmate. God knows who the father was... another inmate, an employee of the asylum..." Doris shuddered, "We took the baby to the nuns at Newtown Orphanage. The situation of being incarcerated in an asylum, the treatment of the inmates... it was all so appalling, so frightening!"

Doris gazed into space pensively for a few moments. Everyone was equally lost in thoughts of being trapped in an asylum.

"Beautiful gardens though," Doris added on a brighter note.

She looked towards Emma, who was now looking rather anxious.

"Oh, come on, this is a terrible conversation to have on such a beautiful afternoon! Let's go inside and have dinner and talk about more civilised topics! Go and choose a bottle of wine from the cellar, you two boys, and Emma and I will go and see how dinner is coming along and choose a record for the gramophone!"

She hooked an arm through Emma's, and they strolled off to the house.

CHAPTER 37

The doctor calls

Dr Woods had clashed with Governor Wicks before on the subject of prisoner management. Woods was committed to prison reform but felt that he was alone in his views in Albury, as none of his recommendations to the Department and specifically, to Governor Wicks had been adopted in the past eighteen months since he had become the gaol's visiting Government Medical Officer.

"Batson is fragile. He is out of his environment. He was suffering extreme exposure and sepsis when first presented and now you are torturing him with solitary confinement and sensory exclusion. He has suffered a severe impact to his skull during the altercation in the exercise yard and before he has a chance to recover, you have him back into solitary. This is inhumane!" fumed Woods.

Wicks gazed across the desk at the doctor impassively.

"This is not a hotel. The inmates are not normal people..."

Wicks was unable to finish his sentence as Woods cut in savagely, "Not normal? They are never going to be normal or rehabilitated if they are treated in a manner which further unhinges their minds!"

"Batson attacked another prisoner. He attacked my guards. He is dangerous. In situations like this with new prisoners, we need to exert our authority, demonstrate that bad behaviour carries consequences," Wick said emphatically.

"I can only see that this excessive treatment will shatter an already broken man," growled Woods.

"Do I have to remind you that Batson is here because he murdered a man and he shot at three others with intent," declared Wicks.

"So, you are judge and jury?" spat Woods, "Batson is here on remand. He is the accused, not the convicted. Granted, his charges are serious, and injuries inflicted on a fellow prisoner were severe, but he should be punished with confinement to his cell, not restrained in a straitjacket and a padded cell."

Wicks glared back at the doctor but said nothing.

"I will take this up the chain and make a complaint, if Batson is not presented to me for an assessment and then returned to his remand cell, without a straitjacket," warned Woods.

It was Woods's turn to glare. The two men faced off at one another.

"Very well, I will have the guards return him to his cell. Go and see him there, if you wish. He will be excluded from work details, the exercise yard and dining hall for a week. Solitary in his cell," growled Wicks.

The doctor considered it to be a win.

"Good day, Governor, I will send a report on my findings."

Wicks nodded and muttered "Good day," before he returned to the paperwork on his desk.

Woods saw himself out of the office.

Woods went to the infirmary and collected his doctors' bag.

"They won't let you take a bag into the cell," advised the infirmary attendant who was mopping the floor.

"Bugger, of course, they won't!" said Woods with a sigh of frustration.

Woods slammed down his bag and took some pills from a vial and slipped them into an envelope. He also selected a small vial of liquid medication. He put the medication and his notebook in his jacket pocket and set off towards the cells. By the time he arrived at the remand cell block, Batson had been reinstated in his cell. The guards were curt and disrespectful to Woods but let him into Batson's cell to review his patient.

Batson stood at the back of the cell as the doctor entered. He looked haunted and wild eyed.

"Sit down, Claude," said Woods calmly.

The man slumped onto the bed and sat hunched over.

"The dark, hate the dark, please, please … not again…" muttered Batson.

"I have done what I can, Claude. You must behave well. They are going to keep you on your own for a few days, so nobody will bother you."

Woods examined the man from a distance and after a moment he concluded that the man was already broken.

"Let me have a look at you. Has the wound on your head been stirred up?" asked the doctor gently.

He approached Batson and put a hand on his shoulder. Batson flinched.

"It is alright now, Claude, let me look at your head," murmured Woods.

Batson swung his face to look up at the doctor, he appeared startled, his eyes skittered across the doctor's face and then he dropped his head again. The bandage was grubby and loose, so Woods began to gently remove it from the prisoner's head. He looked at the matted mess which obscured the wound.

"The injury is no longer bleeding, and the scab is holding the wound closed. Don't pick at it, mind. When they let you go for a shower, just let the water loosen the scab," Woods advised, before continuing, "How are you otherwise, Claude?"

"Hurts…. Here," Batson screwed up his eyes and held his forehead, "Tired…. Don't let them… no dark!"

Woods was concerned; sensory deprivation had wreaked havoc with Batson's fragile psyche. He looked Batson in the eyes and saw dilated pupils and an inability to meet and maintain eye contact.

"Here, Claude, I have some medicine for you. Take two of these," he handed Batson the two pills and the mug of water he had brought in with him. Batson obediently downed the pills.

"And drink this," he checked the volume in the vial and handed it over to Batson.

Again, Batson took the medication.

"Now, I want you to sleep it off, I will be back to check on you tomorrow," the doctor said and smiled gently at the tormented man.

Batson nodded morosely. Woods left the cell with a deep sense of foreboding.

CHAPTER 38

Evidence and egos

Sergeant Kersley examined the handgun which had been sent down to Albury Police Station by the Drummond brothers. It had arrived at a fortunate moment, since Kersley was in the process of reviewing the items of evidence, depositions and statements and overall, satisfying himself that the prosecution was prepared for the next court hearing in relation to the matter of Claude Batson vs the Crown.

"Do we have any clue if this is the handgun with which Batson threatened the Emerson lad?" Kersley asked Detective Cleaver.

"Batson told Constable Jolly where it was hidden, so we can assume it is one and the same," suggested Cleaver.

"We shall have to call Emerson in and see what he thinks," said Kersley thoughtfully as he slid the handgun back into its labelled bag. He checked to ensure the evidence coding matched the evidence log.

"Do we have any news on the three hospitalised victims? Will they be ready for a court appearance on 30 March?" asked Kersley.

"I enquired yesterday and was informed by the doctor in charge that although all were significantly injured, they are now on the mend. There was some concern that Charles Gainer might have to lose his leg, but a consultant arrived from Melbourne this week and there seems to be a more positive slant on his progress, although they expect him to be a patient for months and permanently lame. Richard King has had no further complications and is sitting up in a chair but still not able to walk far because he is short on breath. So, those two will not be in court in person. William McGrath, on the other hand, is a war horse! He has a splint on his wrist to support the fractures but was discharged from hospital on Monday, 8 March. He will be available for the hearing," reported Cleaver.

"Do we have any loose ends, Detective?" asked Kersley.

"The only aspect, which is uncertain, would appear to be Batson. He has been causing some trouble in the Albury Gaol. The warders have had him in solitary confinement. Dr Woods asked if you might return his telephone call to discuss Batson's treatment."

Kersley looked sharply at Cleaver.

"Do you think Batson is playing the *on the grounds of insanity* card?" he asked.

Cleaver shrugged.

Kersley picked up the telephone on his desk and then almost immediately, replaced the handset in the cradle.

"I think we might be best going to Dr Woods' office in person," he said to Cleaver.

The two officers gathered their hats and stepped out of the police station. They made their way up Dean Street on foot. It was a pleasant Autumn afternoon, and it wasn't far to Dr Woods' rooms at Valetta House on Swift Street.

Fortunately, Woods was in his office completing some paperwork when Cleaver and Kersley found their way to his door.

"Good afternoon, Doctor, we wondered if we might have a word?" announced Kersley as he stepped into the office.

"I am glad you dropped by; I was about to telephone your office," said Dr Woods with a serious expression.

He gestured that the police officers take a seat. Cleaver shut the door before sitting.

"Please, Doctor, you go ahead - what do you have to report?" Kersley suggested.

"As you are aware, I have been monitoring Claude Batson since his admission to the Albury Gaol. Initially it was in relation to a concurrent case of sepsis and exposure and obviously, the wounds to his feet. More recently, I have been trying to mediate on his behalf," said Woods with a frustrated expression.

"How so, Doctor?" asked Cleaver.

"If the man wasn't deranged on admission, he will be shortly! The treatment he is receiving as a remand prisoner is inhumane!" spat Woods.

Woods was usually a mild-mannered man, but today, he was fired up with the passion of a crusader. His pale face was flushed with emotion and his moustache seemed to bristle.

"Go on," encouraged Kersley.

"Wicks has had Batson trussed up in a straitjacket and confined to a padded cell, excluded from light and sound. Sensory deprivation it is called .... Chinese torture!" said Woods.

"I understand that Batson attacked a fellow prisoner and inflicted a very serious injury..." Kersley tried to suggest.

"But what initiated the incident? Maybe Batson felt under threat? Either way, the degree of punishment was excessive for a first offence. Since he has been tortured in this manner, Batson's behaviour has changed markedly. Sometimes he is practically incoherent - he seems terrified of the dark, claustrophobic!" Woods said in a frustrated tone.

"I see," said Cleaver looking to Kersley, "In your opinion, Dr Woods, do you think this behaviour is genuine? Have you considered that Batson may have decided that an asylum is the better option than the noose or a lifetime of incarceration?"

Woods was annoyed, "Batson is no actor, Sir. This treatment is designed to unhinge a prisoner. It has been successful!"

"We may have to get Sir John MacPherson back to assess Batson. In the meantime, what would you suggest we do to get Batson to trial? It would be no comfort to Mrs Sheppard if her husband's killer is not brought to justice," said Kersley carefully.

"Have you been to an asylum, Sergeant Kersley? It is no picnic..." Woods looked embarrassed that he chosen such a poor analogy.

"I mean, the dehumanising treatment in most criminal asylums is far worse than Wicks' treatment of prisoners. That being said, I would hope that pressure can be brought to bear to improve the treatment of all prisoners in Albury Gaol," declared Woods.

"So, what do you suggest in relation to Batson, Doctor?" asked Cleaver manoeuvring the conversation away from prison reform and back to the accused.

"Certainly, no straitjacket and no padded cell," said Woods emphatically, "In addition, he needs exercise in the sunshine, a worthwhile task to distract him and a small amount of supervised social interaction."

"Can this be achieved at the Gaol?" asked Kersley carefully.

"I believe so. Batson was a well-behaved, compliant prisoner before the incident. If you can assist me to convince Governor Wicks of the necessity to ensure Batson is exercised on his own, provided with a low-risk task in the work details and then kept in the remand cell on his own, I am sure he will revert and be suitable to stand trial."

"Very well, sounds reasonable. Perhaps you might like to accompany us up to the Gaol and we can review Batson and talk to Wicks," suggested Kersley.

"We will have to muster Colonel Wilkinson, so that Batson has legal representation when we interview him," advised Cleaver, I will just call his rooms, if you agree, Sergeant Kersley?"

Kersley nodded and Cleaver asked to use the telephone on Woods' desk.

By the time arrangements had been made, it was late afternoon. The police officers, Batson's legal representative and Doctor Woods crowded into the Governor of Albury Gaol's office. Wicks was curt and annoyed that his management of prisoners was being called into question.

"As I have advised Doctor Woods, Albury Gaol is not a hotel. Inmates are often dangerous felons, and safety of my officers is my primary concern. If an incident occurs, punishment must be swift and effective," he advised in a bored voice.

"Punishment is one thing, torture is entirely different, Governor Wicks," stated Woods bluntly.

Kersley looked at Woods and said, "One moment, Doctor, I understand your point of view," he swivelled his gaze to Wicks, "I understand too, that Batson has been managed in a manner that it has impacted negatively upon his mental state. He may now be in a condition judged unsuitable to stand trial. He might escape justice!"

Colonel Wilkinson looked shocked, "I spoke to Batson on Friday, and have another appointment with him tomorrow. When we last spoke, I felt he was communicative and sound. In what condition is he now?"

"Perhaps, we should go and find out," suggested Kersley darkly.

"Have Batson brought to the interview room, and we will review his condition and report back with our recommendations," he added to Wicks.

Wicks frowned at the group, "You don't have the authority to advise me on how to manage prisoners under my care ..."

"Care?" spat Woods and laughed hoarsely.

"If the prisoner is too much for you to handle, Wicks, I shall have him transferred to another facility," said Kersley tersely.

Batson was brought into the interview room. He was manacled and a chain around his waist connected to the manacles to further restrict his hands. He shuffled into the room. He didn't make eye contact. He was dishevelled, pale and when his eyes flitted around the room, they were wild and unnervingly unseeing.

"Take a seat, Claude," said Doctor Woods in his calm voice.

Batson's eyes flicked to Woods' face and connected for a moment. He settled into the indicated chair and rested his hands on the table in front of him. One guard stood immediately behind him, the other left the interview room but hovered near the observation window.

The men studied Batson; he shifted uncomfortably as if he felt their eyes prickling along his flesh.

"Tell me Ba..., Claude," asked Cleaver quietly, "how are you holding up?"

As if shocked by the kindly tone, Batson's eyes swept up to meet the detective's eyes. He held the gaze, and the observers could see that he struggled to find an answer.

After a prolonged pause he offered, "Awright....as long as they don't truss me up and throw me in the dark... can't do the dark..., please!"

The sentence ended in a whine and his eyes skittered around the faces, before settling on Woods, "Please can you tell the guv'nor? Please?" Batson pleaded.

Wilkinson spoke for the first time, "Claude, I understand that you committed a violent act in the exercise yard... 'Hurt a fellow prisoner."

Batson looked confused. He thought about the statement and then dropped his head and said, simply, "Dunno."

Woods attempted to reassure Batson, "Look Claude, if you can do as you are asked, and do not, under any circumstances, inflict harm on anyone, Governor Wicks has assured me that, although you will be confined to your cell, he will allow an exercise period ... on your own. And a job to keep your mind off things. How does that sound?"

Batson shook his head. His lank dark hair swayed as a mass, from side to side. His fingers flexed and then steepled, repetitively and his body jiggled.

Kersley and Cleaver frowned at one another.

"We did come here today to ask you about something, Claude," said Kersley, "I have shown this photograph to your solicitor, Mr Wilkinson, and he has approved that I show it to you now."

Batson stopped his repetitive movement and looked up with inter-est.

"I have been told that you described where you had hidden this object to Senior Constable Bunworth and Constable Jolly when you were arrested. It has subsequently been recovered, and we have it in police custody. Please can you look at this picture and tell me if you recognise it."

Kersley took a photograph from his satchel and pushed it across the table. Batson poked at it with a finger, sliding the photograph around on the table so that he could see it better. He examined it silently. After a few moments, Cleaver asked quietly, "Do you recognise it, Claude"

"It's a pistol!" said Batson eagerly.

"Very good," said Cleaver, "Is it yours?"

"It's a Webley" advised Batson.

"Good, but is it yours?" said Cleaver, his patience evaporating.

"It is a picture!" said Batson with cunning, "I don't own any pictures."

"If we were to show you the object in that picture, would you recognise it?" persisted Kersley.

"Maybe, if it were mine," agreed Batson.

"So, you are saying that you owned such a handgun," asked Cleaver.

"No," Batson shook his head.

Kersley took another tack, "When you met with young Percy Emerson last Tuesday morning, you threatened him with a handgun."

Batson gazed at Kersley with a vacant expression, Kersley pressed on, "Was it a model of handgun such as this in the photograph?"

Batson thought a while and then said, "I don't remember threatening Emerson. He and me are mates."

Kersley could see the interview was going nowhere, but he was a bit more encouraged that Batson was responding.

"Fair enough Claude, we will show you the actual object in court when you are next called. In the meantime, we will see if Emerson recognises it, too. I reiterate what Dr Woods has advised - behave. No violent outbursts and we will ensure that you are treated fairly and protected from interference from other prisoners," said Kersley.

Batson looked up sharply, roused from his thoughts, "No trussing? No darkness? Please, no dark! The rabbits will get me!"

The guard behind Batson grinned, the others looked alarmed.

Rabbit pairs awaiting collection by the Rabbitoh - Arnold Playle, Man from Snowy River Museum

The Rabbitoh - Arnold Playle collection, Man from Snowy River Museum.

Chapter 39

A Delivery

Albert knocked on Emma's door and excitedly announced, "Here we go! Minnie is having the baby!"

Emma leapt out of bed in a fluster; she wasn't sure if she was equipped to be assistant midwife.

"What do I know about birthing a baby!" she thought to herself, "Maybe I will just get the children ready for school and shoo them away,"

She didn't even know what time it was.

She drew the curtains and discovered that the garden was bathed in inky blackness.

"Heavens, it's probably the middle of the night!"

Emma pulled on the clothes she had discarded on the chair the night before... or was it the same night... She hurried out into the hall and padded up to Minnie and Albert's room, passed the sleeping children's rooms. She cautiously peered in at the door to see Minnie leaning on a chair, her hand in the small of her back, panting.

"Oh, Minnie, what do I do? What do you need?" Emma could hear the panic in her own voice.

Minnie looked up and grinned in a lopsided fashion.

"It is time for women's work, Lass!" she announced cheerfully.

Another contraction powered through her frame and Minnie winced and resumed her position breathing through the pain stoically.

When she was able to talk again, she said quietly, "Towels, get towels and spread them over the bed. Put a pot of water on to boil..."

"What's the water for?" asked Emma as she hastened to spread the towels, which she found atop the blanket box at the foot of the bed.

"No idea... haven't had to use any to date, but the midwife always asks that the kettle be boiled!" Minnie grinned, trying to dispel Emma's obvious fear.

"Where is Albert?" asked Emma as she glanced around the room.

"He is off, riding for the midwife - she doesn't have a telephone. Mrs Karnatz will be here in a jiffy!"

After a pause and another painful contraction, Minnie groaned, "I hope that her bloody horse can fly!"

"Oh Minnie!" wailed Emma, feeling entirely inadequate.

"Everything will be fine!" assured Minnie, "I have done this before! I am a good ol' cow. I haven't been culled yet!"

Emma chuckled at Minnie's attempt at humour at such a dire moment.

"Just remember though, I haven't done this before!" said Emma quietly.

"Just peep in at the bairns and make sure they are still asleep. If they wake, it will be Bedlam!" said Minnie.

Emma laughed, "They were still fast asleep when I came down the hall, but I will check as I go to the kitchen for that pot of boiled water of unknown purpose!"

By the time Emma returned to Minnie's room, she was lying on top of the bedclothes on the layer of towels. Her night dress was hitched up a little and Emma could see her legs were slick with fluid.

"Not to worry, Emma, this little one is just getting itself ready for the world!" said Minnie, her voice tight.

Emma fetched another towel and tenderly wiped Minnie's legs clean and plumped a pillow under her head.

"Oh Emma, darling, just rub my back under my ribs, down to my bottom, it's all tight and ..." Minnie groaned quietly as she rolled onto her side.

Emma did as she was asked and prayed for Minnie, prayed for the baby and most of all, she prayed the midwife would come soon.

The room was warm, and Minnie's face was flushed pink and bathed in sweat.

"Shall I open window? Get a glass of water?" offered Emma.

"No, not the window," she gave Emma a dark superstitious look, "You never know what might come in!"

Emma had no idea what Minnie meant but shuddered involuntarily. She kept kneading Minnie's back and humming in what she hoped sounded like an encouraging manner. She really had no idea.

Emma rolled over awkwardly and slipped her legs over the side of the bed; Emma gave her a hand and helped her to her feet.

"I just have to..." Minnie tried to talk, tried to reassure Emma, but she was wracked with pain.

She stood, stretched her spine and arms up and then turned again to lean over the bed. She bunched her fists into the bedclothes as she leant on her elbows and groaned in a primal fashion.

"He's coming..." Minnie, groaned.

The door burst open, and an older woman bustled in. Her grey hair was tousled and windswept, indicative of the speed at which she had ridden. She carried a small leather bag which she placed on the bedside table.

"Hello, my dear, we meet again," said Mrs Karnatz in a heavily accented but kindly voice.

"We will all meet this little fighter in a minute," grunted Minnie.

Mrs Karnatz squatted and lifted Minnie's nightdress, "Yes, you are right! A towel... now, girl!" she snapped at Emma.

Emma obeyed and handed Mrs Karnatz a blue towel with pink roses carefully embroidered on the hem. Emma was concentrating on the towel, because Minnie's contortions and groans were terrifying to the young woman.

A protracted groan and gush of fluid heralded the arrival of another Drummond. Mrs Karnatz delivered the baby expertly and had him wrapped in the towel before Minnie's legs collapsed. Emma helped Minnie back up onto the bed and the excited mother was reaching for her baby before she was properly settled.

"A boy," announced Mrs Karnatz.

"I knew it!" laughed Minnie, hugging her baby to her breast and kissing him gently on his fuzzy head.

Emma gazed at the scene in awe. She had never experienced anything quite like it before. Emotions of terror, exhilaration and love had all cascaded through her consciousness in rapid succession, she felt exhausted. She could only guess how Minnie felt. Emma moved towards the bed and looked down on the little baby - so little, wrinkled, waxy and smeared with blood... and blue.

Emma shot a look at the midwife and glanced back at her aunt. Minnie was besotted. Mrs Karnatz looked mildly concerned.

"Here, Minnie, give me the child a moment!" said Mrs Karnatz briskly as she reached for the newborn.

Mrs Karnatz spun around, her body obscuring Minnie's view of the baby. She laid the baby over her forearm face down and slapped him deftly between the shoulder blades, before taking the corner of the towel and swabbing his nostrils. She opened his mouth and with her little finger, she swiped across his tongue, dragging out mucous and fluid. She mopped his face and gave him another pat on the back. The baby announced his displeasure at the rough treatment with a howl and the three women all grinned at one another. The baby's cheeks flushed pink and his little, now pink, fists screwed up in rage.

"Now, now you little monster," crooned Mrs Karnatz and handed the baby back to his mother.

The door burst open, and first, Albert peered around the jamb to enquire if he could come in, and then, before he could halt the avalanche, the children all rushed in to meet their new little brother.

Emma was so relieved, so exhilarated, all she could do was laugh.
"I think we all need a cup of tea, now!" she announced.
She had finally figured why she had to boil water.

CHAPTER 40

Descent into madness

The telephone trilled on Kersley's desk. He stretched out a hand and lifted the receiver to his ear, whilst reading through the document on his desk. Before he could announce himself, an anxious voice broke into his thoughts.

"Sergeant Kersley? Governor Wicks here. It's about Batson, Sir. He has been confined to a straitjacket for the past ten days, now. Doctor Woods is badgering me to have him released but invariably once out of restraints, Batson lashes out."

"I thought that this would be the case, Mr Wicks," said Kersley solemnly, "Batson, was a very fractured man when I last clapped eyes on him."

Wicks seemed rattled; he rushed to deliver more evidence as to Batson's deterioration.

"He has lucid moments, but when embroiled by rage he has the strength of ten men. He has hurled bunks and buckets at my guards, and it now takes four guards to restrain him. Between rages he is passive, but more often than not, he is muttering about rabbits and revenge, working himself up to violence."

Kersley sighed, and advised, "The Governor General has finally authorised Batson's transfer to Long Bay Penitentiary. He will be transported in the morning. Please have him ready for, I believe, the 7am train. Long Bay is sending specifically trained and armed guards to facilitate his transfer."

"When do we expect to see them?" asked Wicks.

Kersley checked his notes and replied, "I believe they arrived in Albury this afternoon. I will direct Doctor Woods to prescribe a sedative to make Batson more compliant and to prepare him for transport. Thank you, Mr Wicks."

Kersley put the telephone receiver back in its cradle and put his head in his hands. He was torn between conflicting sentiments: pity for Batson that the system had broken him; disquiet on behalf of the surviving victims of the Jingellic Sniper that they might never be convinced that the perpetrator had been brought to justice, and deep concern that the culture in Albury Gaol was such that the guards were no better that the felons.

Doctor Woods was disappointed that he had been unable to make Batson's period in remand more comfortable. He was frustrated that the medication available to him could not moderate the prisoner's behaviour sufficiently and, in the end, he had been forced to agree to the restraints being applied to Batson for the safety of the guards. With an increasing sense of desperation, he had continued to advocate for Batson. He had saved him from the padded cell and darkness and when Batson refused to eat, Woods had resorted to inserting a naso-gastric tube and providing Batson with sustenance and fluid. This situation created a conflict in his beliefs – was Batson better off dead, rather than having to endure this hellish existence – a scenario that Woods was forced to observe. Woods debated capital punishment versus life imprisonment in his head, but he failed to assuage his reservations either way. He kept reminding himself that Batson seemed to have been convicted without trial.

Sergeant Kersley advised Dr Woods that his patient was to be transferred. Woods was relieved to discharge Batson to the care of the physician at Long Bay. He was desperate to try and rid his conscience of the horror of his daily observations of the man. He knew now that Batson wouldn't stand trial, and that he would be committed to a life sentence to an asylum. Woods was confident that Sir John MacPherson would sign the warrant to transfer Batson to an asylum for the criminally insane.

"He will certainly be punished for his crimes," thought Woods as his mind's eye wandered through the horrific scenes of asylums he had been forced to visit earlier in his career.

Woods was escorted to Batson's cell. He stood at the door and looked in at the wasted man in front of him. The guards had shaved Batson's head because his lank hair had become matted with a foetid mix of faeces and food. Scars and bruises were stark against his pallid pate. Some injuries were self-inflicted, but Woods was convinced that most were administered by the ever-over-zealous prison guards. The straitjacket in which Batson was restrained was equally stained and rank. He sat on the edge of his bunk; his head bowed.

"Claude," called Woods quietly, "Claude, I have come to give you some medicine, some food too, if you will."

Batson was unmoved.

"Claude, I am sorry it has turned out this way for you."

The guards behind the physician snorted.

Woods moved closer towards Batson. He carried a tray with a bowl of food, a spoon and tin cup of water. He placed the tray on the chair and tried again.

"Claude, you are going on a train ride to Sydney. It is a long journey; you need to eat. Here, let me help you."

Woods offered the spoon to Batson. The man looked up suddenly. He had tears in his eyes. He stubbornly held his mouth shut.

Woods tried again, "Come along, Claude, I am sure the guards will not be as accommodating as I, offering you food."

He pressed the spoon against Batson's lips.

Batson looked again at Woods, his expression was stark, his eyes haunted.

"Thank you," he muttered and opened his mouth for the food.

The guards were impatient and grumbled that they still had to get Batson showered, dressed and restrained in a fresh straitjacket before the transport arrived.

Woods ignored the guards and doggedly fed Batson. He held the cup of water to Batson's lips so that he could drink his fill and finally persuaded Batson to take a swig from a vial of laudanum. Woods fervently hoped the drug would provide Batson with an escape from the dreadful reality of his situation.

"Goodbye Claude, I am truly sorry your life has been so hard," he whispered to the wretched form that sat in front of him.

On the 30 March 1924, Claude Valentine Batson was transported from Albury Gaol to Long Bay Penitentiary. He was a guest of the facility for thirteen days before being transferred to Morisset Mental Asylum. On the 17 April 1924, after a rigorous assessment by a panel of criminal psychologists, Batson was declared criminally insane and unfit to stand trial. All charges against him were dropped.

Claude Batson lived out the rest of his life in an asylum and died in Morisset Mental Hospital in Wyong, NSW, aged 70 years, in 1971.

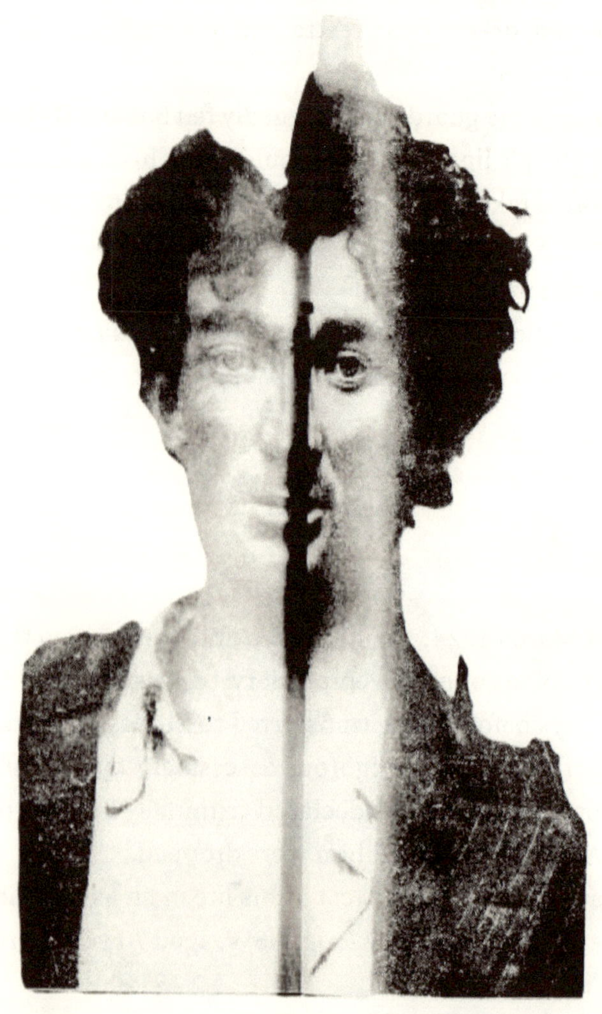

Claude Valentine Batson - Trove, National Library of Australia

So much had happened in such a short time... Emma's head spun when she thought about it. The violence and tragedy of the Botanic Gardens shooting had propelled her into the orbit of Jacob Miller. A holiday in the Upper Murray provided an opportunity to take the relationship so much further, but it was against a background of yet another picnic tragedy. Was this echoing theme a dark omen for a continued relationship with the man with whom she was now so entirely smitten?

Emma shook her head with frustration, and she flung herself down on the bed, staring up at the ceiling and sighing in a dramatically tortured fashion. The sudden upheaval on the bed caused her suitcase to slam shut and there was a bang as her hairbrush flipped off the bed and hit the floorboards.

"Everything all right, Dear?" came a soft voice from the doorway.

Emma rolled over and surveyed her Aunt Minnie solemnly.

"I am put out and perplexed!" Emma declared with a wan smile.

"Oh? Perhaps I can help? Let's go and have a cup of tea... Albert has the children occupied and the little one is asleep, so we have time and privacy. Come on!" Minnie smiled conspiratorially.

In the kitchen, with the obligatory cup of tea at hand, Minnie gazed sympathetically across the table at her niece.

"What's bothering you, Emma?" she asked quietly.

Emma tried to order her thoughts. She picked at the corner of the lace doily on the table and sighed again, although less dramatically this time.

"Do you think I am silly? Have I fallen for Jacob too fast?" she whispered.

Minnie's eyes twinkled and her smile was soft and comforting.

"Oh Emma, my love, you are far from silly! You are a sensible and organised young woman with a heart of gold!" said Minnie vehemently, "Your feelings for a young man, in this case, Jacob, are not something you can control. You two obviously have a deep connection with one another. He is a dependable, gallant and handsome young man. Let your story tell itself!"

Emma smiled, the warmth and glow of rosy emotions lit her eyes.

"So, my plan to go home, pack up my goods and chattels, quit the lease with my landlady, hand in my resignation with the Repat Department and return to Albury to take up a cadetship with The Banner... it isn't just a rash decision?" asked Emma.

"If you put it like that, it sounds like a very solid plan to further your career!" encouraged Minnie.

"And if I add to the mix: commence a serious relationship with Jacob Miller?" asked Emma hesitantly.

"Well, because you have your ducks in a row, you are independent of Jacob. So, your relationship has room to grow!" Minnie stretched out a hand and squeezed Emma's, "You have covered everything, Emma! Propriety by arranging lodgings in a respectable home in Albury, the cadetship will provide a regular income, and you have created the ideal environment to foster a meaningful, respectful and loving relationship with Jacob."

"But it is all so quick... a complete change in the direction of my life in just a few weeks!" cried Emma, gazing at her aunt with worried eyes.

"Seize the day, Emma! Take the opportunity in both hands. We are in an age when women have so much more opportunity, ... you are living proof! And love... well, hearts have a mind of their own! If it is meant to be between yourself and Jacob, then you are certainly giving the relationship the best chance!" said Minnie emphatically.

"Do you think my family will be shocked?" asked Emma carefully.

Minnie laughed and hid a slightly guilty look, as the memory of her last conversation with her sister, Emma's mother, flitted across her mind. They had been discussing Emma's blooming relationship, and they had concluded that Emma had a very sensible choice in friends... and lovers.

"Your family loves you, Emma. They will want what is best for you! If this is the path that you choose, they will be happy and supportive," said Minnie reassuringly.

Minnie squeezed Emma's hand again, cocked her head to one side and smiled at her warmly.

"Anyway, they will meet Jacob in the next few days and welcome him to the family!" she added.

"You make it sound like we are engaged to be married!" laughed Emma.

"I am quite sure it won't be long!" said Minnie firmly.

Emma smiled and took a sip of her tea, whilst regarding her aunt over the rim of the cup. Her expression became serious.

"You are a bit spiritual, Minnie... what about the darkness behind our relationship... the fact that two picnic shootings have been the backdrop to our romance? Will the darkness creep in?" asked Emma fearfully.

Minnie considered the question carefully before leaning over and looking in Emma's teacup.

"Finish your tea, Dear, swirl it around and I will read the leaves for you!" said Minnie brightly.

Minnie then placed both palms flat on the tabletop and adopted a meditative pose. Her eyes were half closed; she was still and focussed.

Emma did as she was told. She looked at the bottom of her cup - the tea leaves were scattered in no discernible shape or pattern. She pushed her cup towards Minnie.

Minnie took the cup, held it in both hands, breathed over the rim and then studied the contents for a few minutes.

Emma fidgeted nervously. She wasn't sure she believed in her aunt's hocus-pocus, but she was willing to try anything to soothe her indecision.

After what seemed to Emma, to be an eternity, Minnie looked up, met Emma's eyes and beamed.

"Oh Emma... you have absolutely nothing to worry about! There is so much positivity in your future!"

Emma grinned happily and was about to ask for details, but Minnie's expression became stern, and she cautioned, "Nothing is ever assured though, so, no complacency, mind, and remember that everything in life needs effort... But in the short term, everything is rosy! Go and finish your packing! Albert will be back soon and then you will be off to Albury!"

Emma was relieved, she wanted to believe. She hopped up, hugged her aunt and rushed off to her room to pack. She didn't notice the cloud that scudded briefly across her aunt's face. There was a wisp of smoke on the horizon for Emma, but Minnie was unable to divine the details.

"Best that you don't know, my Love," she murmured to herself.

❧

THE END

THE FACTS ....

Walwa and Jingellic

The *Australian City Directories and Almanac (1845-1948)* published directions to get to Jingellic and Walwa Creek. (Walwa Creek was the former name of Walwa before it was gazetted as a township in the early 1900's.) The directory noted that the journey to Walwa Creek from Melbourne entailed a train trip of 187 miles to Wodonga, followed by a coach trip of 67 miles to Jingellic and a further 3 miles to Walwa Creek. In this worthy tome Jingellic was noted as being in Shire of Towong, Parish of Jingellic (Often spelt Jinjellic), County of Benambra, State of Victoria. So, the community of- and the geography of the hamlet of Jingellic spanned two states!

The Batson Family Tree:

William Batson (Senior) married Bridget "Biddie" (Murphy) Batson (Bridget died in 1912 and is buried in Walwa Cemetery). Their progeny included Edward A-, William J- (William Batson was a surveyor whose name appears on many Towong Shire locality maps), Thomas H-, James Valentine-, (Bankrupt in August 1923 in Holbrook), Anne J-, Bridget W-, Agnes and Florence.

Florence Batson (1887 - 1950; buried in Bowna) had a brief relationship with Dennis Vincent Kennedy and she fell pregnant with Claude Valentine Batson, born in 1900. Kennedy abandoned Florence and she later married Friedrich C Schreiber in 1902.

Claude Denis Valentine Batson – AKA "Dilly", "Jest" or sometimes "Batty" was born on 29 August 1900 in Albury, NSW. Florence was a young, single woman living in Bowna. She was just 18 years old when Claude was born.

After Kennedy and Florence separated, he went on to have an unsettled life: Kennedy was committed to an asylum in 1902 (24/1/1902 – 31/10/1902). The author discovered two warrants were issued against Kennedy for wife desertion (he was married for just a year in 1908 to Margaret Spillane, 28 years his senior) and there was possibly another case of wife desertion in 1925, in Hay. He served in the AIF in France in 1916 but went AWOL. He was listed as being on charges as a deserter on 10 February 1916. Later, he was committed to an asylum in Goulburn in in 1924, where he died, aged 71, in 1948.

It appears that Florence failed to bond with young Claude. It may have been because he was an embarrassment being a child born out of wedlock, an unwanted pregnancy to a man who had deserted her or who had perhaps, assaulted her. Furthermore, Reginald Valentine Batson, cousin to Claude, stated that Batson was a particularly sickly child so, perhaps Florence was just unable to cope.

Florence married Friedrich C Schreiber in 1902, and they welcomed a daughter, Stella Florence Schreiber on 29 July 1902. Florence went on to have a tribe of children, a total of four girls and seven boys between 1900 and 1923.

Claude was farmed out to a relative in Germanton at an early point in his life as his mother became busy with children born of her new relationship. The spinster aunt, Miss Hitchcock, sent young Claude to school but he was neither compliant, nor interested in an education, and soon spent most of his youth as a truant. His older cousins went to school with him in Germanton (which was renamed Holbrook soon after WWI) His cousins were Reginald and Charles Batson. One of the Bryant girls also remembered Claude Batson as a classmate and considered him to be a "sneaky little brat."

Batson's days as a truant were spent roaming the bush, where he was very comfortable and he became adept at rabbit trapping and bush craft. He apparently suffered a Red Belly Black snake bite as a child, most likely a dry bite, which caused him to hate, but not fear snakes. He and his young friends were inspired by stories of bushrangers and played around Morgan's Lookout, the bushranger's hide-out in the hills West of Holbrook. This was a favourite spot for the children to explore. The boys reenacted the stories of *Mad Dog* Morgan and Ned Kelly's gang from the era of bushrangers in the late 19th Century. A particularly favourite scenario was that of the ambush of Constable Maginnity: Morgan shot the Constable and left him for dead in the bush between Tumbarumba and Holbrook. There were numerous tales of Ned Kelly in Walwa – it was rumoured that the Kelly gang was harboured by Eliza Dunn at the Jingellic Wine Shanty (Redbank Hotel) in the 1880's. Another rumour linked the Coughlans of Walwa Creek with prototypes of Ned's armour.

Eliza Dunn's Redbank Hotel - State Library Victoria

Batson was heard to encourage a friend to accompany him to go "Bush ranging" in 1919. This friend may well have been "Dickie" Richard/Raymond White AKA Edgar Raymond Joseph Farrell, as the two had some association soon after White's arrival in the Upper Murray. (Refer to Janice Newnham's book *White Lies – Where There Is Smoke*)

Superintendent SI Rootes (ex-Officer In Charge of Tumbarumba Police Station) reported that Batson's uncle was involved in a horse stealing case in the 1880's and was sentenced to serve time in the Tumbarumba gaol. His wife smuggled tools into the gaol during a visit, and he used them to remove the bolts of the gaol door, and he escaped for a short time before being recaptured under arms. Perhaps Batson looked up to his uncle in much the same way he viewed his bushranger heroes.

Batson remained with his aunt in Holbrook for five years. Miss Hitchcock described Batson as an honest lad, but he was frequently bullied by his peers, and he would hold grudges and take his revenge in a determined fashion on all those who crossed him. When Batson was 16, Miss Hitchcock reported Batson to the Tumbarumba policeman, Sergeant Graham. Details of his misdemeanour are unclear, but soon afterwards, the lad left to find work in the Walwa-Jingellic district. Miss Hitchcock stated that Batson was illiterate, and she doubted the claim made by police, that he had written the note found in Barber's house. She was also dismissive of the claim on the grounds that Batson had no affection for his mother, so why would he have addressed the letter to "Mother dear."

As a young man, Batson was employed by farmers in the Walwa district as a dairy hand, general labourer and rabbit trapper. He had strong associations with Charles and Ruth Barber (they had known one another for 6 years). Batson was employed by Charles Barber for a few years prior to 1922 and then intermittently since September 1923. Ruth had a soft spot for the troubled lad and would provide him with meals and short-term accommodation long after his employment on their property was over. Batson completed odd jobs for the Barbers in the years preceding the picnic shooting. In October 1923, Batson had asked Barber to consider a share farm agreement with him, but Richard King was already contracted with the Barbers in a tobacco share farming arrangement and Barber refused. This might have been another "slight" against Batson with King at the core.

In 1923, Batson was employed by Barrow Brothers' Butter Factory, Jingellic, (located on the Victorian side of the river) for a short period, but was fired as his work ethic and performance were not up to the standard required by David Sheppard, the new manager. Again, he was bullied by other young men at the Butter Factory, and they nicknamed him "Dilly". Batson was resentful of his treatment.

Batson was also employed by Alf Lawrence primarily as a rabbit trapper and he occupied a slab hut on Lawrences' hill overlooking Walwa with his sandy coloured mongrel dog, "Ding" (as in dingo) or "Dink" (as in "fair dinkum").

In June 1923, Alf Lawrence sued William Thomas Newton Rae, the lessee of his Walwa property, for a breach of lease agreement. Rae had a four-year lease on 800 acres from Lawrence. Lawrence claimed negligence and costs arising from poor maintenance of fences, uncontrolled weeds and vermin, and damage to an orchard. During the dispute, Lawrence had employed Batson to regain some control over the rabbit population, and he claimed, in his evidence to the court, that Batson had killed 4000 rabbits and dug out 800 burrows. Batson, Charles Barber, Jack Cook and John Johnson also provided evidence to support Lawrence's case. The judge found in favour of Lawrence and awarded costs of £32 against Rae.

Locals considered Batson to be "stupid" (as described by Mounted Constable Ellery Murray) and eccentric but despite this, he was actually well liked, although he was often the butt of jokes and pranks. For example: he bought a new suit and later found that someone had cut the legs off the pants. He abstained from drinking alcohol and was usually well behaved, although he bore grudges against those who had slighted him for years. He was jealous and judgemental about persons who had done well for themselves. He hated David Sheppard because, although he was a *Johnny-come-lately*, he was charismatic, popular and successful. Sheppard was strong and active, and a wrestler in his youth. His party trick was to pick up a box of butter in each hand and raise them from shoulder height to above his head several times. Each box weighed 56lb.

Under Sheppard's management, the butter factory accelerated production. Sheppard was firm friends with William McGrath, another recent settler to the district. Sheppard helped his friend to purchase his property on Jingellic Creek from Barrow Brothers. This fact may have also made McGrath a target in Batson's warped view as he resented successful people.

Limited education implies that Bason was illiterate. Mr JF Davis (administrator at the Butter Factory) noted that Batson was unable to sign his payslip, and Batson had confessed to him that he was unable to read and write. Ellery Murray also claimed that Batson was unable to write. A E Hastain employed Batson on his dairy in Walwa for 8 months in1921-22. He was convinced that Batson was illiterate and recollected that if he showed Batson a newspaper article which revived historical anecdotes about Ned Kelly or other bushrangers, Batson would ask Hastain to read it to him. Hastain emphasised Batson's fascination with Bushrangers and noted that he had a grudge against society in general and wealthy folk specifically. On the other hand, some other erstwhile friends of Batson suggested he was keen on reading lurid novels, "penny awful paperbacks" featuring gangsters and lawless American cowboys. Ruth Barber admitted that she had spent a bit of time trying to teach Batson to read and write. So, the jury is out on Batson's capacity in relation to literacy and specifically whether he actually wrote the "suicide note" or whether an associate wrote it on his behalf to throw the police off Batson's scent. This fuelled the police officers' suspicion that Batson was being aided by community members to avoid capture.

Batson was a member of the Walwa Gun Club and was an excellent marksman. An article in a newspaper of the era described Batson's prowess with his rifle at a shooting competition in which he won a gold bangle with a score of 78/80.

After WWI, every village and locality had a rifle club. It was an initiative of the RSL and Department of Defence to train men to shoot and ensure that Australia would be ready for a future war. Similarly, the Lighthorse regiments continued their activities and training in rural centres. In Walwa, all the equipment for the 8th Lighthorse training days was stored in one of Hugh Hanna's houses (situated second last on the right in Hanna Street). According to the Kelly brothers, Batson visited their camp on Lawrences' Hill early on the Sunday morning before the picnic shooting. He was carrying a rifle and bragged about his prowess with the weapon. To demonstrate, he aimed at small target at 150 yards range and hit it true. This makes one conclude that he may well have hit his initial victims at the picnic by accident, which is tragic, or perhaps with more interest in maximising pain rather than killing outright, which is sinister.

Senior Constable Bunworth had known Batson since he was a child. He was awed by the man's knowledge of bushcraft and commented that Batson and his rifle were inseparable he was quoted as saying: "He considered his rifle to be a lifelong friend and would never part from it."

Lawrence and Batson applied for a patent on a rabbit extermination formula in August 1923. Patent application 13853 – Rabbit Exterminator. The patent was never granted with the reason cited that the invention was too similar to a previous application. Batson thought that someone had sold him out and stolen his idea.

The rabbit poison may have been associated with cyanide or a delivery mechanism for a gaseous version of cyanide. (Hydrocyanic acid gas mixed with Carbon bisulphite in a cartridge) In October 1923, representatives of the Department of Agriculture, Lands Board and farmers gathered to witness a demonstration of the Batson-Lawrence soon-to-be-patented technique and product, but the demonstration was a disaster, and Batson was stung by derisive laughter and enthusiastic negative reporting in the newspapers.

Desperate to erase the doubt relating to his invention, Batson appealed to the government officials, pleading for recognition and saying he would prove himself by eradicating rabbits on a 600-acre property with no charge, providing they ratified his invention. The offer was refused.

Charles Barber stated during police interviews and under oath, that Batson's demeanour and attitude changed dramatically in late 1923 and he considered him to be erratic and odd. After his arrest, Batson was charged and arraigned but after a perceived mental deterioration in gaol, he was found unfit to stand trial and was committed to a mental institution in April 1924. He lived out his days at Morisset Mental Hospital in Wyong, NSW, where he died, aged 70 years, in 1971. (Reg 41307 / 1971).

Mike Willesee created a documentary *Inside Morisset Hospital 1983* – it is available on YouTube. It is quite startling; Batson's incarceration must have been a never-ending nightmare.

Batson's missing handgun: Batson stated under oath that he had hidden two handguns of which only one was recovered. One was near Drummond's dairy (Possibly on *Bona Vista* which Albert Drummond leased from Joseph Hanna, and later became part of *Croyland*, HP McKenzie McHarg's property or perhaps at *Glen Alva* which was operated by J Drummond and sons) and one near Barber's dairy (It is unclear where this dairy was since Charles Barber owned property at *Redbank* (titles indicate his property was adjacent to the Butter factory), but he also leased *Springfield* land from Robert Hanna from 1918. It is my opinion that it is most likely that Barber milked on his own property and cropped and pastured dry cows at *Springfield*).

Attendees at the Jingellic Creek picnic on 10 February 1924

- David Thomas Sheppard 42 years, Manager of Barrow Bros. Walwa Jingellic Butter Factory from mid-1923.

- Mrs Alice Sheppard – wife to David

- The Sheppards' child - name and gender unknown

- Charles Barber (1884 - 03/03/1959) Dairy farmer with property at Redbank and leasehold at Hanna's *Springfield*. He also farmed tobacco with Richard King on the Jingellic river flats.

- Ruth Barber (Died 16/07/1958 aged 73years) – wife to Charles

- Major William Lachlan (Lachie/y) McGrath Ex- 8th Lighthorse Major, a decorated war hero in Gallipoli and Palestine campaigns. A farmer at Jingellic Creek, site of the picnic. He had purchased his property from Barrow Bros, (owners of the Jingellic Butter Factory) assisted by David Sheppard. He was hospitalised for injuries inflicted by Batson from 11/2/1924 until 8/3/1924 in Albury District Hospital. He was forced to give up his farm due to the extent of injuries inflicted during the event and left the Jingellic district in April 1925. He returned to Melbourne to take up his profession as an accountant. On 5 February 1925, William McGrath was awarded a Silver medal by the Royal Humane Society and a silver lifesaver medal from the Royal Shipwreck Relief & Humane Society of NSW for his heroics. The latter organisation felt that the water in the creek made his efforts align to the category of "Lifesaver and shipwreck". McGrath enlisted again in World War Two, serving firstly as second in command of Broadmeadows Camp and later second in command to the Officer Commanding 12th Garrison Battalion.

- Lizzie Ethel McGrath (Died in 1965, aged 75, buried in Walwa Cemetery) – wife to Lachie

- Jean McGrath (Toddler at the time)- child of the McGraths

(Later married Cleaver Gadd. Died in 1992, aged 71, buried in Walwa Cemetery)

- Bill McGrath (13 years) (Died in 1991, aged 80, buried in Walwa Cemetery) – eldest child of the McGraths. He served in WWII and returned to the Upper Murray to live with his sister until early 1970's.

- Charles Gainer - Brother to Lizzie McGrath. Visitor to the district and a farmer from near Broken Hill. Hospitalised in Albury District Hospital from 11/2/1924 until 8/10/1924. His leg injury was so dire that he came close to losing his leg.

- Gwendoline Ursula Irene Gainer - wife to Charles.

- Gainer child name and gender unknown.

- Richard King (60 years) Share farmer with Charles Barber – Grew Tobacco on Jingellic flats. He had been residing with the Barbers for 12 months prior to the incident. A widower and possibly once a manager of the Jingellic Tin Mine.

- Harry Poyntz (15 years) Nephew to Charles Barber

- George Poyntz (8 years) Nephew to Charles Barber

Witnesses to the events and local characters:

William (Bill) Hore (22 years) Dairyman employed by Albert and Alexander Drummond.

Robert Percival (Percy) Emerson (20 years) Dairyman employed by Charles Barber and Albert and Alexander Drummond.

Percy Barber (*The Prince*) an elderly gentleman, brother to Charles Barber. Lived in Jingellic.

Harriet Georgina Bryant - *Bannockburn,* Lankeys Creek. Involuntary host of Batson's overnight stay in Lankeys Creek after the picnic shooting. Margaret and Annie were her daughters.

Charles Edward Coysh - Secretary to Walwa-Jingellic Rifle Club – supplied Batson with a rifle.

Leslie Osborne - Farm hand at Alexander and Albert Drummond's property who rode to alert the police to the fact that Batson had been captured.

Albert WA Ashcroft - driver of the motor lorry which carried freight between Albury and Jingellic. He transported the victims to hospital and identified Sheppard's body at the morgue.

Professor Sir John MacPherson *Alienist* (Psychologist consultant to the Police), born in Scotland 1857, knighted in 1922 and took up the chair of Psychiatry at Sydney University. He was once the *Commissioner in Lunacy* for Scotland!

"PROFESSOR SIR JOHN MACPHERSON." The Sydney Morning Herald (NSW: 1842 - 1954) 5 June 1922: 7. Web. 30 Jan 2025 <http://nla.go v.au/nla.news-article16005933>.

Dr Conway M MacKnight - (Attending physician / Surgeon Albury Hospital) – medical officer who attended victims of Jingellic shooting and conducted the autopsy on David Sheppard.

Dr Cleaver Woods – Government Medical Officer (attended Batson in Albury Gaol). An influential member of the Albury Community. He was an Alderman for decades until 1925 and had two spells as Mayor of the young city. In 1888 he built and managed the Burnley Private Hospital behind his magnificent home on Swift Street Albury, Valetta House. He introduced X-ray technology to Albury Hospital. In 1886 he authored a thesis on the relationship between sheep, dogs and hydatid cysts in humans (Although the cycle was not officially described until 1930.)

Constable Richard Henry Percival Jolly – stationed in Walwa (married to Grace and had two children). He transferred away from Walwa in 1925.

Constable Cecil Rice – NSW Police force, stationed at Jingellic Police station on Redbank, Jingellic (Vic).

Sergeant Tom Morris, Holbrook - The first Australian recommended for a Victoria Cross in the Boer war. He was the best shot in the Riverina Rifle Club in 1924.

Constable Rowlands, Holbrook

Sergeant John Patrick O'Connor, Tumbarumba

Sergeant O'Neil, Police Depot, St Kilda Road Police Station

Constable Ellery Murray, St Kilda Road Police Station (born in Walwa)

Constable Stanley Murray, St Kilda Road Police Station (born in Walwa)

Constable JJ McCarthy, St Kilda Road Police Station

Constable RL Johns, St Kilda Road Police Station

Constable S Foote, St Kilda Road Police Station

Senior Constable D Bunworth OIC, Bourke Street West Police Station ex-Jingellic Police station (for 6 years)

Detective Cleaver Albury - OIC of the search initially but was transferred to the investigation relating to coronial inquiry into death of DT Sheppard.

Sergeant Cooper, Albury - accident prone! Tipped out of boat and had a motor vehicle accident after Batson was captured.

Superintendent Cook, Albury - OIC Communications and logistics, Albury

Inspector OH Parker, Wagga Wagga - the second NSW OIC

Senior Constable Comrie, Gippsland Police – Vic OIC

Constable Finlayson, Gippsland Police

Constable Lucas, Gippsland Police

Constable Newton, Gippsland Police

Constable Clermann, Gippsland Police

Constable MacPherson, Gippsland Police

Sub Inspector Connelly, Wangaratta Vic – second Vic OIC - Batson's arresting officer.

Constable Glowaski, Wodonga Police prosecutor.

Other minor characters and incidental history:

Postmistress and exchange operator at Walwa in 1924: Amy May Hughes.

Postmistress and exchange operator at Jingellic: 1912 May Smith took over from her mother Frances. She married in 1911 and became May Griffiths, and Miss Frances Margh Consta (Connie) Smith (May's sister) worked for May and became post mistress in 1928. Irene King was listed as postal assistant in Jingellic.

Jingellic Store was initially owned by J Medcalfe (or Metcalf) when he was publican of Bridge Hotel / Jingellic Travellers' Rest. (Burnt down in 1896 and rebuilt shortly afterwards.) Subsequent licensees of the hotel at its original site, (on *Darcy's,* a few miles up-river of current site) also ran the onsite store. When the new Bridge Hotel was built (construction commenced in 1925 and officially opened in 1928) the store moved to a site on the river side of the new pub (on the footprint of current beer garden), and it was operated by the Wilson family from late 1920's.

Hotel Licensee Walwa, 1924: Walter Trevalyn John (and brother George) both buried in Walwa cemetery.

Hotel Licensee of Jingellic, 1924: Finlay Smith (Brother to May Griffiths). His father, John Morrison Smith, was a manager of the Jingellic Tin mine and held liquor licenses for the "Jingellic Tin Mines Hotel", a period in the Redbank Hotel and took over the Jingellic Hotel in 1910.

Walwa General Store owned by John Brindley in 1924.

John Kennedy was the Walwa Store Manager.

Alec Thomas a storekeeper at Walwa (c1921-1924).

John Kennedy - Mail run contractor Bowna- Jingellic-Ournie in 1924

Mr Robert "Bob" Grey was mail coach driver between Jingellic and Holbrook He declared that he knew Batson well and gave evidence that he saw Batson walking towards the picnic site on the Sunday, armed to the hilt.

Baker in Walwa: Alfred Leschke 1921, Charles Burgess, a bit later (Bakery was, at that stage adjacent to Walwa Store).

William Coysh was a saddler in Walwa

Stephen Phillip Everard was a teamster

John Duncan Fraser was a cheesemaker

John Kelly was one of the Kelly brothers mentioned in this novel. They were prospectors and had a hut in the hills above Walwa.

Michael Kelly was a shearer, unsure if brother or father to John Kelly.

Hugh Patrick McKenzie McHarg was a cheesemaker; he initially managed Walwa Creek and then built a second Cheese factory at *Croyland* initially in partnership with Allan Purss.

Blacksmiths were plentiful:

Blacksmiths at the forge at Redbank (opposite the current era Golf Course) included:

- Martin Egan was blacksmith before 1911

- Arthur Stephenson 1912 -

- Donald Andrew Hore

- In addition, at different locations were: William Plunkett and Charles Thurling

- Ruston Stephenson at the Bridge Hotel, Jingellic, was a smithy and built sulkies. 1900-1903, before moving his forge to Redbank with his brother.

- Ernest Murray - Wheelwright and blacksmith (and undertaker) (corner of Shelley Road and Walwa Main street)

John Ulysses McCallum - Walwa Bank Manager, Bank of Australasia

Douglas Salmon – Bank of Australasia bank clerk

Tobacco: Chinese miners started growing tobacco successfully in the Upper Murray in the 1890's and it was considered profitable at 10 3/4d/lb. Over the next couple of decades, tobacco escalated in price to 3 Shillings/lb in 1924. I read that a blue fungus arrived and could not be controlled and destroyed the industry.

Border Morning Mail was started in 1903 by brothers Hamilton and Decimus Mott (later the Justice who heard the Inquest into Sheppard's death), the Mott family continued the business for several decades.

William Corbett succeeded David Sheppard as Jingellic Butter Factory manager 1924. Corbett was a witness in the Coronial inquest into Elizabeth White's death. She died in association with a fiery car crash and suspicion was, that her husband Richard / Raymond (Dickie) White, was culpable.

Richard (Dickie) White was listed on electoral rolls in 1925 as a labourer at Mt Alfred and his address was Burrowye Station in 1924. His story expanded from 1925 to 1939 when he became associated with- and later married one of the Brennan sisters in Walwa. He was later to become the topic of much gossip and rumour and was accused of deliberately killing his wife Elizabeth (Brennan) White in a car accident and fire in February 1939. He is the subject of Janice Newnham's first novel: White Lies – Where There is Smoke.

Livestock sales in the 1920's occurred on the 3rd Thursday of the month, conducted at John's saleyards North of Walwa Hotel (current Walwa Recreation Reserve.)

Allan Purss and Co. were the stock agents in the 1920's and Weir Hanna was an auctioneer.

Jingellic saleyards was owned and operated by the two hotels; Redbank and Bridge Hotel, so the name of the yards reflected this, until Redbank closed in 1918 (e.g. Redbank and Metcalf saleyards, Jingellic.)

There were calls for recognition of bravery for the two dairymen who apprehended Batson: Robert Percy Emerson and William (Bill) Hore, and for William McGrath's heroics at the picnic when he ran for his rifle.

In addition, Sister Martin's dedication to duty, demonstrated by her attending the scene of the picnic shooting incident when there was a potential for the sniper to return, was lauded. Also, mention was made of Mrs Judith Hanna (an ex-AVA nurse) who also attended the victims of the shooting.

Newspaper reports highlighted the need for assistance for Batson's victims. William McGrath and Charles Gainer were invalided and were no longer able to work in a farming capacity. Sergeant Cooper and Detective Cleaver organised a fund raiser for the pair and successfully raised £56 on 31 October 1924.

The Drummonds:

The author took liberties with details of the Drummond family members and residences. In truth, this is what I know of the Drummonds:

Albert Burns Drummond (1882- 1968) married Minnie Beatrice Wilson (1886 – 1985) Children included: Kathleen Mary (1915 -), Edna Beatrice (1917 -?) and Ronald James (1919 – 2016)

Alexander James Drummond (1894 - 1958) brother to Albert.

There were many other Drummonds, who failed to find a place in this novel, sorry.

And now my confession... the Drummonds referred to in this novel certainly existed, but I have used their names in an entirely fictitious manner. I was tempted to give them pseudonyms but since the family name was integral in Batson's capture, I opted to identify them.

Emma Payne is entirely a figment of my imagination, as is Jacob Miller and Phillip Hardwick, the journalist.

Despite my best efforts, I have not been able to definitively locate where Albert Drummond and Charles Barber's houses or their dairies were in 1924. These locations were scenes during the actual event and subsequently in my novel, so in the text, I have merely suggested the locations.

The Drummond homestead, *Glenalva* was built in 1912, I believe, and in my novel, I have loosely based Albert and Minnie's home on that location. Drummond relatives assure me that Ivon Drummond was master of that property in 1924, not his older brother, Albert. However, I understand that when James, the Drummond patriarch, was in the twilight of his life, the Drummonds ran *Glenalva* as a partnership (James, Ivon, Alexander and Albert) and I found a reference that indicated after James' death, the "fine dairy herd" was dispersed by the Drummond brothers in 1925. So perhaps I can stretch the connection!

I have discovered cadastral maps of the Walwa-Jingellic district and, although I can locate numerous Drummond and Barber holdings on the maps, I cannot reconcile the locations on the maps with newspaper reports and descriptions as to scenes of the action. So, I have used a bit of creative licence!

The scene of the picnic: I think I have located that! McGrath's house is long gone (Possibly where Hicks' Hay shed is now, west of Jingellic Creek and behind the existing house near the Jingellic Creek.) The beach and the embankment from which Batson fired on the picnic party is about 400m from the Jingellic Creek bridge on Talmalmo / River Road.

Please don't trespass to go and have a look!

I am always grateful to receive feedback from readers, particularly if you have identified a mistake or if you are willing to contribute additional information. You can make contact via my website or social media platform.

www.janicenewnhamauthor.com

Thank you so much for reading *A Sandwich Short of a Picnic*, I hope you have enjoyed reading it as much as I enjoyed writing it!

Feel free to provide a review on platforms such as Goodreads, Amazon, and social media platforms. Every bit of promotion helps and encourages me to seek out other skeletons in the closet to write about!

Janice Newnham - Author

9 781764 030205